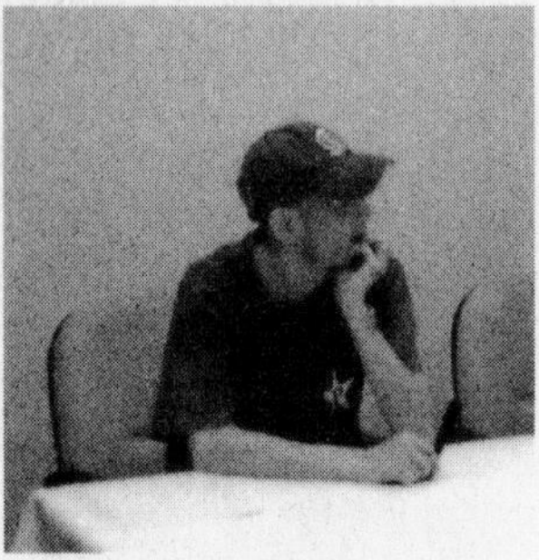

桂　正和

Masakazu Katsura

A year has passed since *I"s* began. This means that a year has passed inside the manga. The cover illustration is of Iori surrounded by cherry blossoms in full bloom. What? Her face isn't realistically drawn, you say? Sorry, please forgive me. It takes a lot of effort to do that. What? You say you've seen a picture just like it on the color title page? I apologize. But really, it's a brand new drawing. I like doing color work, but it takes a lot of time. That's the difficulty of doing a weekly series.

When Masakazu Katsura was a high school student, he entered a story he had drawn into a manga contest in hopes of winning money to buy a stereo. He won the contest and was soon published in the immensely popular weekly manga anthology magazine *Weekly Shonen Jump*. Katsura was quickly propelled into manga-artist stardom, and his subsequent comic series, *Wingman*, *Video Girl Ai*, *DNA²*, and *Shadow Lady* are perennial fan favorites. *I"s*, which began publication in 1997, also inspired an original video series. Katsura lives in Tokyo and possesses an extensive collection of Batman memorabilia.

I"s
VOL. 7: SPANK
The SHONEN JUMP ADVANCED Manga Edition

STORY AND ART BY
MASAKAZU KATSURA

English Adaptation/Arashi Productions
Translation/Arashi Productions
Touch-up Art & Lettering/Deron Bennett
Design/Hidemi Sahara
Editor/Jonathan Tarbox

Managing Editor/Elizabeth Kawasaki
Director of Production/Noboru Watanabe
Vice President of Publishing/Alvin Lu
Vice President & Editor in Chief/Yumi Hoashi
Sr. Director of Acquisitions/Rika Inouye
Vice President of Sales & Marketing/Liza Coppola
Publisher/Hyoe Narita

Printed in the U.S.A.

Published by VIZ Media, LLC
P.O. Box 77010
San Francisco, CA 94107

SHONEN JUMP ADVANCED Manga Edition
10 9 8 7 6 5 4 3 2 1
First printing, May 2006

www.viz.com

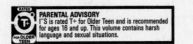

PARENTAL ADVISORY
I"S is rated T+ for Older Teen and is recommended
for ages 16 and up. This volume contains harsh
language and sexual situations.

THE WORLD'S MOST
CUTTING-EDGE MANGA
SHONEN JUMP ADVANCED
www.shonenjump.com

SHONEN JUMP ADVANCED MANGA

I"s™

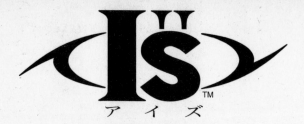

アイズ

Vol. 7
SPANK

STORY & ART BY

MASAKAZU KATSURA

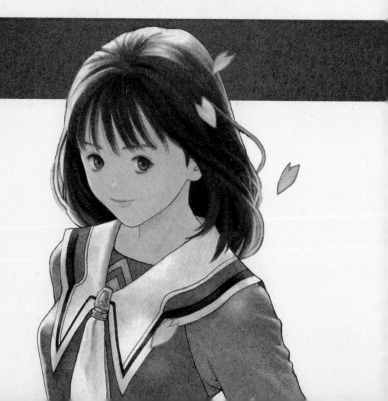

I"s
アイズ

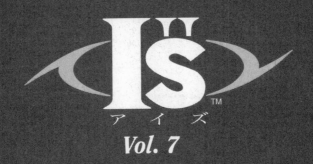

Vol. 7

CONTENTS

READ THIS WAY

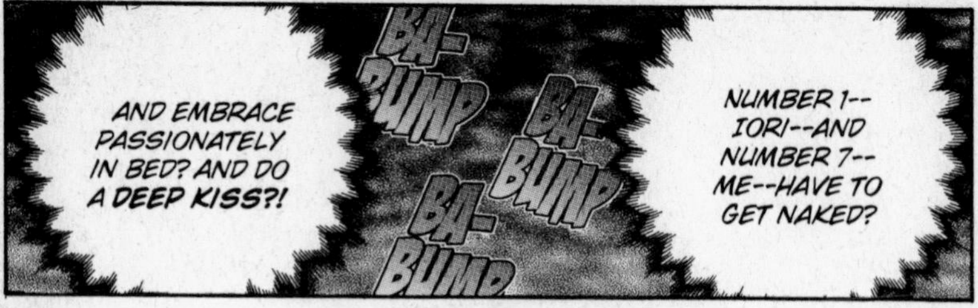
NUMBER 1-- IORI--AND NUMBER 7-- ME--HAVE TO GET NAKED?
BA-BUMP
BA-BUMP
BA-BUMP
AND EMBRACE PASSIONATELY IN BED? AND DO A DEEP KISS?!

Chapter 55: In the Dark

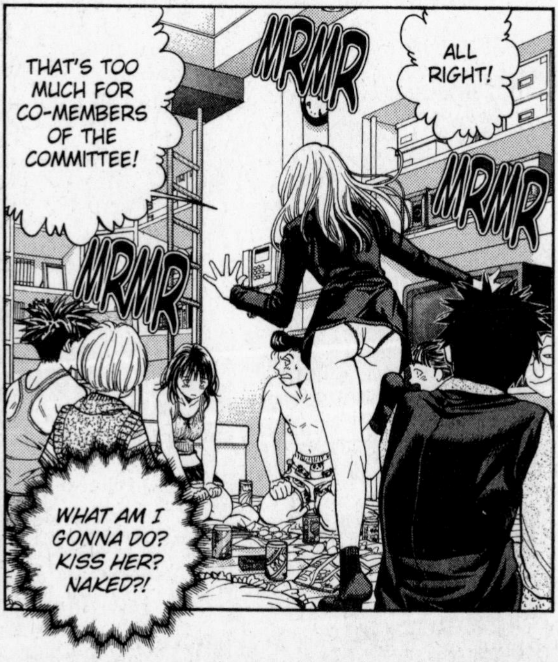
ALL RIGHT!
MRMR
THAT'S TOO MUCH FOR CO-MEMBERS OF THE COMMITTEE!
MRMR
MRMR
WHAT AM I GONNA DO? KISS HER? NAKED?!

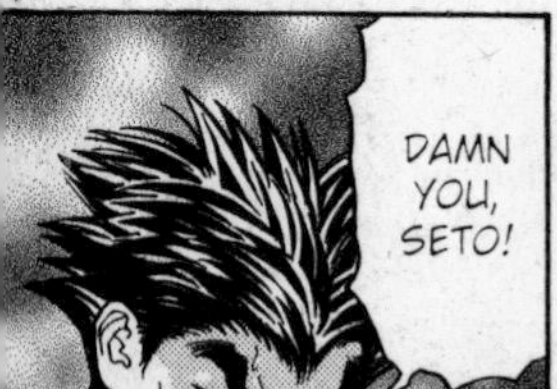
DAMN YOU, SETO!

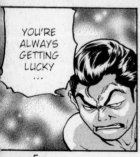

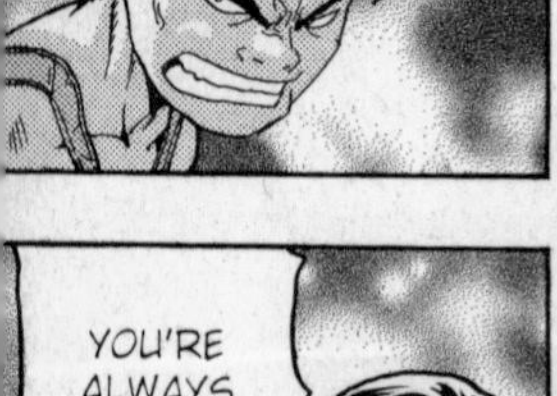
YOU'RE ALWAYS GETTING LUCKY ...

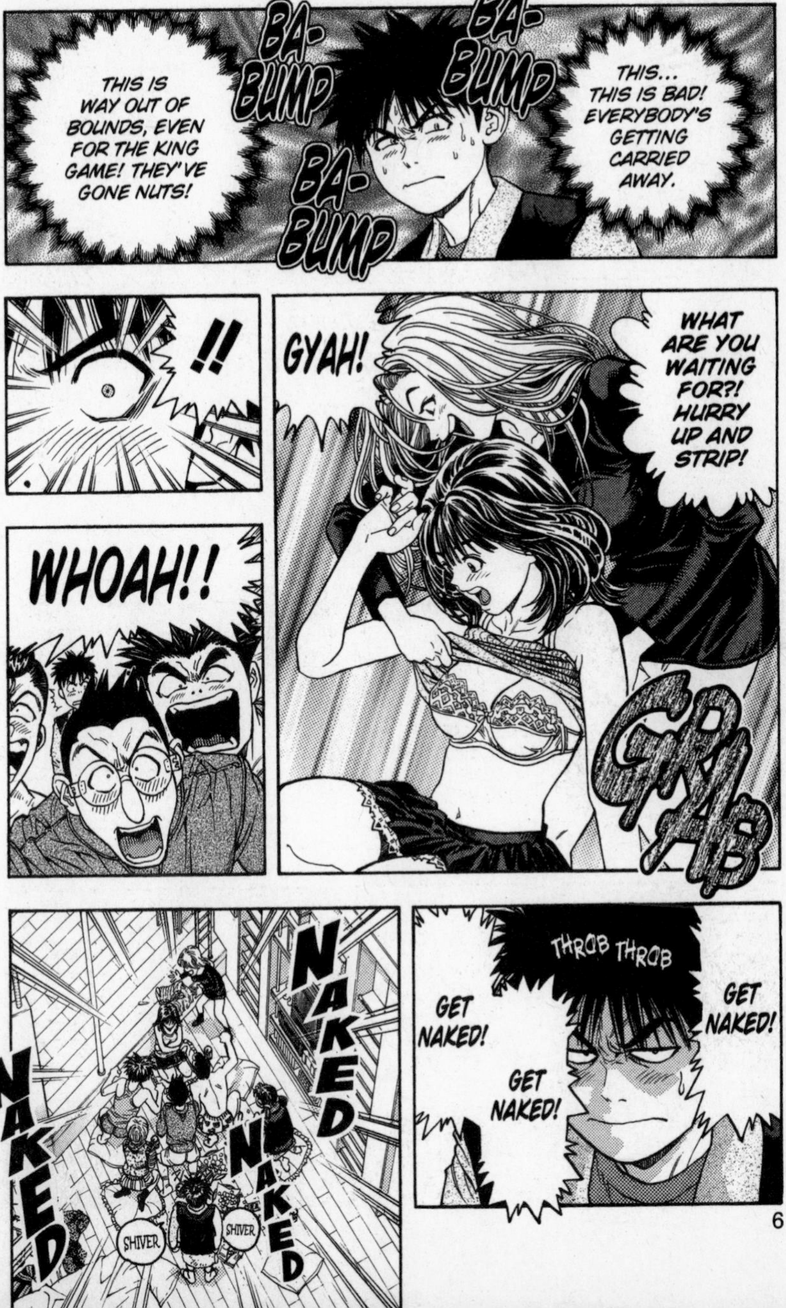
BA-BUMP
THIS... THIS IS BAD! EVERYBODY'S GETTING CARRIED AWAY.
BA-BUMP
BA-BUMP
THIS IS WAY OUT OF BOUNDS, EVEN FOR THE KING GAME! THEY'VE GONE NUTS!
WHAT ARE YOU WAITING FOR?! HURRY UP AND STRIP!
GYAH!
GRAB
!!
WHOAH!!
THROB THROB
GET NAKED!
GET NAKED!
GET NAKED!
NAKED
NAKED
NAKED
SHIVER
SHIVER

READ THIS WAY

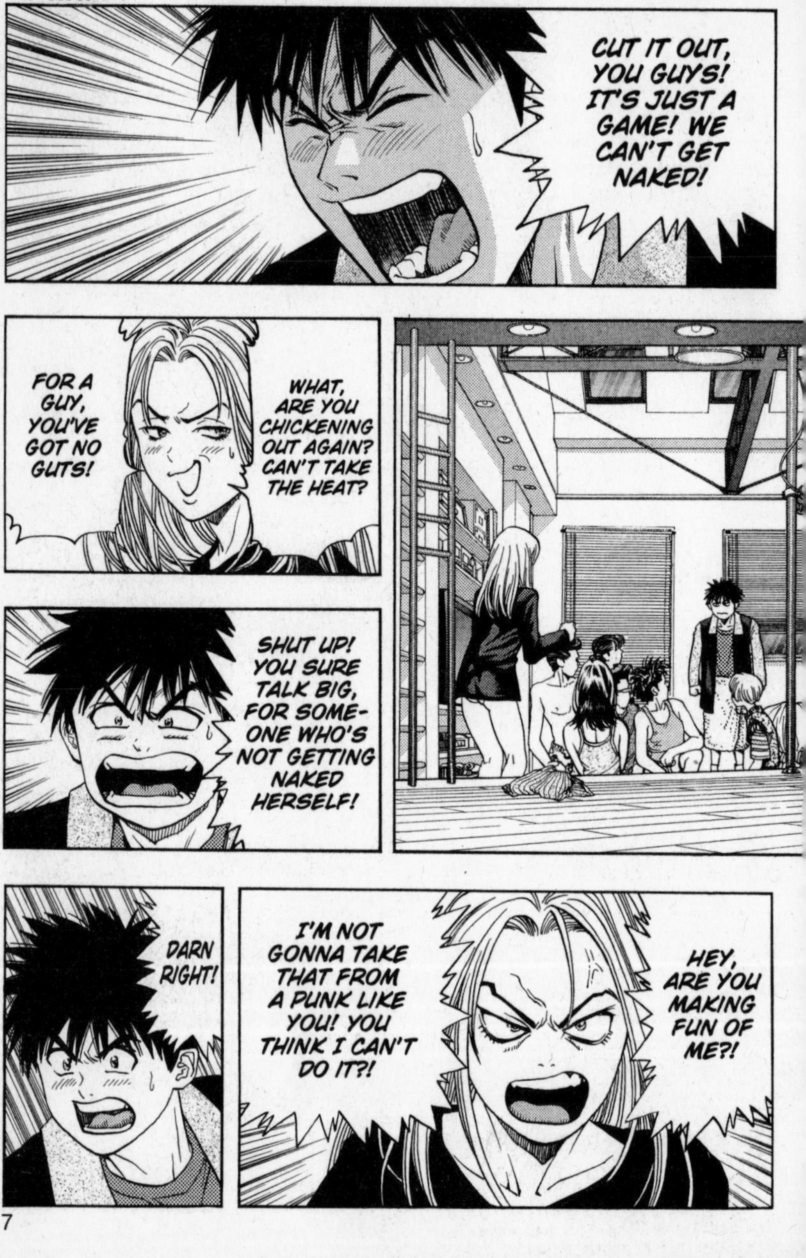

CUT IT OUT, YOU GUYS! IT'S JUST A GAME! WE CAN'T GET NAKED!
WHAT, ARE YOU CHICKENING OUT AGAIN? CAN'T TAKE THE HEAT?
FOR A GUY, YOU'VE GOT NO GUTS!
SHUT UP! YOU SURE TALK BIG, FOR SOME-ONE WHO'S NOT GETTING NAKED HERSELF!
HEY, ARE YOU MAKING FUN OF ME?!
I'M NOT GONNA TAKE THAT FROM A PUNK LIKE YOU! YOU THINK I CAN'T DO IT?!
DARN RIGHT!

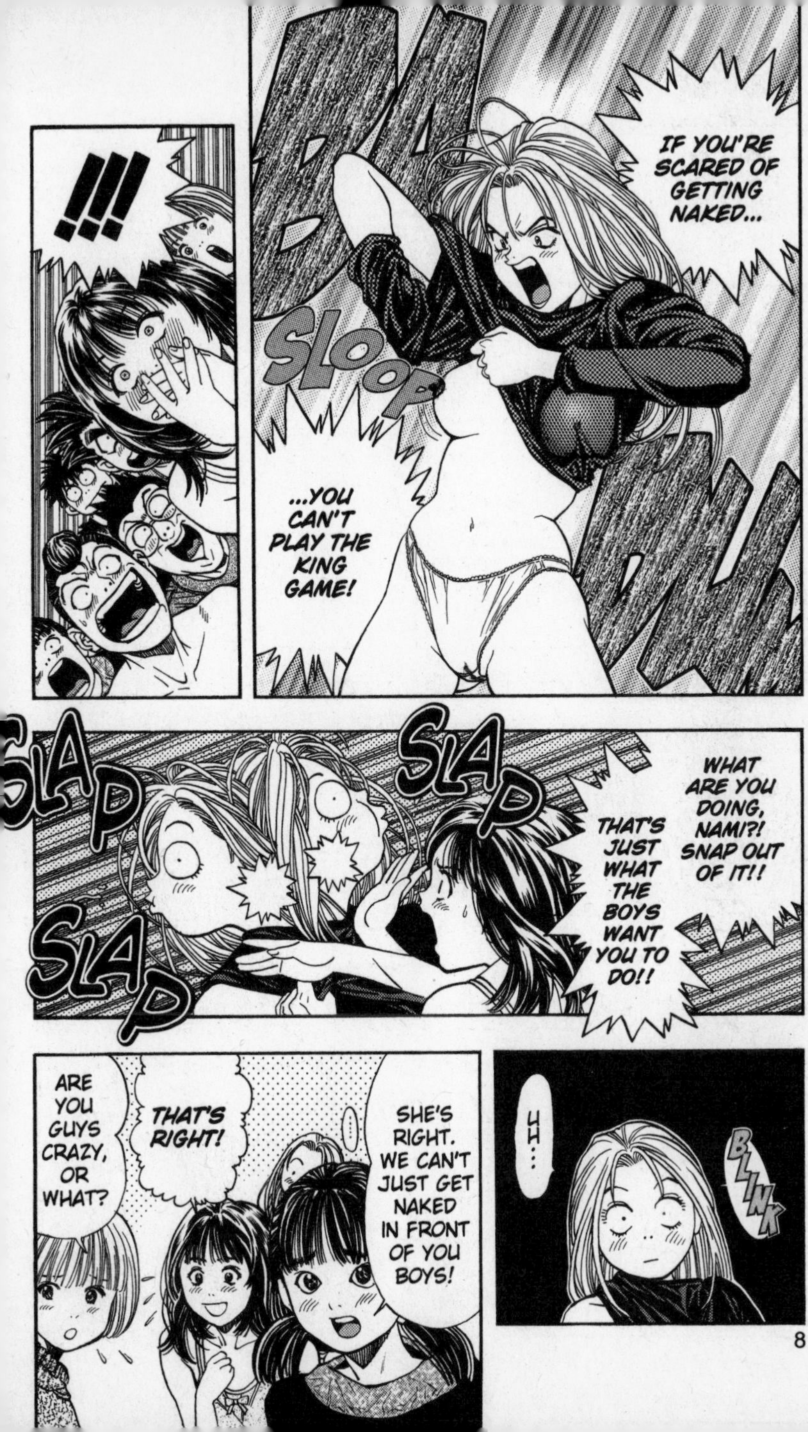
IF YOU'RE SCARED OF GETTING NAKED...
SLOOP
...YOU CAN'T PLAY THE KING GAME!
!!!
WHAT ARE YOU DOING, NAMI?! SNAP OUT OF IT!!
THAT'S JUST WHAT THE BOYS WANT YOU TO DO!!
SLAP
SLAP
SLAP
UH...
BLINK
SHE'S RIGHT. WE CAN'T JUST GET NAKED IN FRONT OF YOU BOYS!
...
THAT'S RIGHT!
ARE YOU GUYS CRAZY, OR WHAT?

READ THIS WAY

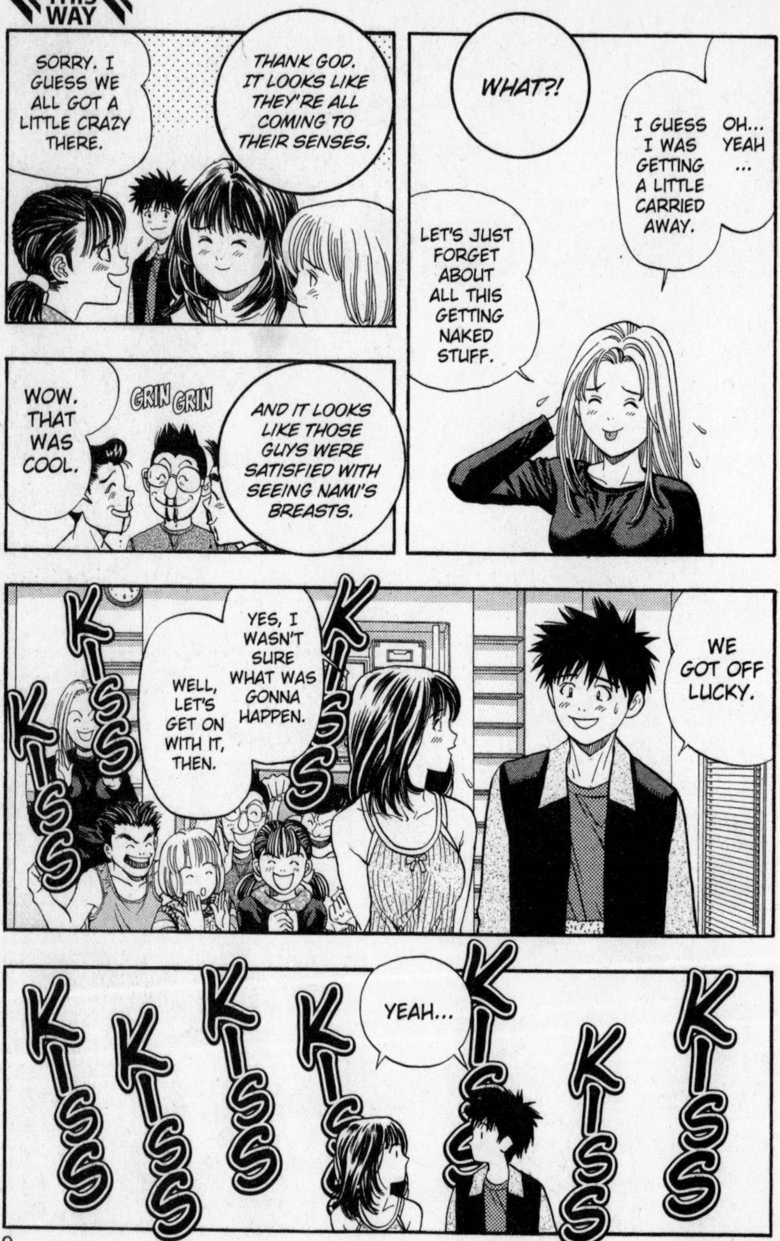
OH... YEAH ...
I GUESS I WAS GETTING A LITTLE CARRIED AWAY.
WHAT?!
LET'S JUST FORGET ABOUT ALL THIS GETTING NAKED STUFF.
THANK GOD. IT LOOKS LIKE THEY'RE ALL COMING TO THEIR SENSES.
SORRY. I GUESS WE ALL GOT A LITTLE CRAZY THERE.
AND IT LOOKS LIKE THOSE GUYS WERE SATISFIED WITH SEEING NAMI'S BREASTS.
GRIN GRIN
WOW. THAT WAS COOL.
WE GOT OFF LUCKY.
KISS
YES, I WASN'T SURE WHAT WAS GONNA HAPPEN.
WELL, LET'S GET ON WITH IT, THEN.
KISS KISS
KISS KISS KISS
YEAH...
KISS KISS KISS KISS

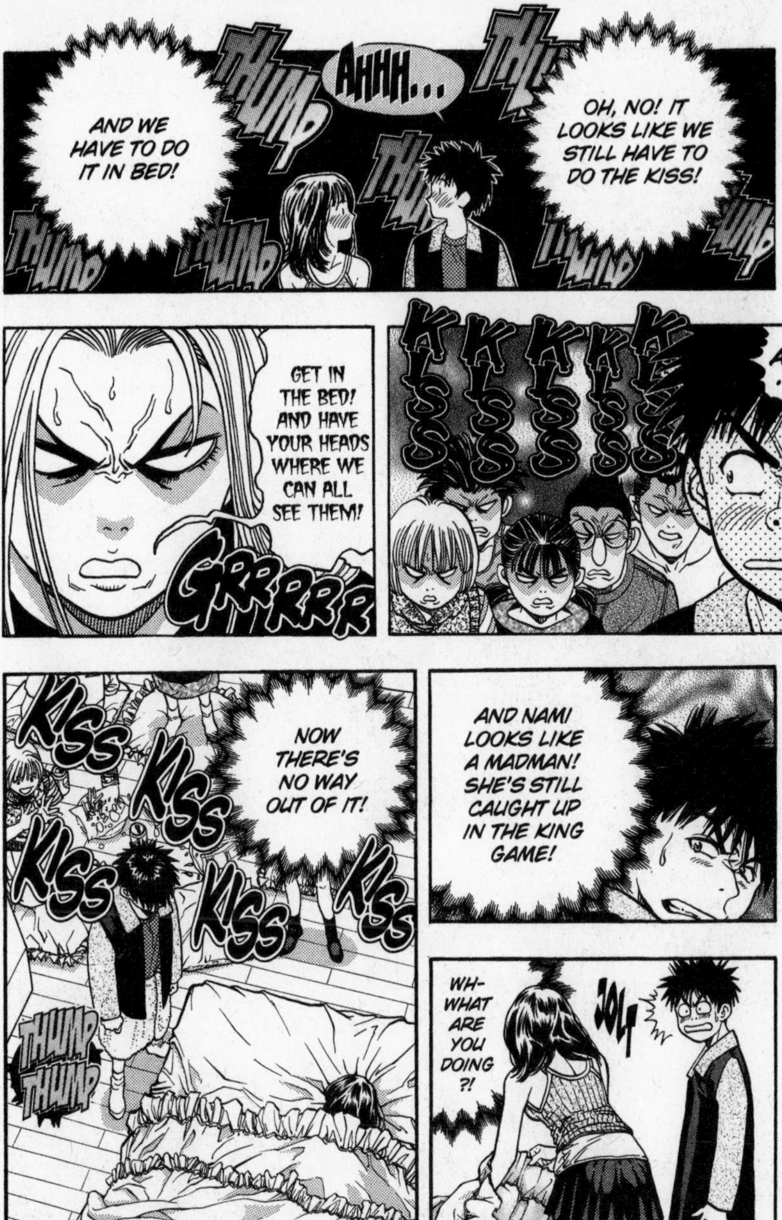
OH, NO! IT LOOKS LIKE WE STILL HAVE TO DO THE KISS!
AHHH...
THUMP
AND WE HAVE TO DO IT IN BED!
AH ...
KISS KISS KISS KISS KISS
GET IN THE BED! AND HAVE YOUR HEADS WHERE WE CAN ALL SEE THEM!
GRRRRR
AND NAMI LOOKS LIKE A MADMAN! SHE'S STILL CAUGHT UP IN THE KING GAME!
JOLT
WH- WHAT ARE YOU DOING ?!
NOW THERE'S NO WAY OUT OF IT!
KISS KISS KISS KISS KISS
THUMP THUMP

READ THIS WAY

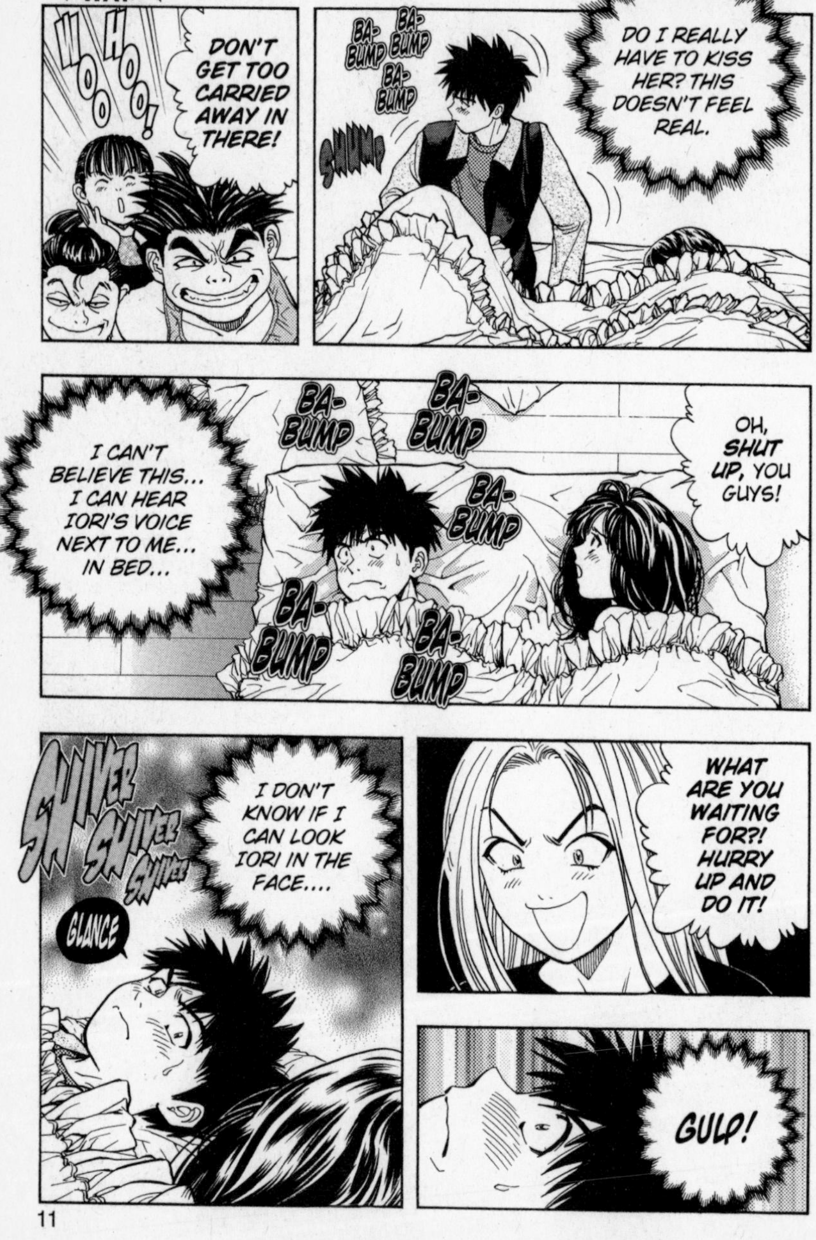

BA-BUMP
BA-BUMP
BA-BUMP
SHUMP
DO I REALLY HAVE TO KISS HER? THIS DOESN'T FEEL REAL.
WOOHOO!
DON'T GET TOO CARRIED AWAY IN THERE!
OH, SHUT UP, YOU GUYS!
BA-BUMP
BA-BUMP
BA-BUMP
BA-BUMP
BA-BUMP
I CAN'T BELIEVE THIS... I CAN HEAR IORI'S VOICE NEXT TO ME... IN BED...
WHAT ARE YOU WAITING FOR?! HURRY UP AND DO IT!
GULP!
SHIVER SHIVER SHIVER
I DON'T KNOW IF I CAN LOOK IORI IN THE FACE....
GLANCE

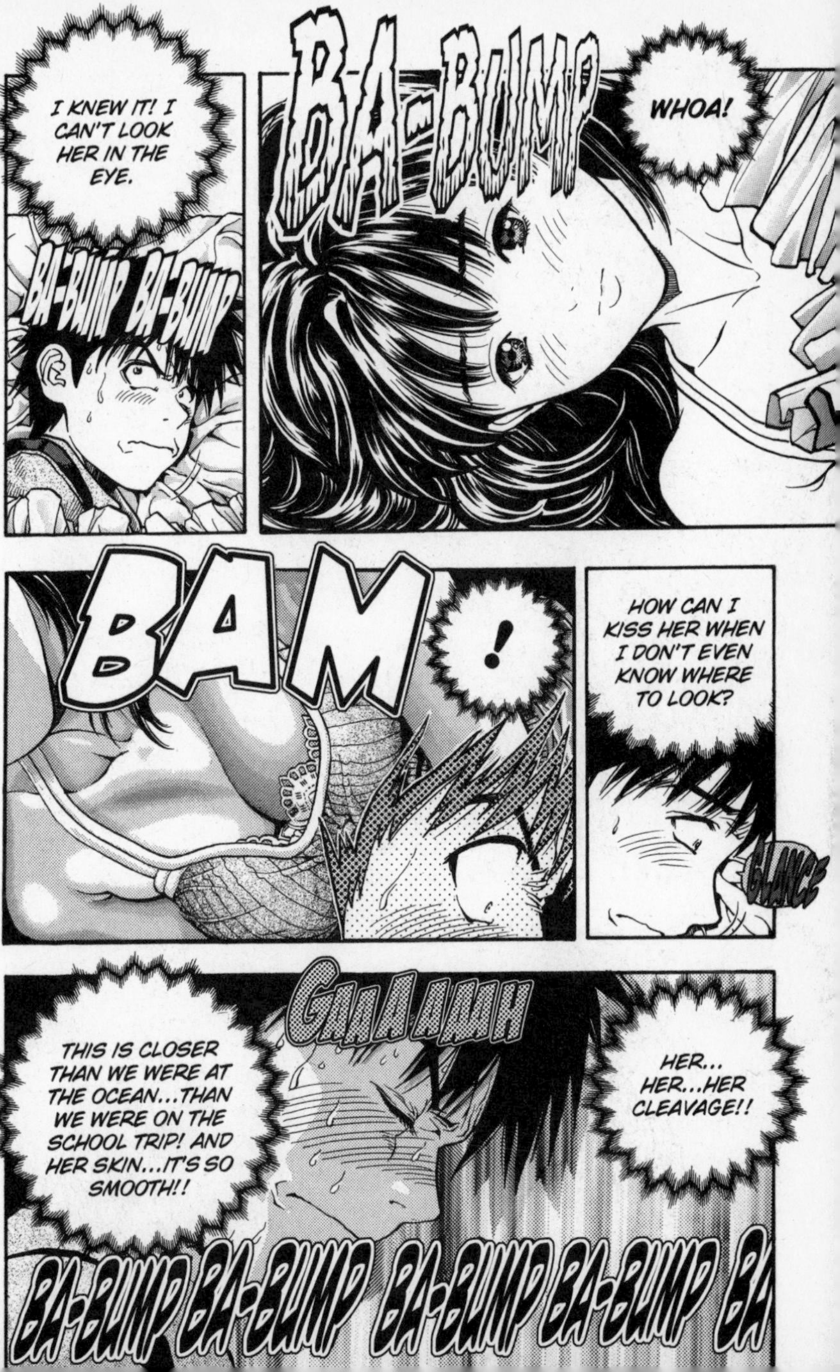
WHOA!
BA-BUMP
I KNEW IT! I CAN'T LOOK HER IN THE EYE.
BA-BUMP BA-BUMP
HOW CAN I KISS HER WHEN I DON'T EVEN KNOW WHERE TO LOOK?
GLANCE
!
BAM
HER... HER...HER CLEAVAGE!!
THIS IS CLOSER THAN WE WERE AT THE OCEAN...THAN WE WERE ON THE SCHOOL TRIP! AND HER SKIN...IT'S SO SMOOTH!!
BA-BUMP BA-BUMP BA-BUMP BA-BUMP BA

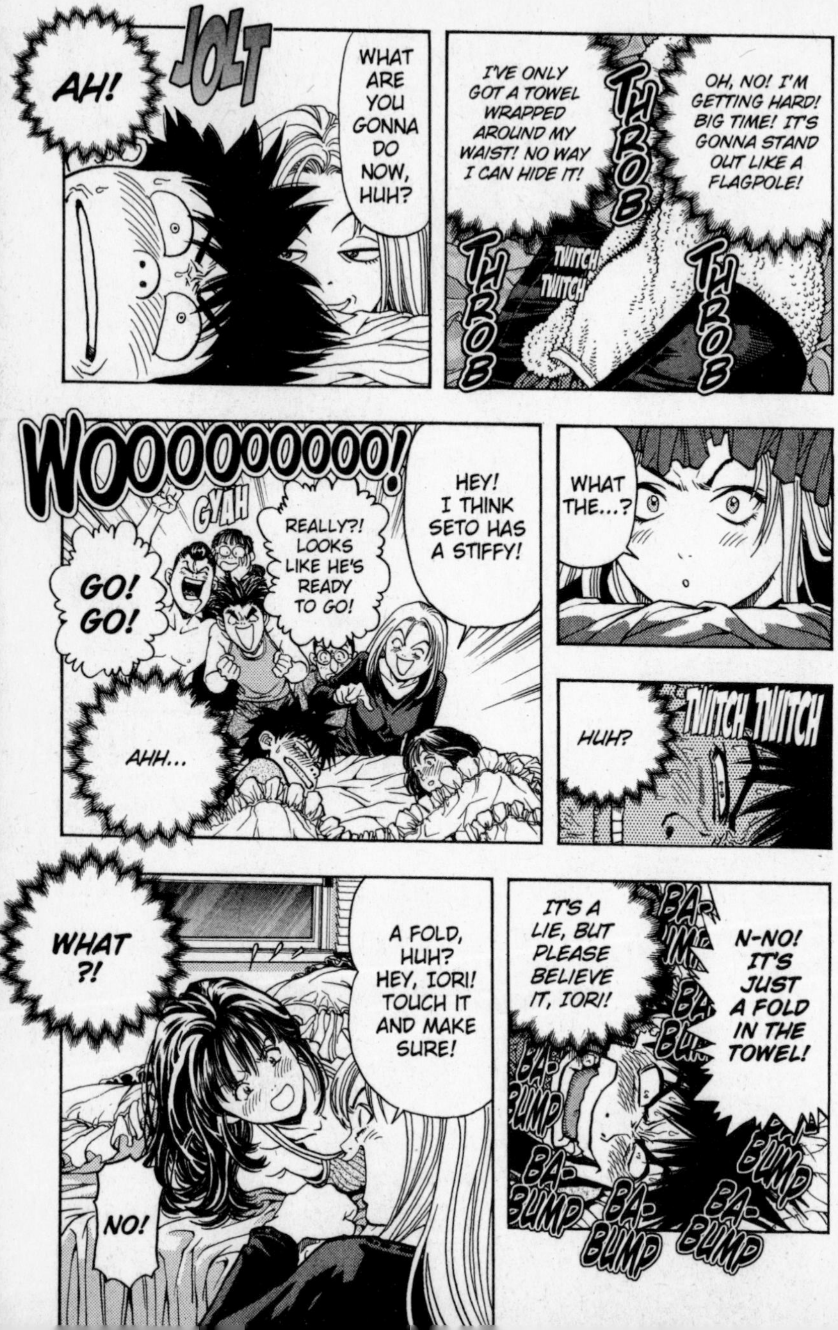
OH, NO! I'M GETTING HARD! BIG TIME! IT'S GONNA STAND OUT LIKE A FLAGPOLE!
THROB
I'VE ONLY GOT A TOWEL WRAPPED AROUND MY WAIST! NO WAY I CAN HIDE IT!
THROB
TWITCH TWITCH
THROB
WHAT ARE YOU GONNA DO NOW, HUH?
JOLT
AH!
WHAT THE...?
TWITCH TWITCH
HUH?
WOOOOOOOOO!
HEY! I THINK SETO HAS A STIFFY!
REALLY?! LOOKS LIKE HE'S READY TO GO!
GYAH
GO! GO!
AHH...
N-NO! IT'S JUST A FOLD IN THE TOWEL!
BA-BUMP BA-BUMP
IT'S A LIE, BUT PLEASE BELIEVE IT, IORI!
BA-BUMP BA-BUMP BA-BUMP BA-BUMP BA-BUMP
A FOLD, HUH? HEY, IORI! TOUCH IT AND MAKE SURE!
WHAT?!
NO!

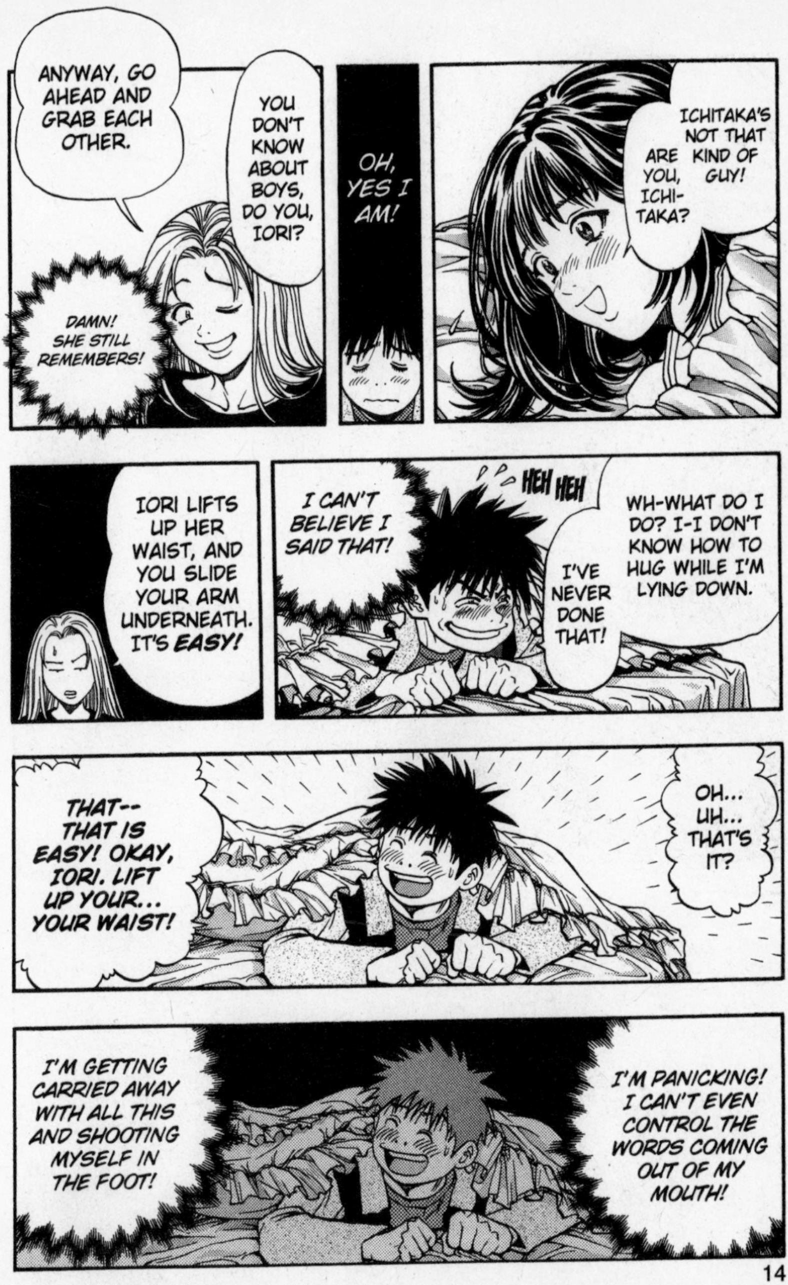
ICHITAKA'S NOT THAT KIND OF GUY!
ARE YOU, ICHITAKA?
OH, YES I AM!
YOU DON'T KNOW ABOUT BOYS, DO YOU, IORI?
ANYWAY, GO AHEAD AND GRAB EACH OTHER.
DAMN! SHE STILL REMEMBERS!
HEH HEH
WH-WHAT DO I DO? I-I DON'T KNOW HOW TO HUG WHILE I'M LYING DOWN.
I'VE NEVER DONE THAT!
I CAN'T BELIEVE I SAID THAT!
IORI LIFTS UP HER WAIST, AND YOU SLIDE YOUR ARM UNDERNEATH. IT'S EASY!
OH... UH... THAT'S IT?
THAT-- THAT IS EASY! OKAY, IORI. LIFT UP YOUR... YOUR WAIST!
I'M PANICKING! I CAN'T EVEN CONTROL THE WORDS COMING OUT OF MY MOUTH!
I'M GETTING CARRIED AWAY WITH ALL THIS AND SHOOTING MYSELF IN THE FOOT!

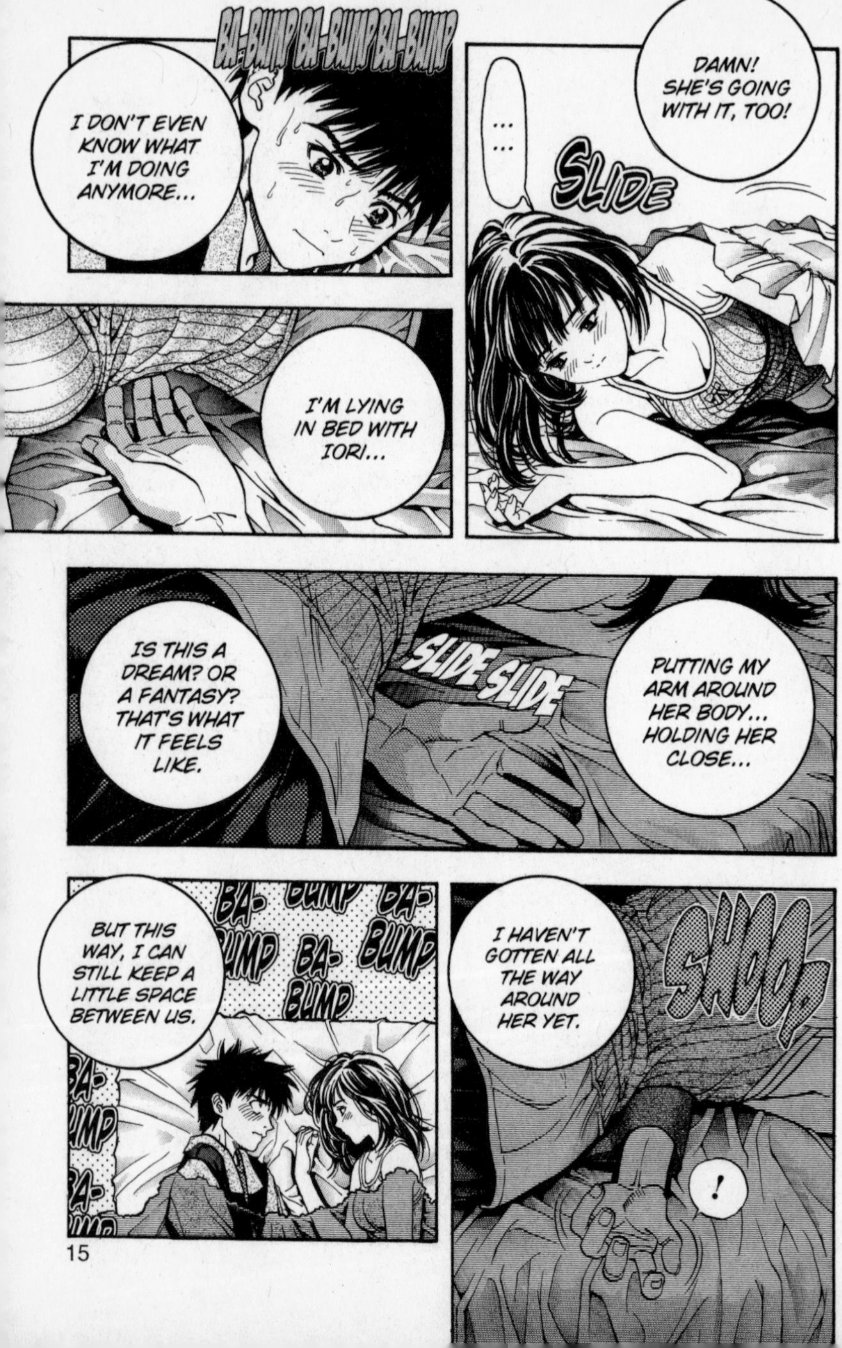
DAMN! SHE'S GOING WITH IT, TOO!
... ...
SLIDE
BA-BUMP BA-BUMP BA-BUMP
I DON'T EVEN KNOW WHAT I'M DOING ANYMORE...
I'M LYING IN BED WITH IORI...
PUTTING MY ARM AROUND HER BODY... HOLDING HER CLOSE...
SLIDE SLIDE
IS THIS A DREAM? OR A FANTASY? THAT'S WHAT IT FEELS LIKE.
SHOOP
I HAVEN'T GOTTEN ALL THE WAY AROUND HER YET.
!
BA-BUMP BA-BUMP BA-BUMP
BUT THIS WAY, I CAN STILL KEEP A LITTLE SPACE BETWEEN US.
BA-BUMP BA-BUMP

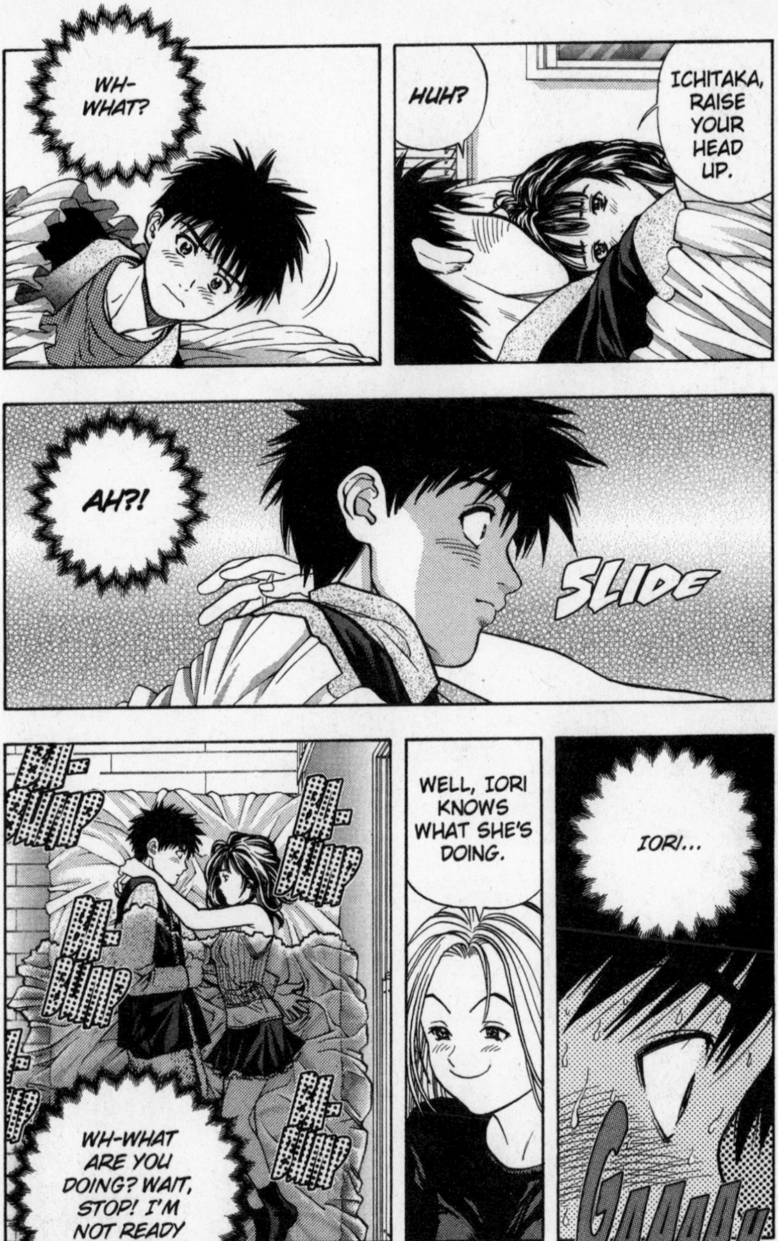
ICHITAKA, RAISE YOUR HEAD UP.
HUH?
WH- WHAT?
AH?!
SLIDE
IORI...
GAAAAH
WELL, IORI KNOWS WHAT SHE'S DOING.
WH-WHAT ARE YOU DOING? WAIT, STOP! I'M NOT READY FOR...

READ THIS WAY

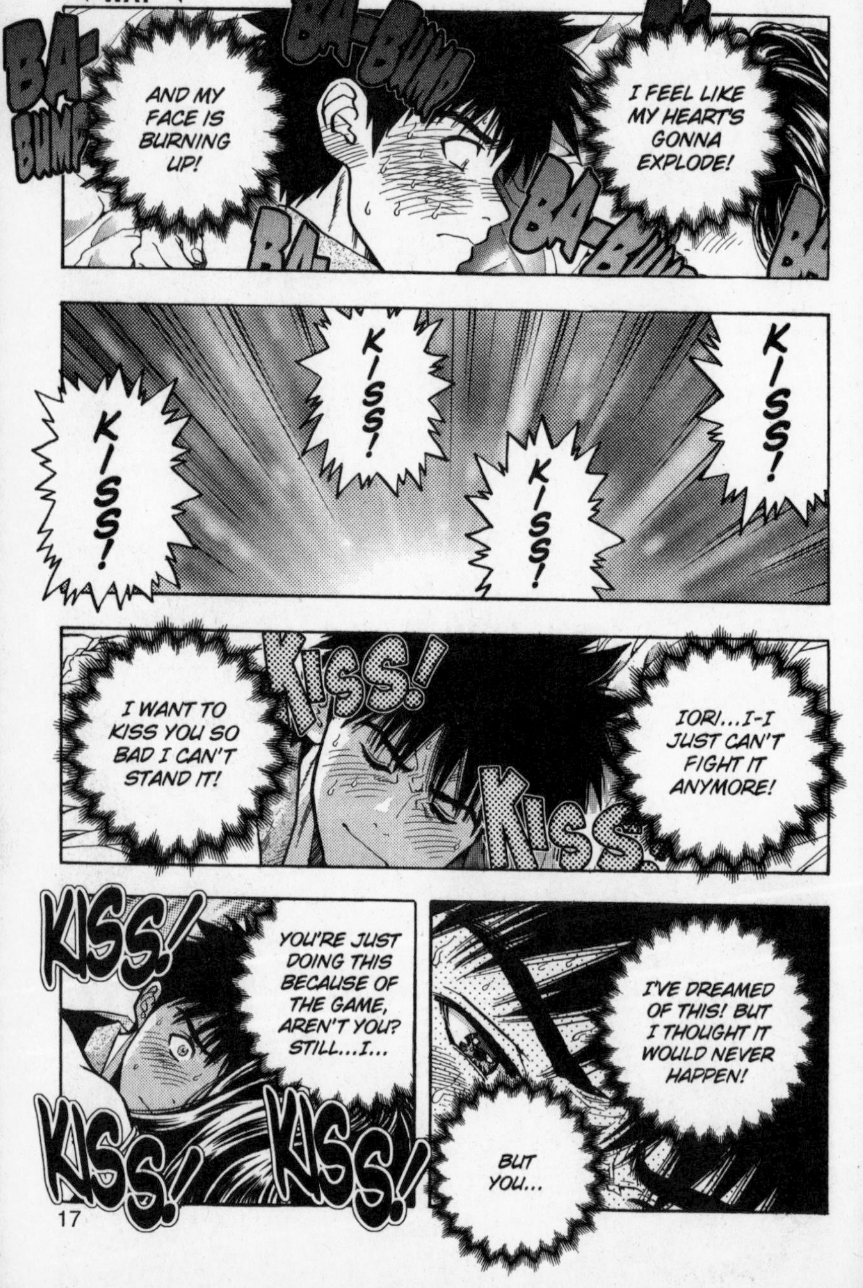

I FEEL LIKE MY HEART'S GONNA EXPLODE!
BA-BUMP
AND MY FACE IS BURNING UP!
BA-BUMP
KISS!
KISS!
KISS!
KISS!
IORI...I-I JUST CAN'T FIGHT IT ANYMORE!
KISS
KISS!
I WANT TO KISS YOU SO BAD I CAN'T STAND IT!
I'VE DREAMED OF THIS! BUT I THOUGHT IT WOULD NEVER HAPPEN!
BUT YOU...
YOU'RE JUST DOING THIS BECAUSE OF THE GAME, AREN'T YOU? STILL...I...
KISS!
KISS!
KISS!

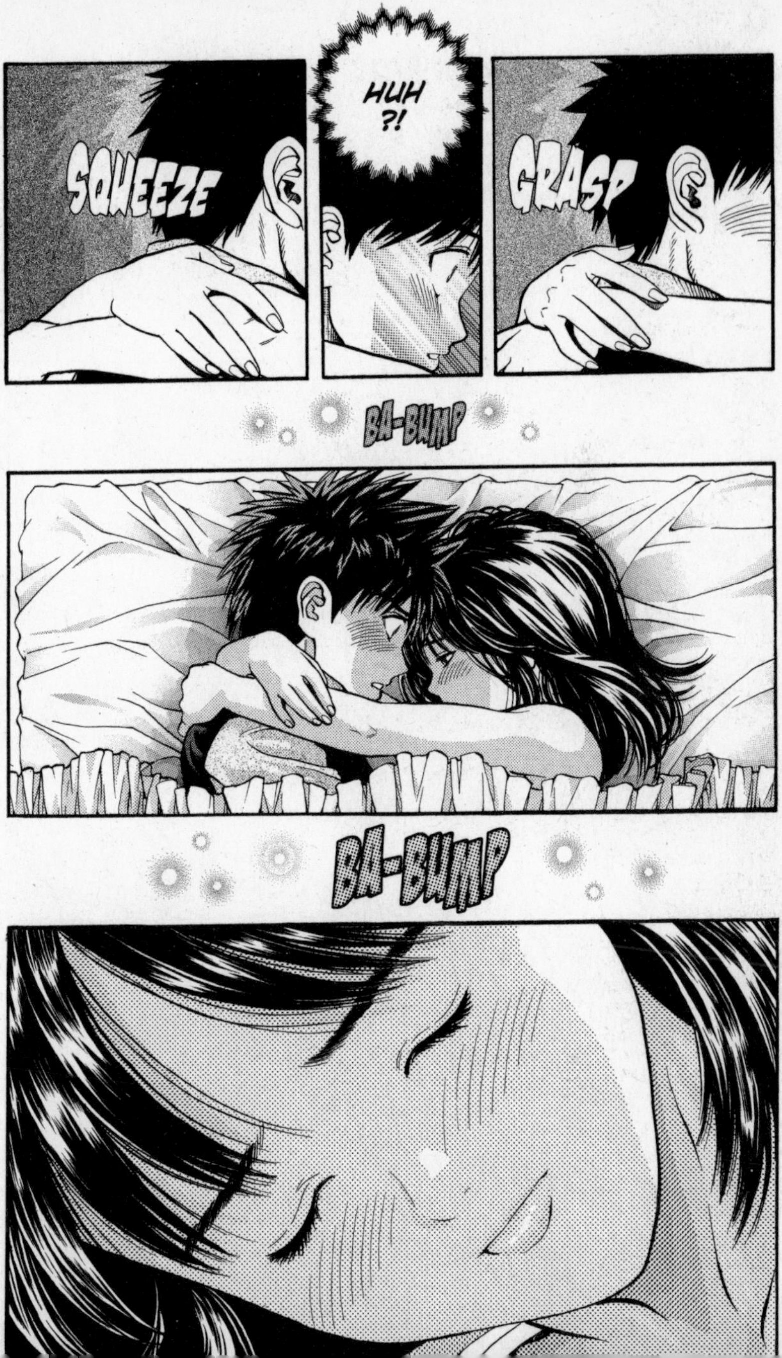
GRASP
HUH ?!
SQUEEZE
BA-BUMP
BA-BUMP

READ THIS WAY

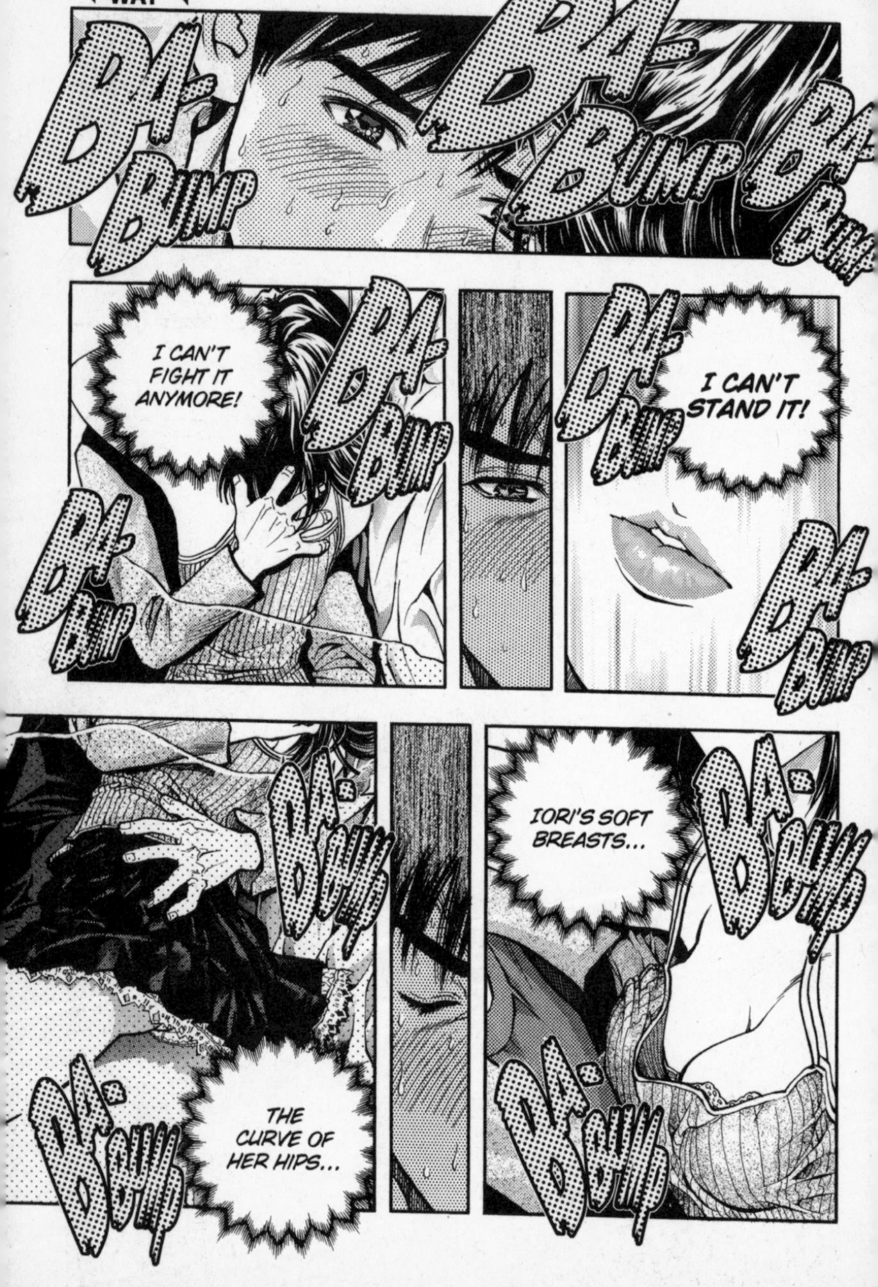
DA-BUMP
DA-BUMP
DA-BUMP
I CAN'T STAND IT!
I CAN'T FIGHT IT ANYMORE!
IORI'S SOFT BREASTS...
THE CURVE OF HER HIPS...

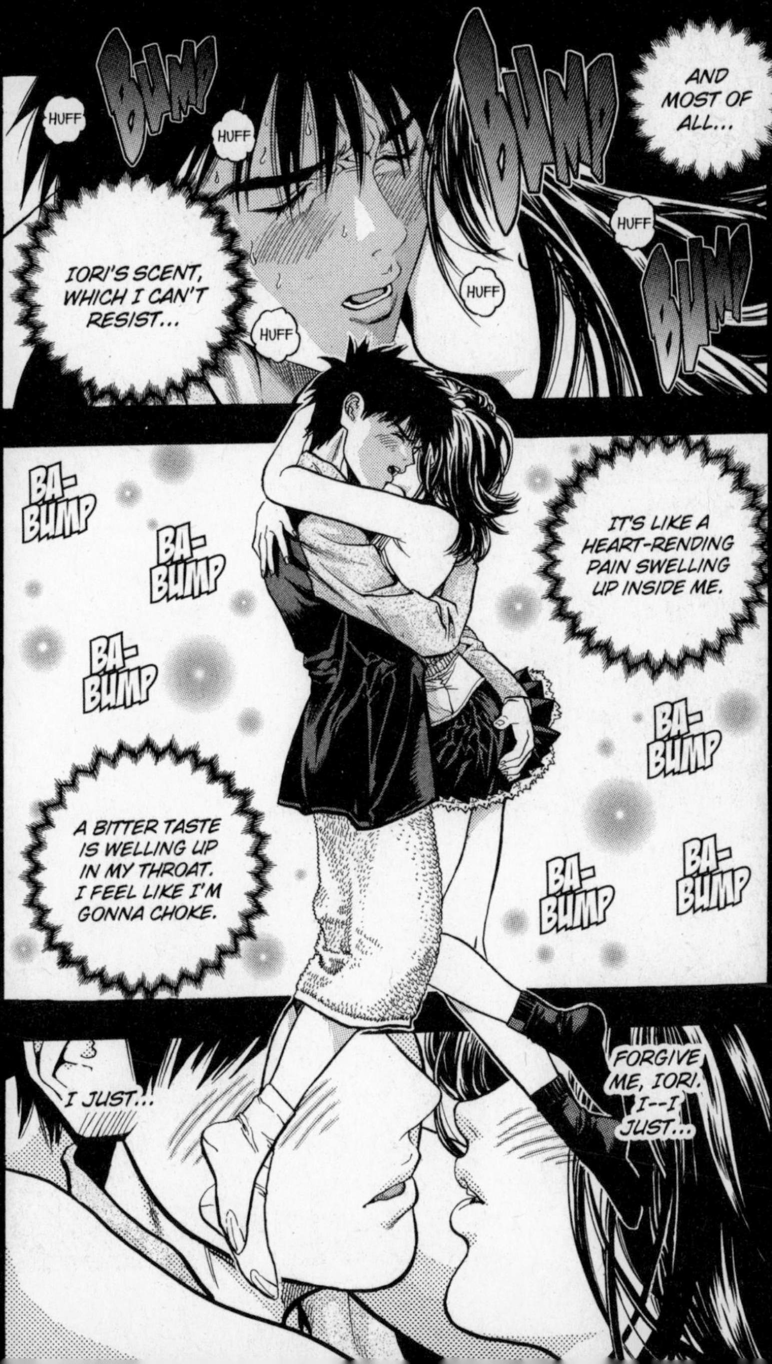
AND MOST OF ALL...
BUMP
HUFF
BUMP
HUFF
BUMP
HUFF
HUFF
HUFF
IORI'S SCENT, WHICH I CAN'T RESIST...
IT'S LIKE A HEART-RENDING PAIN SWELLING UP INSIDE ME.
BA-BUMP
BA-BUMP
BA-BUMP
BA-BUMP
BA-BUMP
BA-BUMP
BA-BUMP
A BITTER TASTE IS WELLING UP IN MY THROAT. I FEEL LIKE I'M GONNA CHOKE.
FORGIVE ME, IORI. I--I JUST...
I JUST...

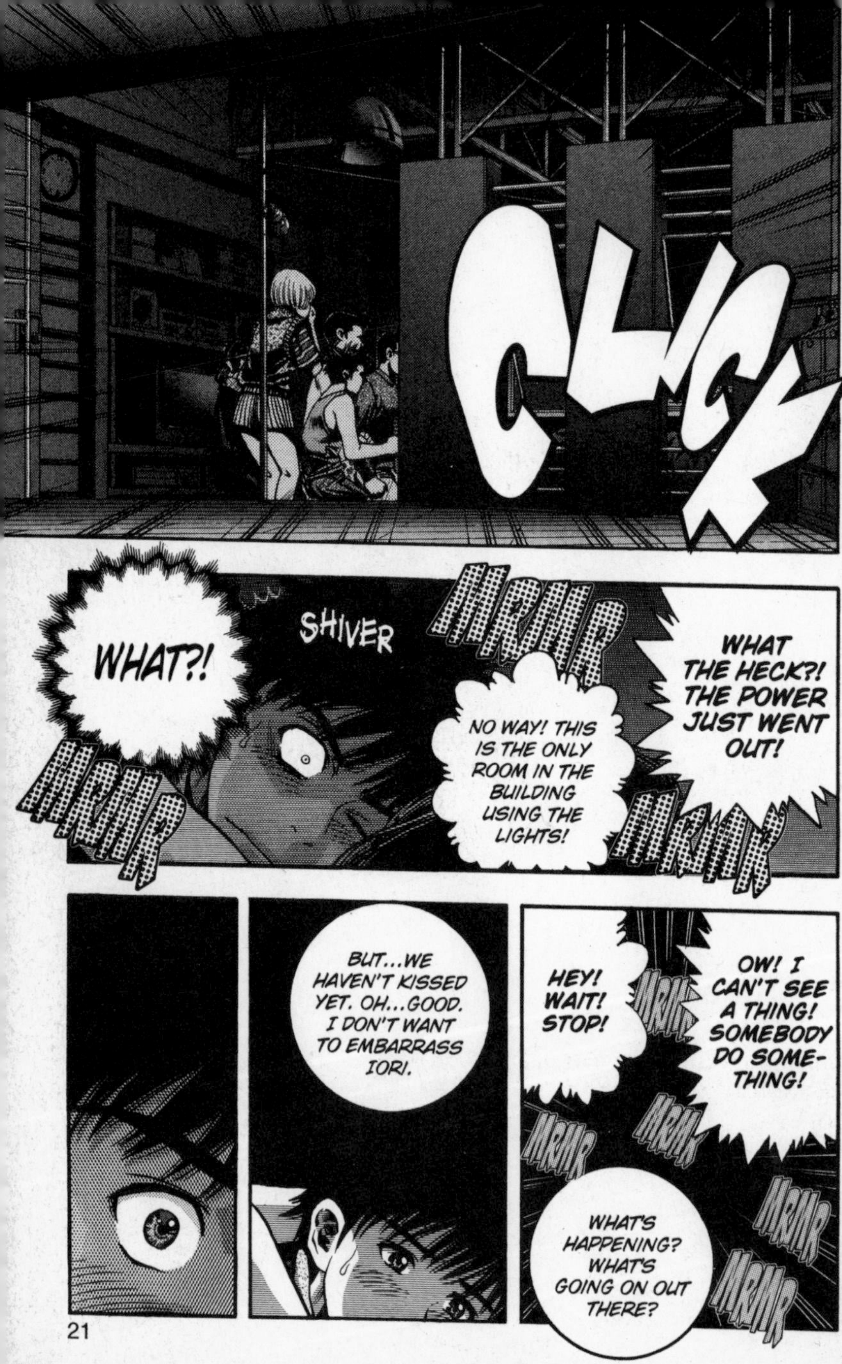
CLICK
WHAT THE HECK?! THE POWER JUST WENT OUT!
NO WAY! THIS IS THE ONLY ROOM IN THE BUILDING USING THE LIGHTS!
SHIVER
WHAT?!
OW! I CAN'T SEE A THING! SOMEBODY DO SOME-THING!
HEY! WAIT! STOP!
WHAT'S HAPPENING? WHAT'S GOING ON OUT THERE?
BUT...WE HAVEN'T KISSED YET. OH...GOOD. I DON'T WANT TO EMBARRASS IORI.

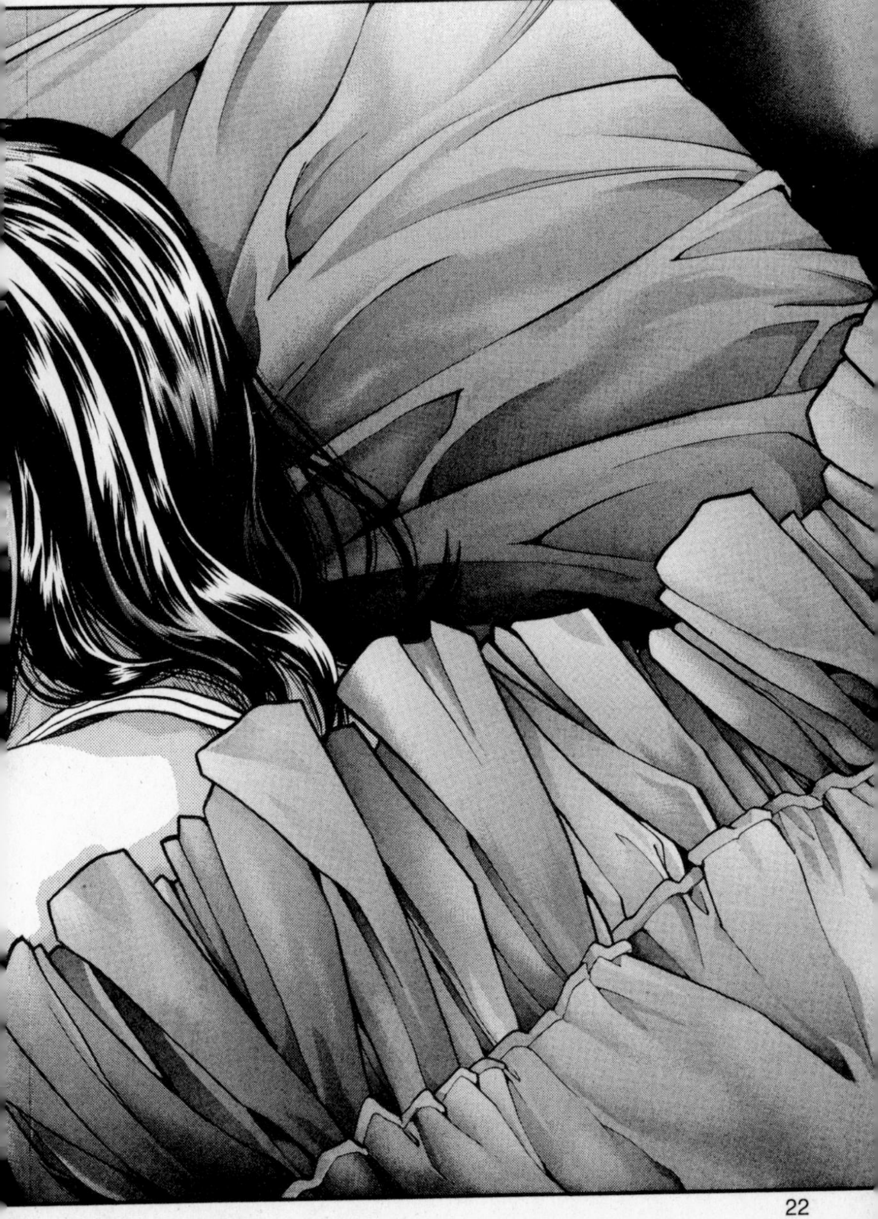

READ THIS WAY

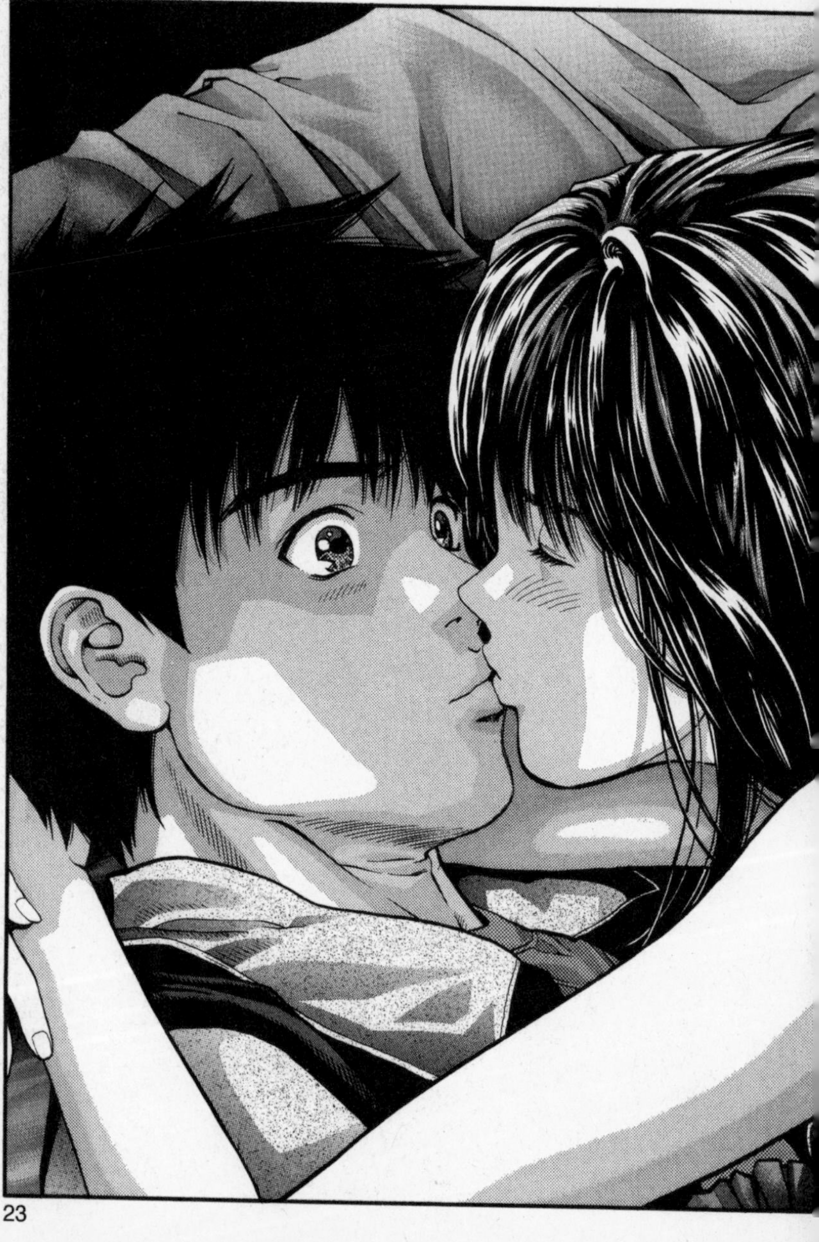

Chapter 56: Reaction

HOW MUCH OF THIS IS REAL? I CAN'T REALLY BELIEVE IT.

IORI HAS HER ARMS WRAPPED AROUND MY NECK.

THIS CLOSENESS... THIS WARMTH...

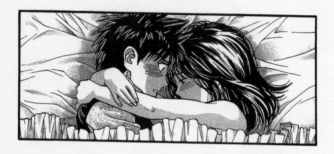

I'M BEING ATTACKED BY A VIOLENT STIMULATION THAT I'VE NEVER FELT BEFORE.

MY MIND HAS GONE COMPLETELY BLANK.

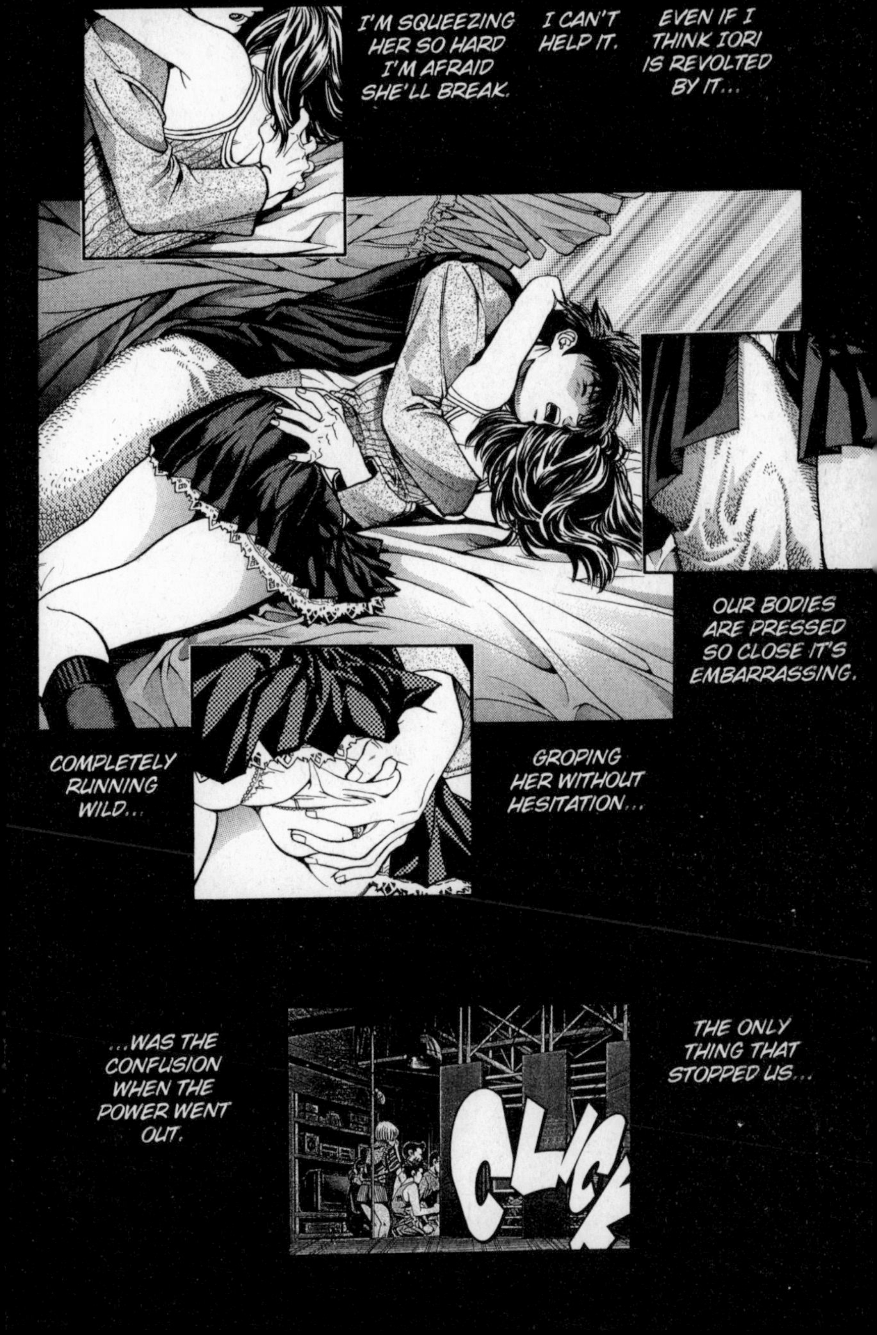
EVEN IF I THINK IORI IS REVOLTED BY IT...
I CAN'T HELP IT.
I'M SQUEEZING HER SO HARD I'M AFRAID SHE'LL BREAK.
OUR BODIES ARE PRESSED SO CLOSE IT'S EMBARRASSING.
GROPING HER WITHOUT HESITATION...
COMPLETELY RUNNING WILD...
THE ONLY THING THAT STOPPED US...
CLICK
...WAS THE CONFUSION WHEN THE POWER WENT OUT.

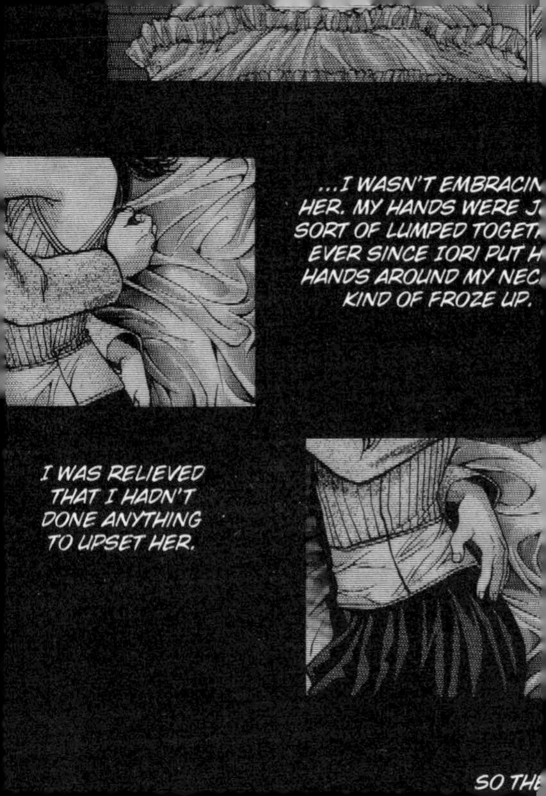
...I WASN'T EMBRACIN HER. MY HANDS WERE J SORT OF LUMPED TOGET EVER SINCE IORI PUT H HANDS AROUND MY NEC KIND OF FROZE UP.
I WAS RELIEVED THAT I HADN'T DONE ANYTHING TO UPSET HER.
SO THE

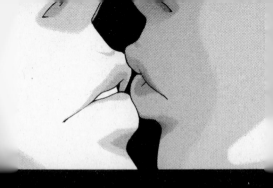

THAT SOFT FEELING
OF TOUCHING HER
LIPS, JUST FOR AN
INSTANT...

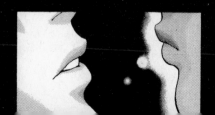

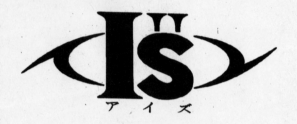

Chapter 56:
Reaction

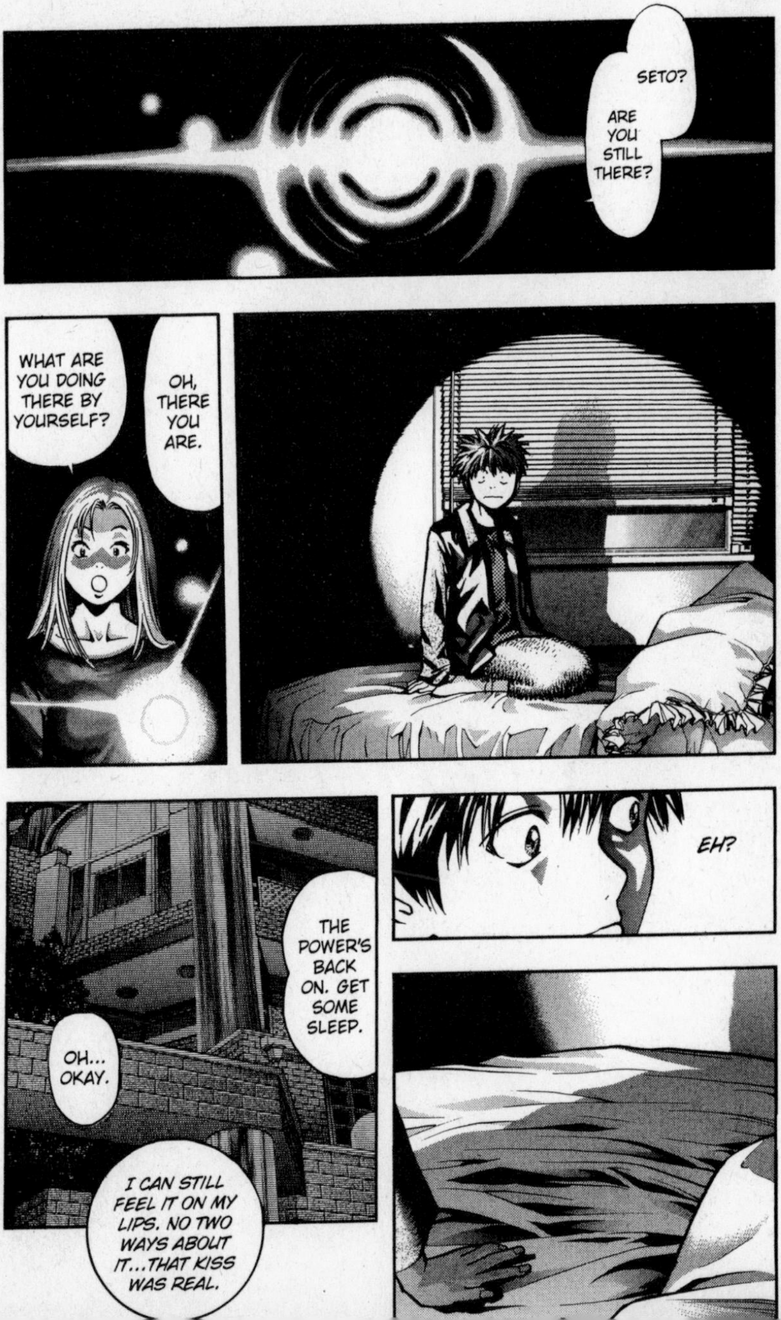
SETO?
ARE YOU STILL THERE?
OH, THERE YOU ARE.
WHAT ARE YOU DOING THERE BY YOURSELF?
EH?
THE POWER'S BACK ON. GET SOME SLEEP.
OH... OKAY.
I CAN STILL FEEL IT ON MY LIPS. NO TWO WAYS ABOUT IT...THAT KISS WAS REAL.

READ THIS WAY

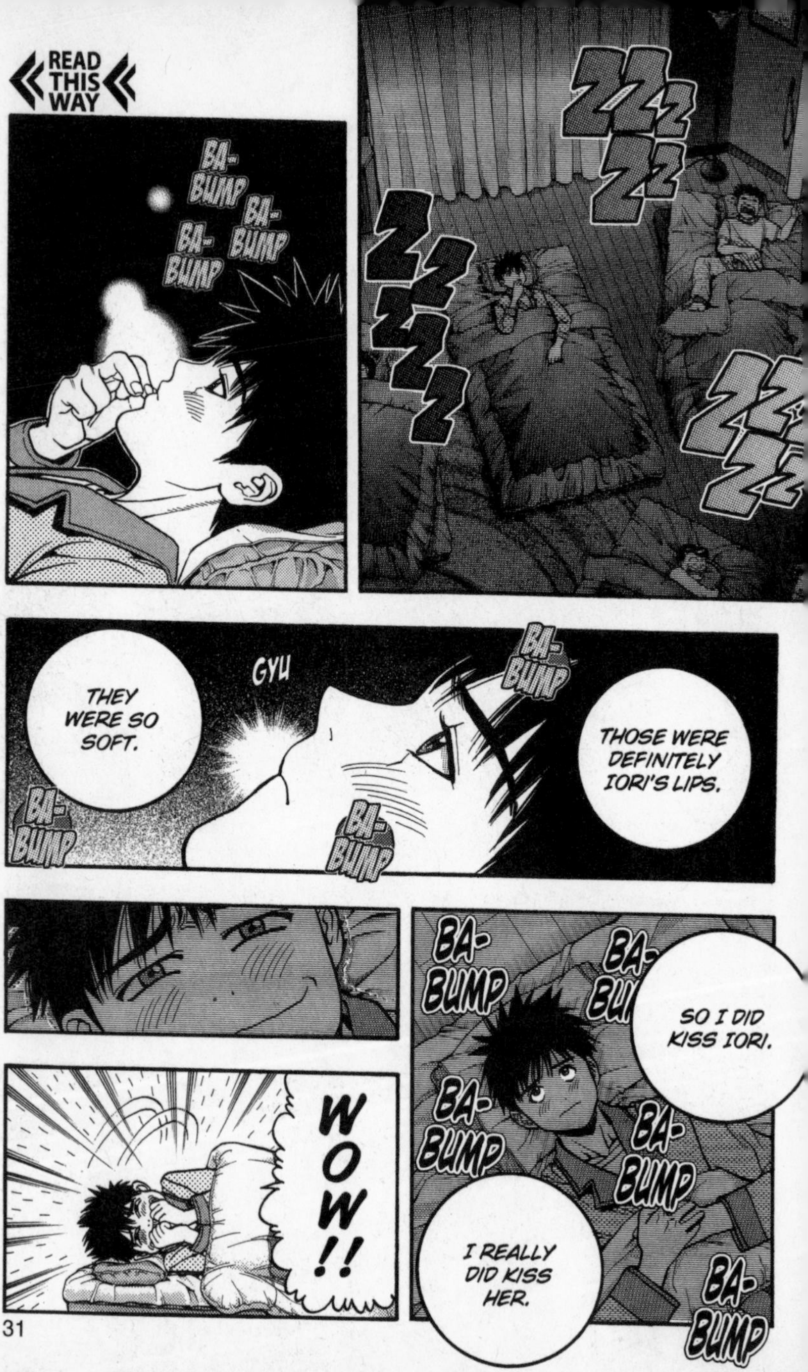

ZZZZZ
ZZZZZZ
ZZZZZ
BA-BUMP
BA-BUMP
BA-BUMP
BA-BUMP
THOSE WERE DEFINITELY IORI'S LIPS.
GYU
THEY WERE SO SOFT.
BA-BUMP
BA-BUMP
BA-BUMP
BA-BUMP
SO I DID KISS IORI.
BA-BUMP
BA-BUMP
I REALLY DID KISS HER.
BA-BUMP
WOW!!

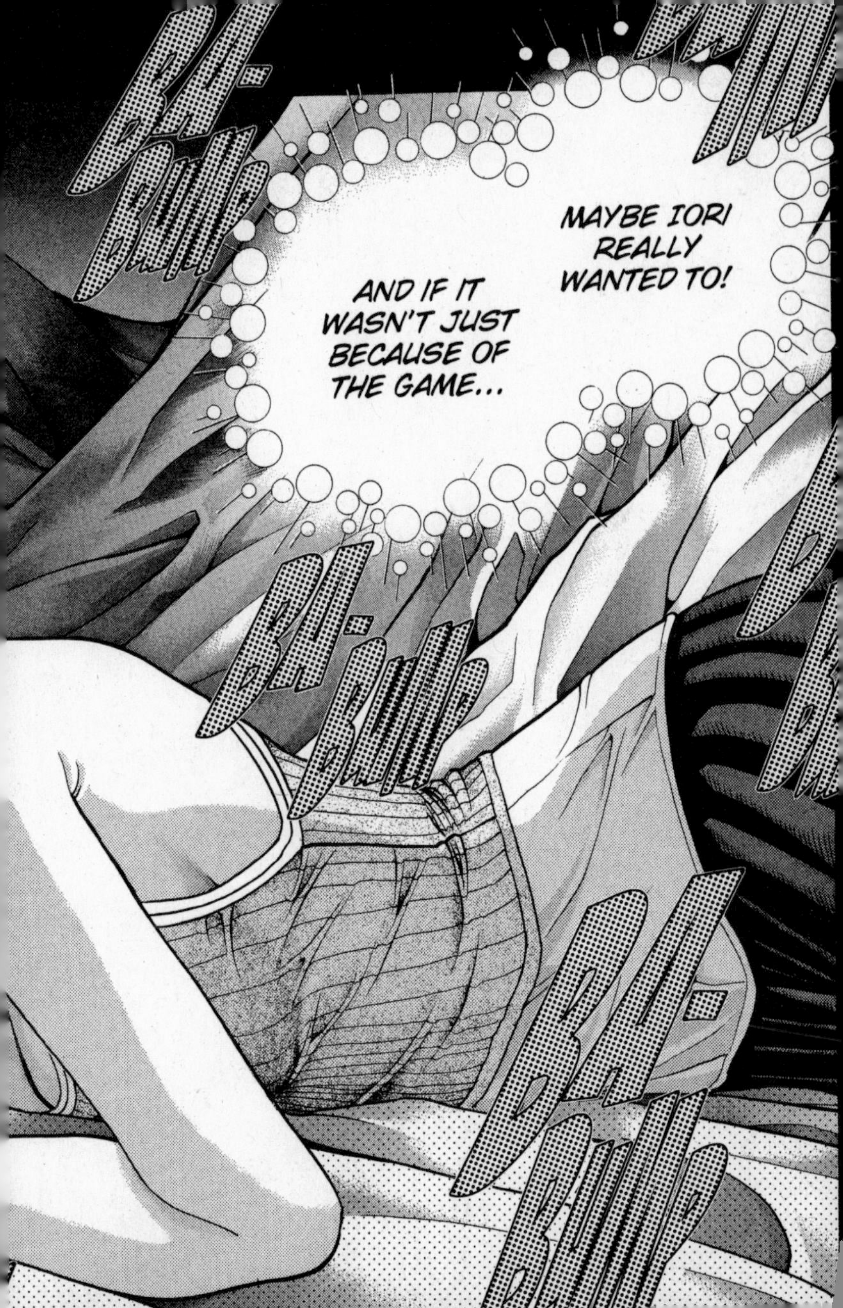
MAYBE IORI REALLY WANTED TO!
AND IF IT WASN'T JUST BECAUSE OF THE GAME...

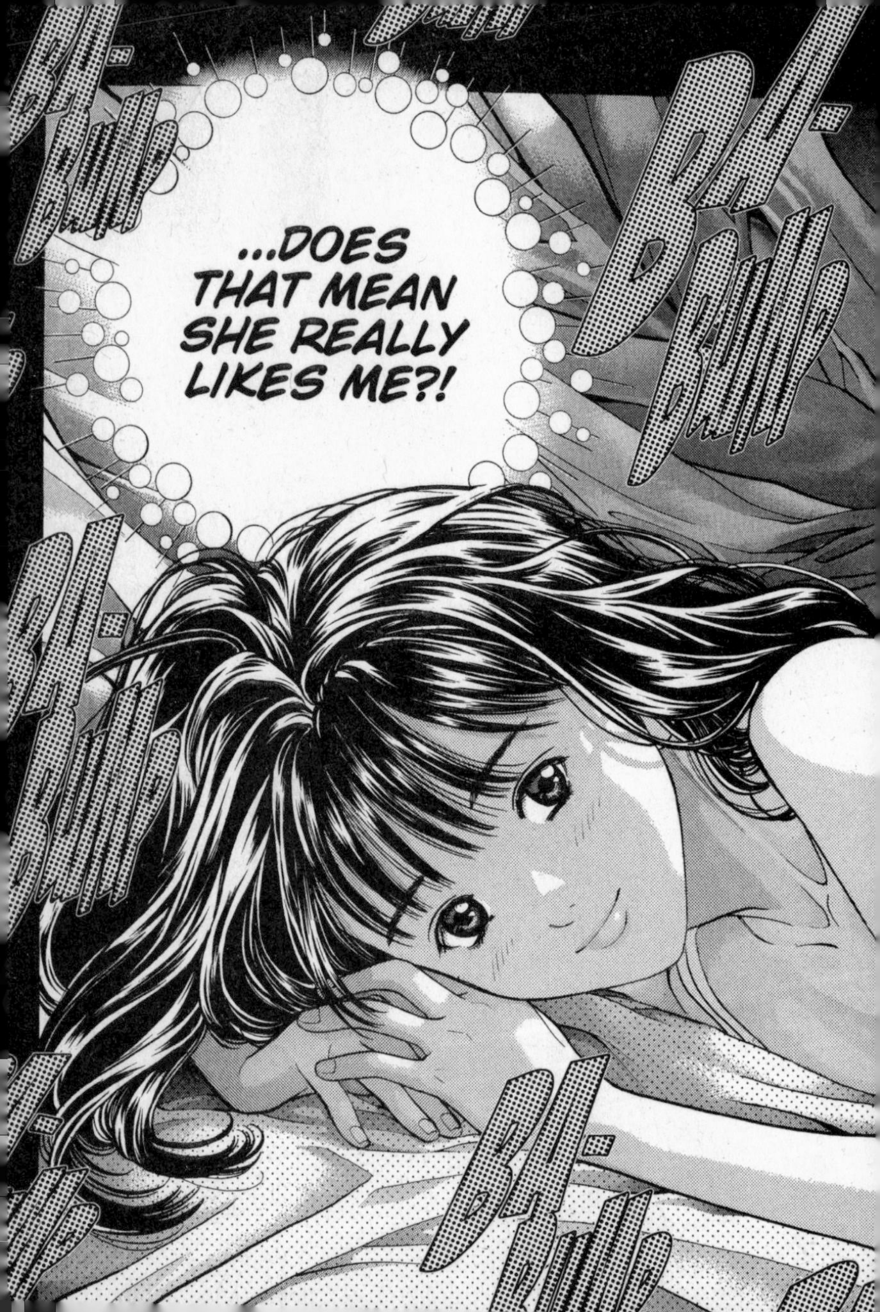
...DOES THAT MEAN SHE REALLY LIKES ME?!

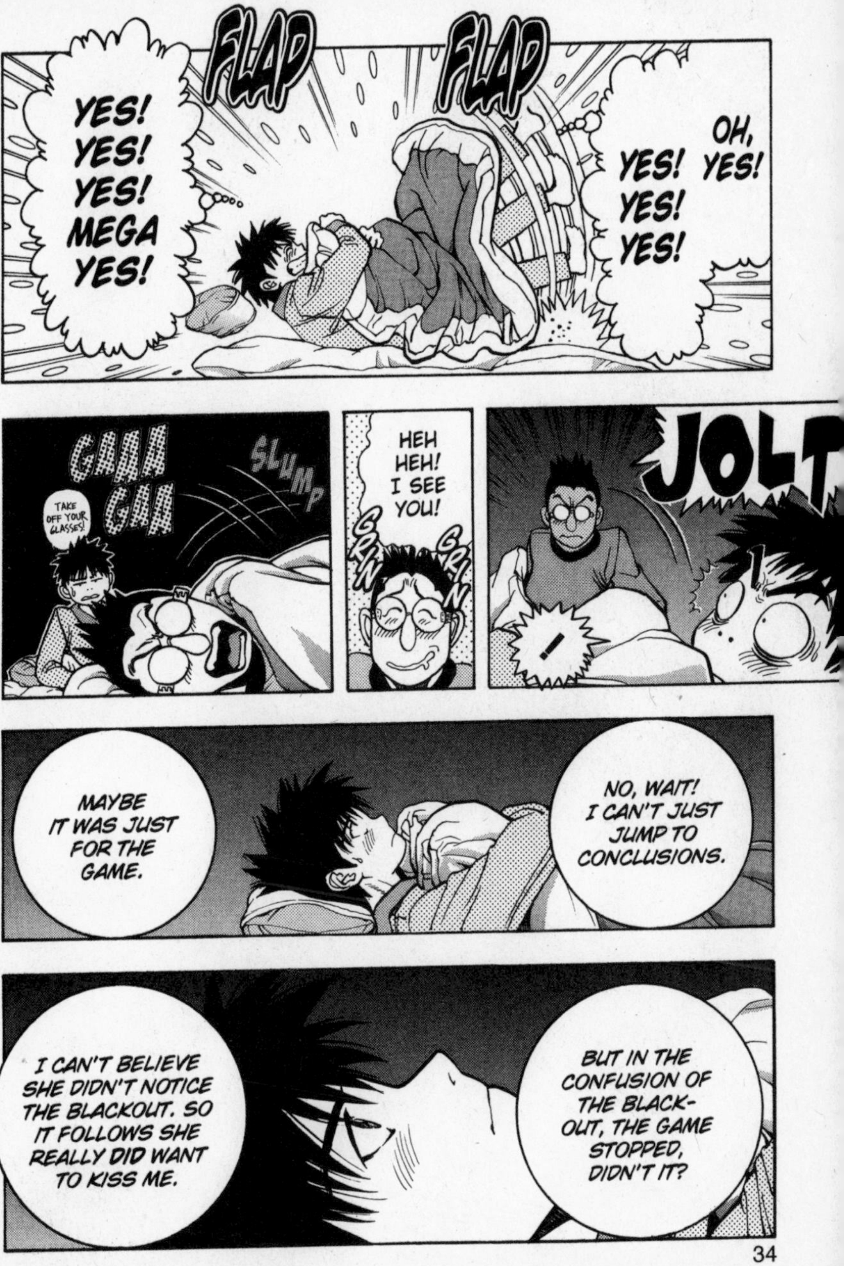
FLAP
FLAP
OH, YES!
YES! YES! YES!
YES! YES! YES! MEGA YES!
JOLT
!
HEH HEH! I SEE YOU!
GRIN GRIN
SLUMP
GUAA GUA
TAKE OFF YOUR GLASSES!
NO, WAIT! I CAN'T JUST JUMP TO CONCLUSIONS.
MAYBE IT WAS JUST FOR THE GAME.
BUT IN THE CONFUSION OF THE BLACK-OUT, THE GAME STOPPED, DIDN'T IT?
I CAN'T BELIEVE SHE DIDN'T NOTICE THE BLACKOUT. SO IT FOLLOWS SHE REALLY DID WANT TO KISS ME.

READ THIS WAY

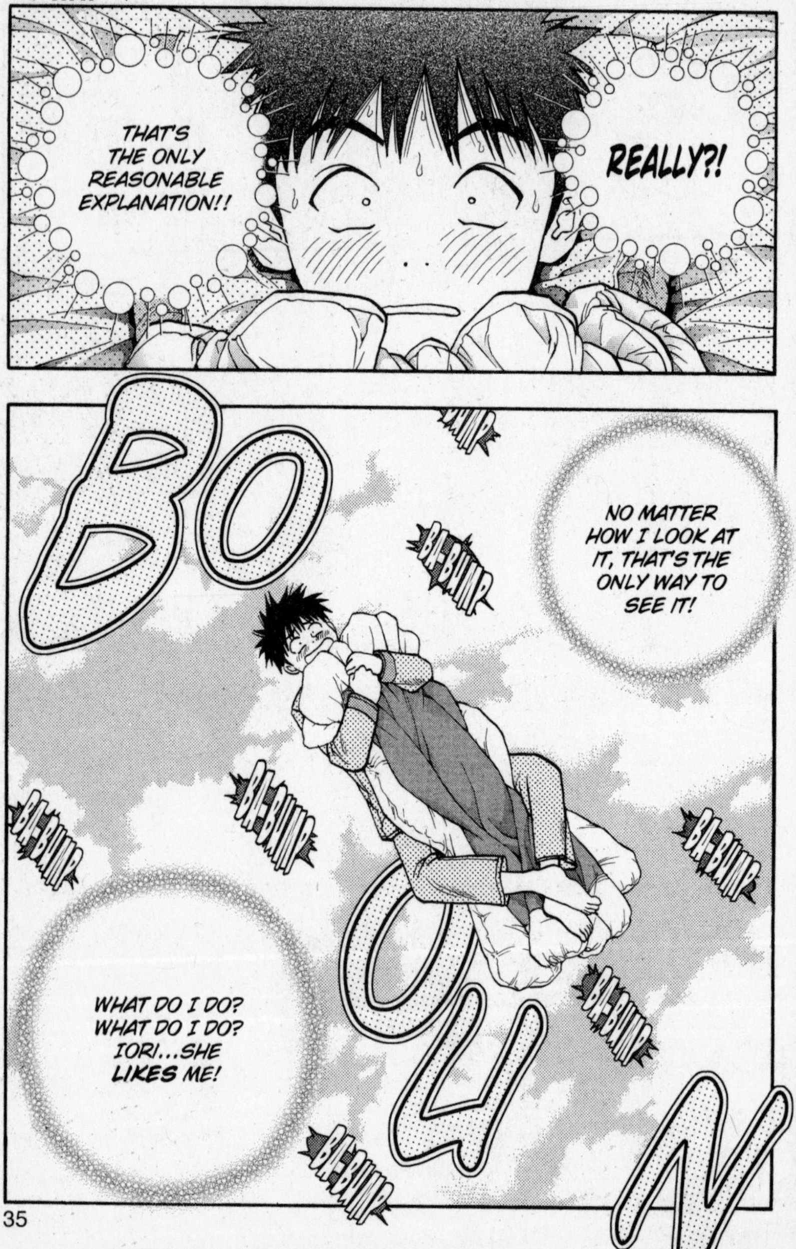
REALLY?!
THAT'S THE ONLY REASONABLE EXPLANATION!!
BA-BUMP
NO MATTER HOW I LOOK AT IT, THAT'S THE ONLY WAY TO SEE IT!
BA-BUMP
BA-BUMP
BA-BUMP
BA-BUMP
BA-BUMP
WHAT DO I DO? WHAT DO I DO? IORI...SHE LIKES ME!
BA-BUMP

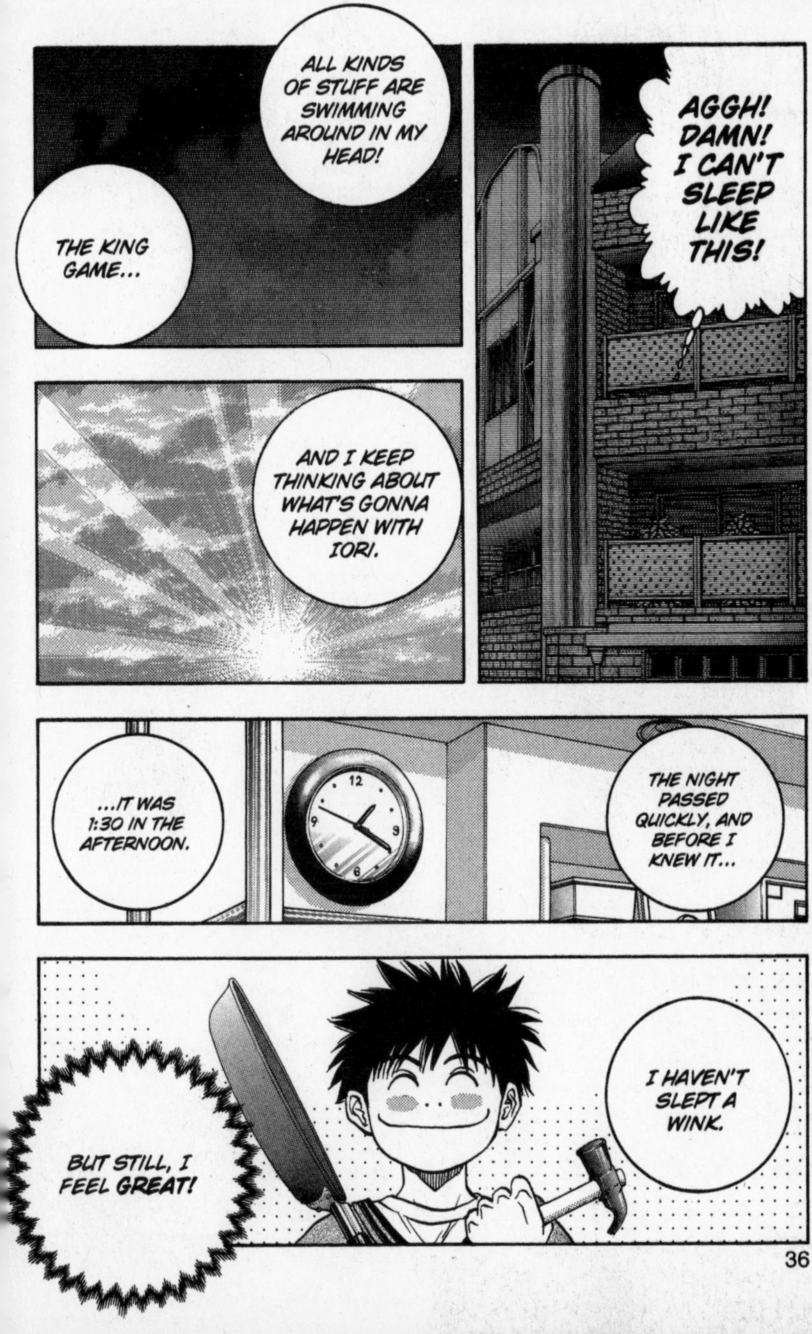
AGGH! DAMN! I CAN'T SLEEP LIKE THIS!
ALL KINDS OF STUFF ARE SWIMMING AROUND IN MY HEAD!
THE KING GAME...
AND I KEEP THINKING ABOUT WHAT'S GONNA HAPPEN WITH IORI.
THE NIGHT PASSED QUICKLY, AND BEFORE I KNEW IT...
...IT WAS 1:30 IN THE AFTERNOON.
I HAVEN'T SLEPT A WINK.
BUT STILL, I FEEL GREAT!

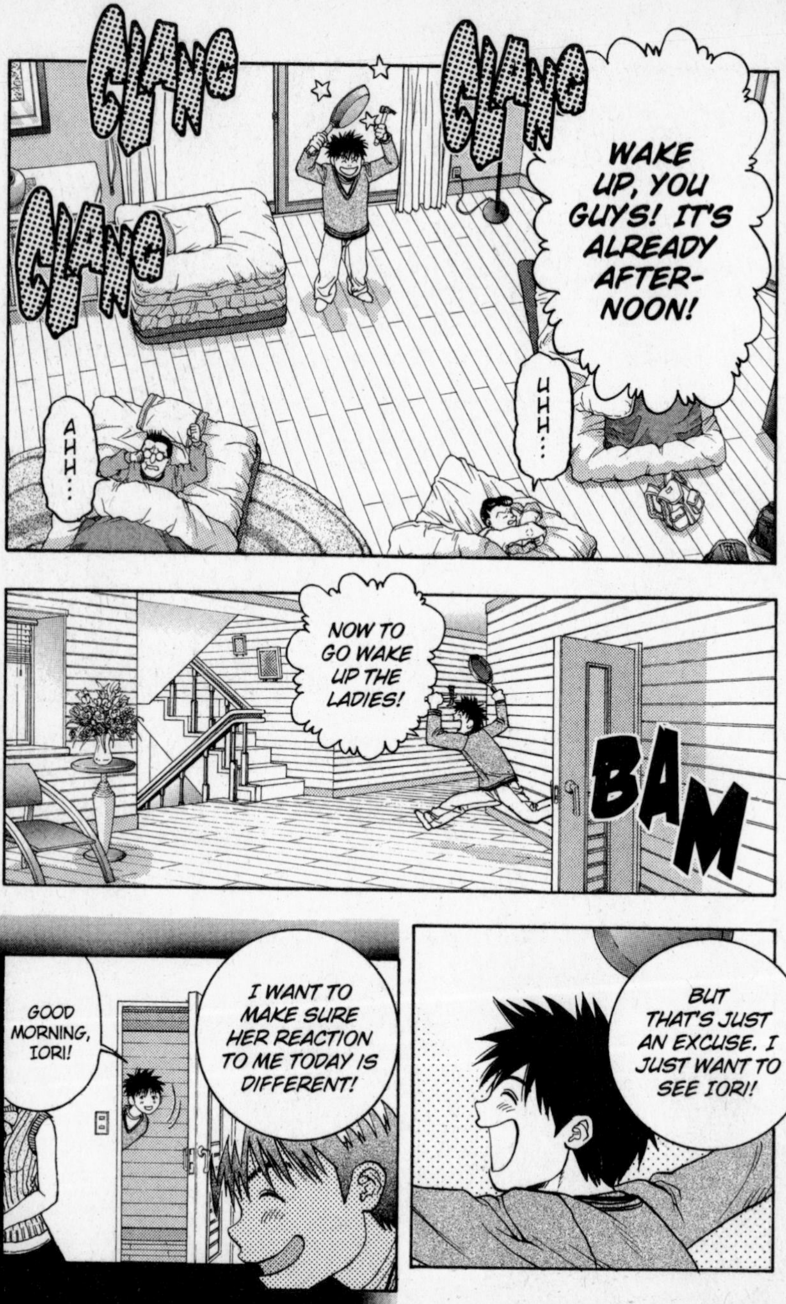
CLANG
CLANG
CLANG
AHH...
UHH...
WAKE UP, YOU GUYS! IT'S ALREADY AFTER-NOON!
NOW TO GO WAKE UP THE LADIES!
BAM
GOOD MORNING, IORI!
I WANT TO MAKE SURE HER REACTION TO ME TODAY IS DIFFERENT!
BUT THAT'S JUST AN EXCUSE. I JUST WANT TO SEE IORI!

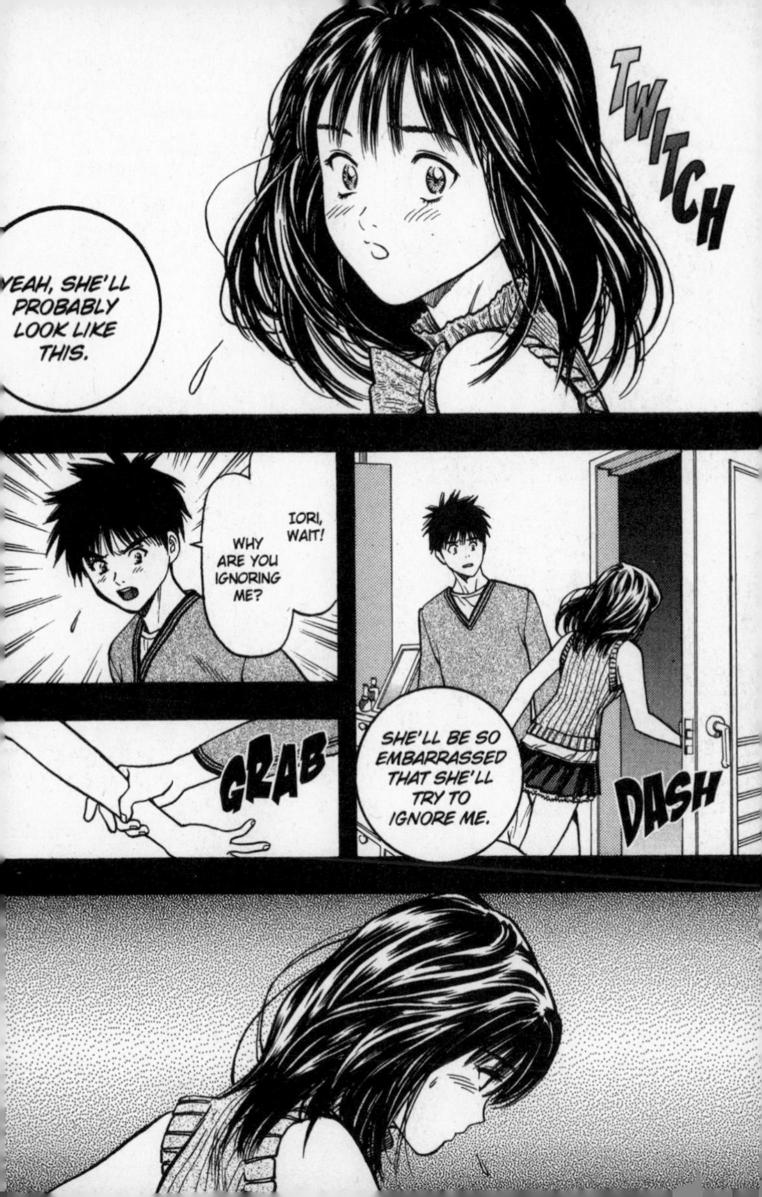
TWITCH
YEAH, SHE'LL PROBABLY LOOK LIKE THIS.
SHE'LL BE SO EMBARRASSED THAT SHE'LL TRY TO IGNORE ME.
DASH
IORI, WAIT!
WHY ARE YOU IGNORING ME?
GRAB

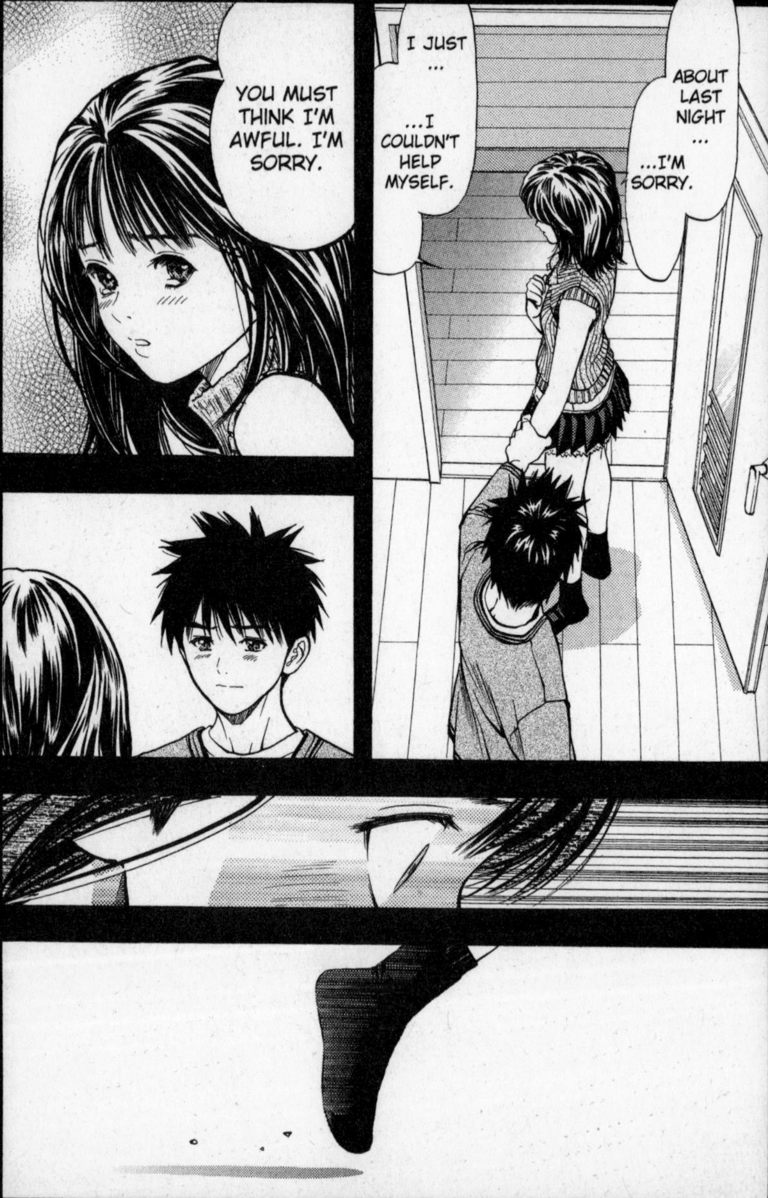
ABOUT LAST NIGHT ... ...I'M SORRY.
I JUST ... ...I COULDN'T HELP MYSELF.
YOU MUST THINK I'M AWFUL. I'M SORRY.

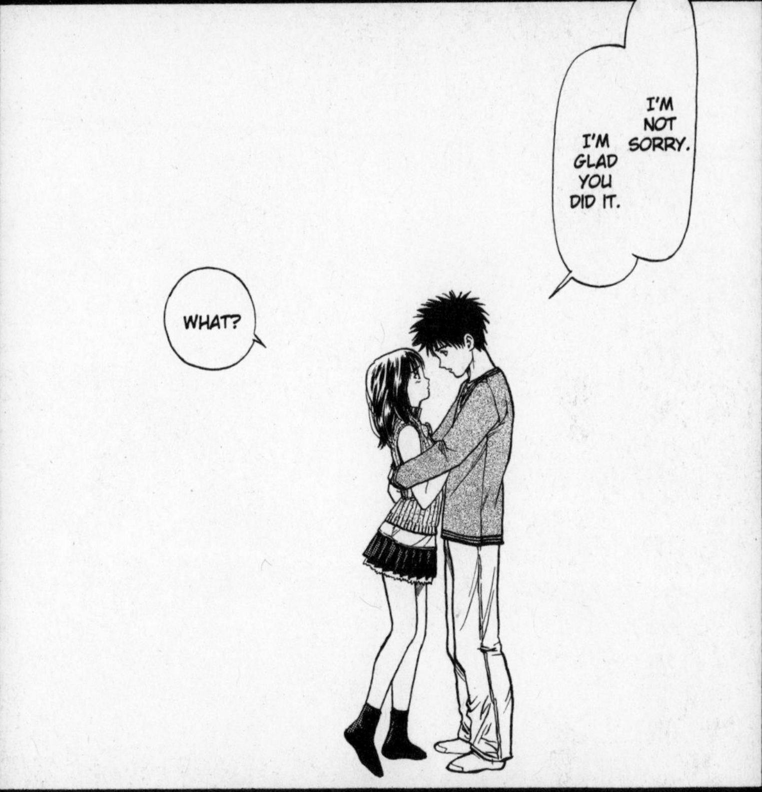
I'M NOT SORRY.
I'M GLAD YOU DID IT.
WHAT?
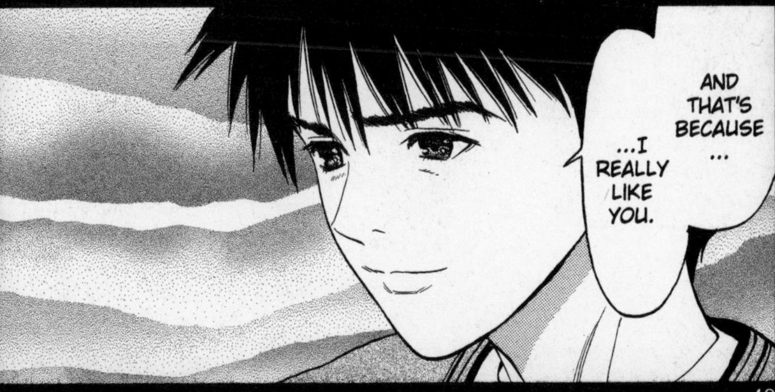
AND THAT'S BECAUSE ...
...I REALLY LIKE YOU.

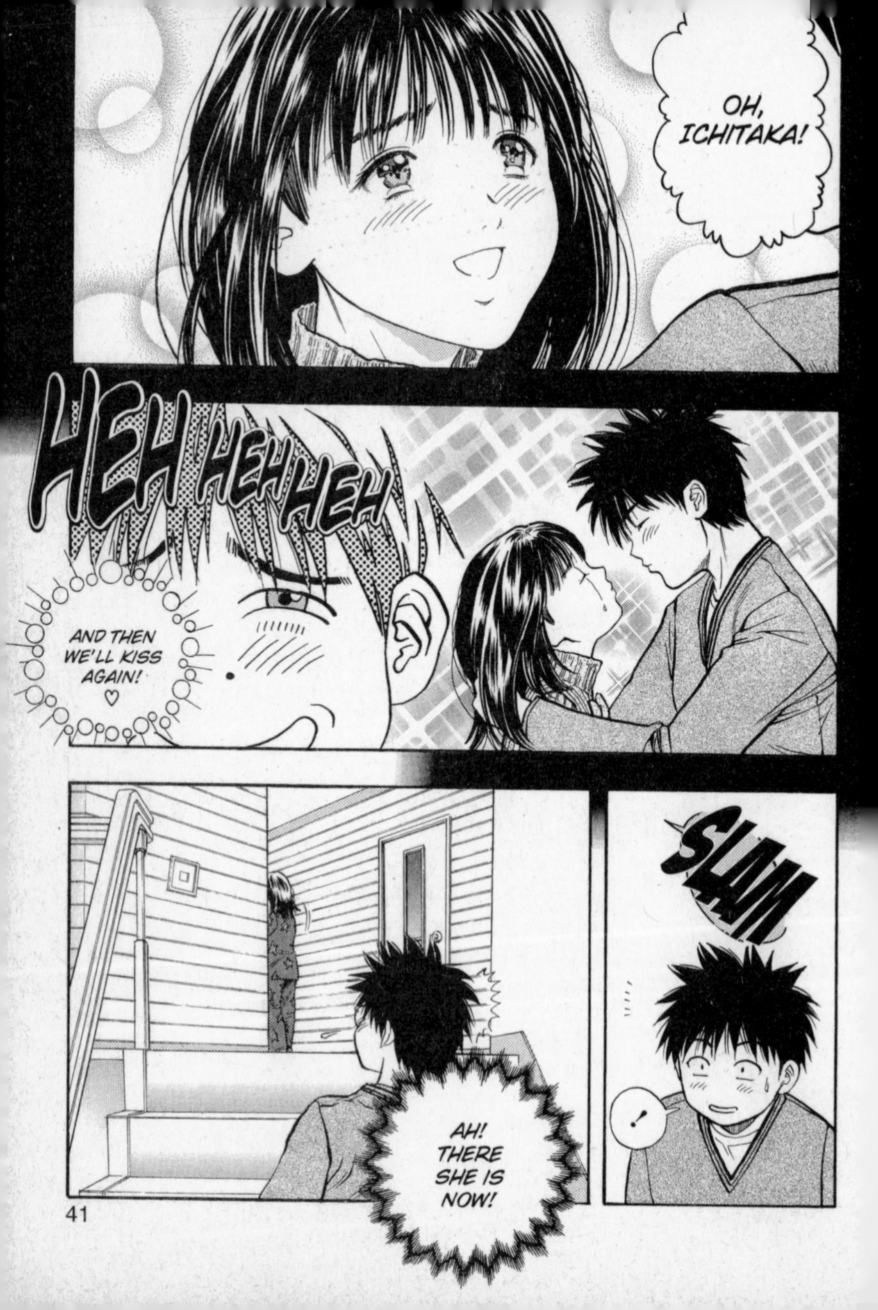
OH, ICHITAKA!
HEH HEH HEH
AND THEN WE'LL KISS AGAIN! ♡
SLAM
...
!
AH! THERE SHE IS NOW!

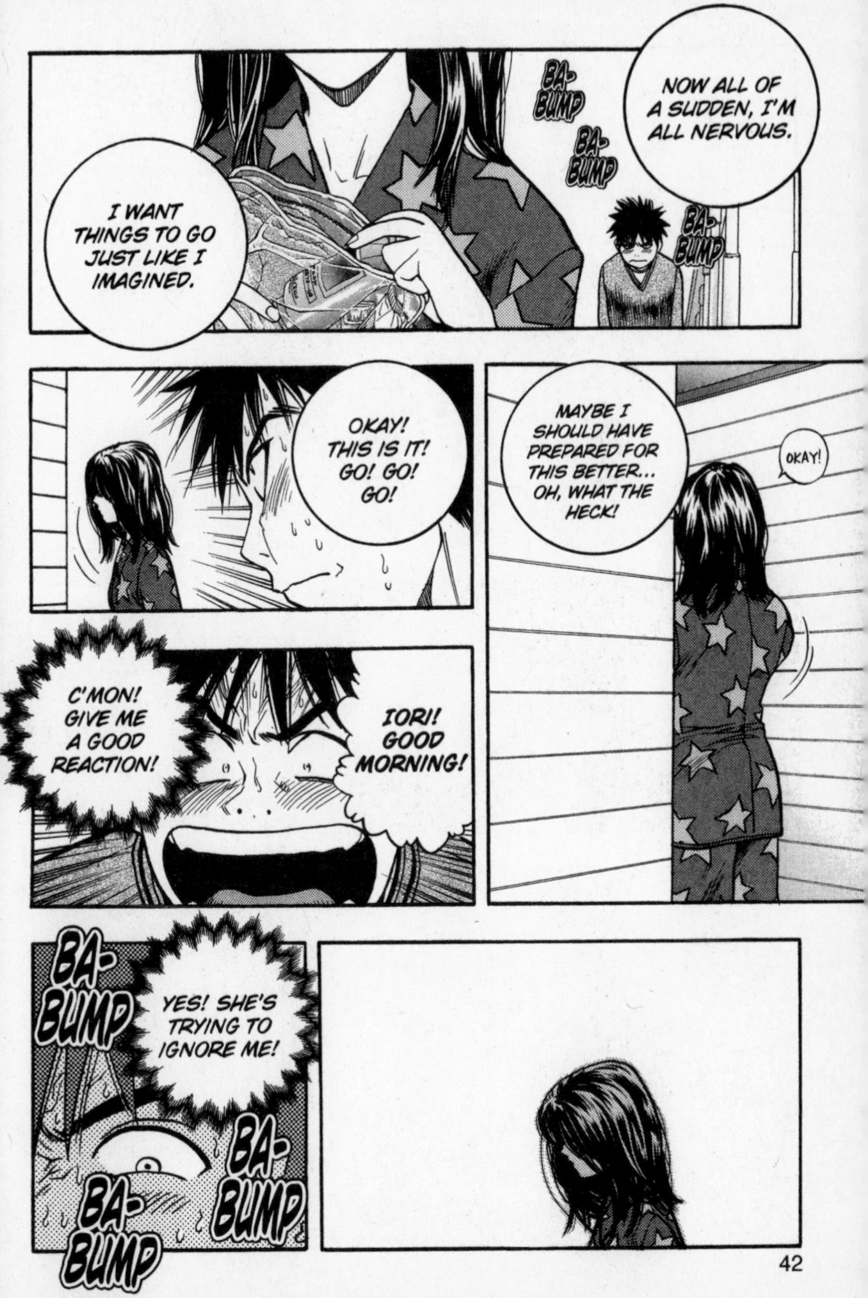
NOW ALL OF A SUDDEN, I'M ALL NERVOUS.
BA-BUMP
BA-BUMP
BA-BUMP
I WANT THINGS TO GO JUST LIKE I IMAGINED.
MAYBE I SHOULD HAVE PREPARED FOR THIS BETTER... OH, WHAT THE HECK!
OKAY!
OKAY! THIS IS IT! GO! GO! GO!
IORI! GOOD MORNING!
C'MON! GIVE ME A GOOD REACTION!
BA-BUMP
YES! SHE'S TRYING TO IGNORE ME!
BA-BUMP
BA-BUMP

« READ THIS WAY «

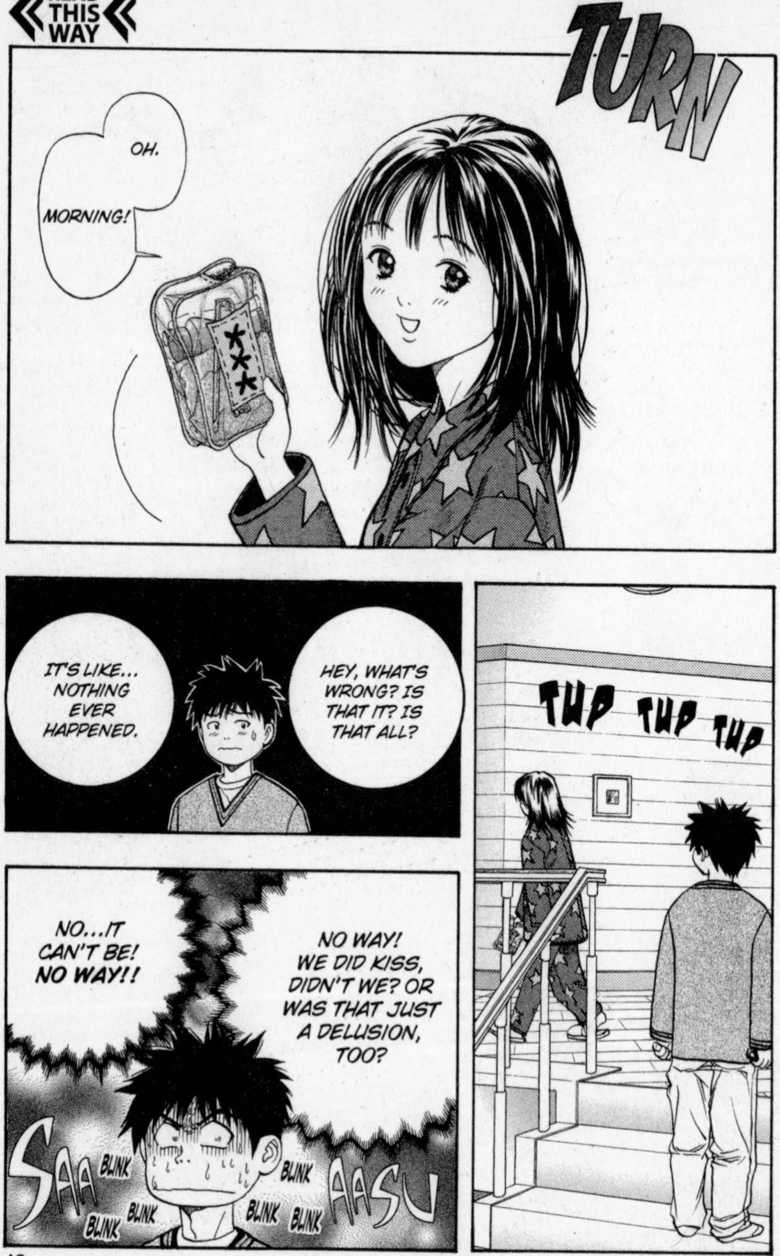
TURN
OH.
MORNING!
TUP TUP TUP
HEY, WHAT'S WRONG? IS THAT IT? IS THAT ALL?
IT'S LIKE... NOTHING EVER HAPPENED.
NO WAY! WE DID KISS, DIDN'T WE? OR WAS THAT JUST A DELUSION, TOO?
NO...IT CAN'T BE! NO WAY!!
SAA AASU
BLINK BLINK BLINK BLINK BLINK BLINK

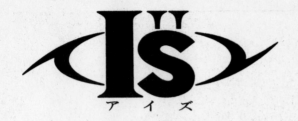

Chapter 57:
Teratani's Scenario

READ THIS WAY

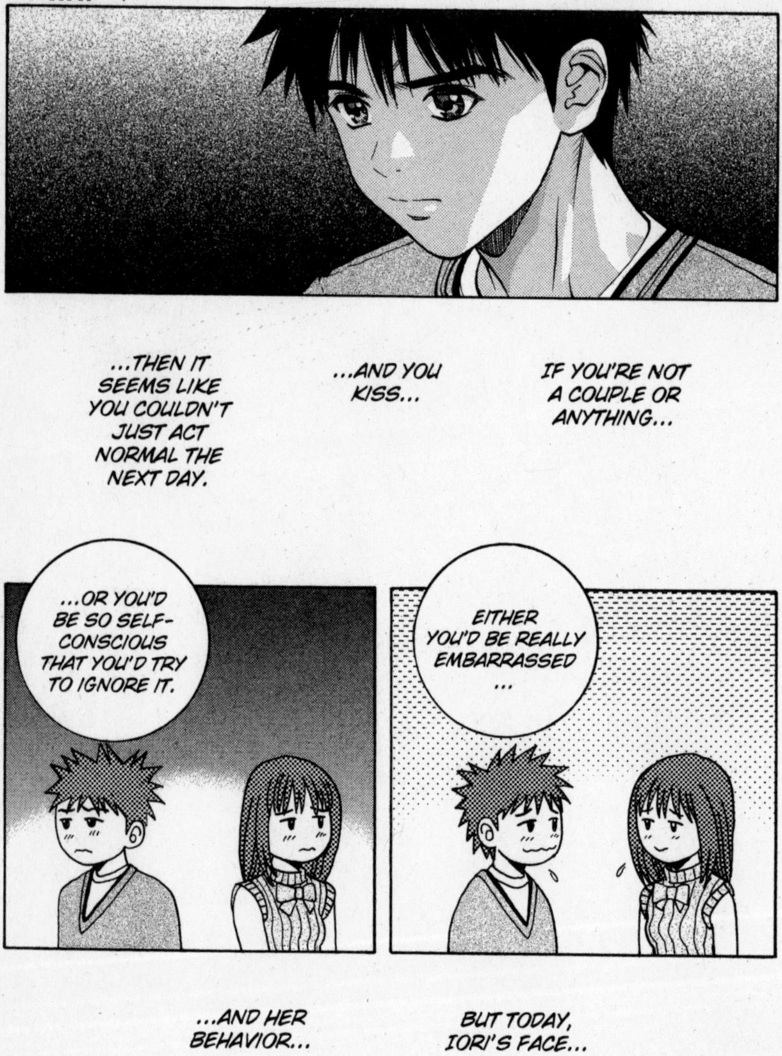

IF YOU'RE NOT A COUPLE OR ANYTHING...
...AND YOU KISS...
...THEN IT SEEMS LIKE YOU COULDN'T JUST ACT NORMAL THE NEXT DAY.
EITHER YOU'D BE REALLY EMBARRASSED ...
...OR YOU'D BE SO SELF-CONSCIOUS THAT YOU'D TRY TO IGNORE IT.
BUT TODAY, IORI'S FACE...
...AND HER BEHAVIOR...

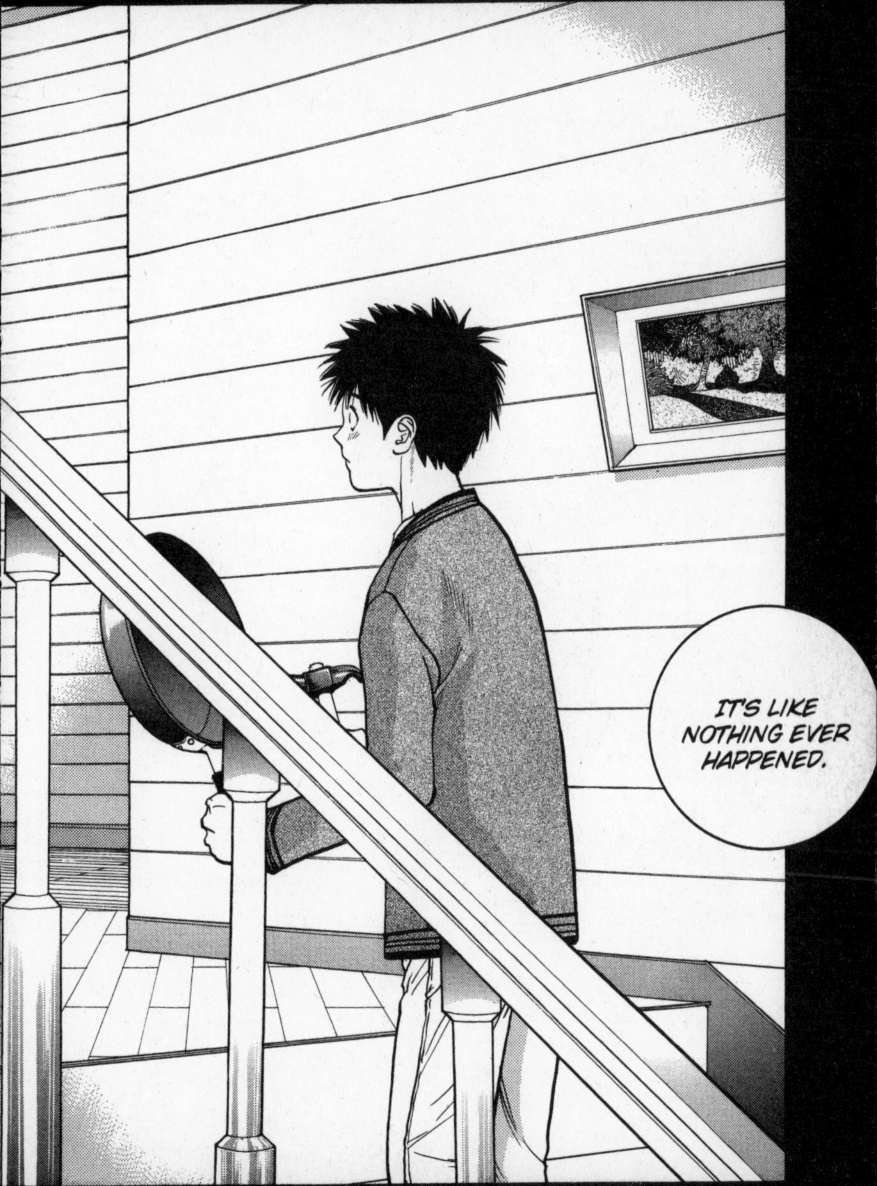
IT'S LIKE NOTHING EVER HAPPENED.

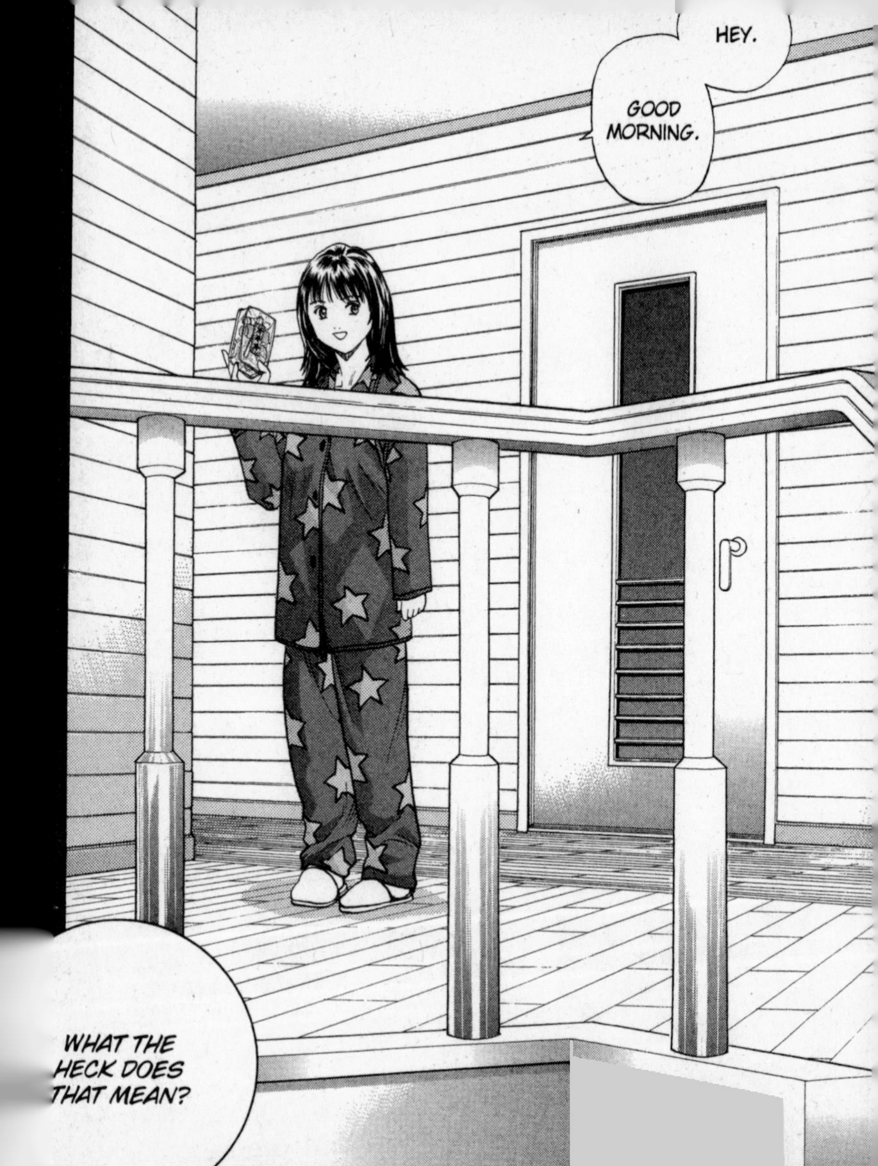
HEY.
GOOD MORNING.
WHAT THE HECK DOES THAT MEAN?

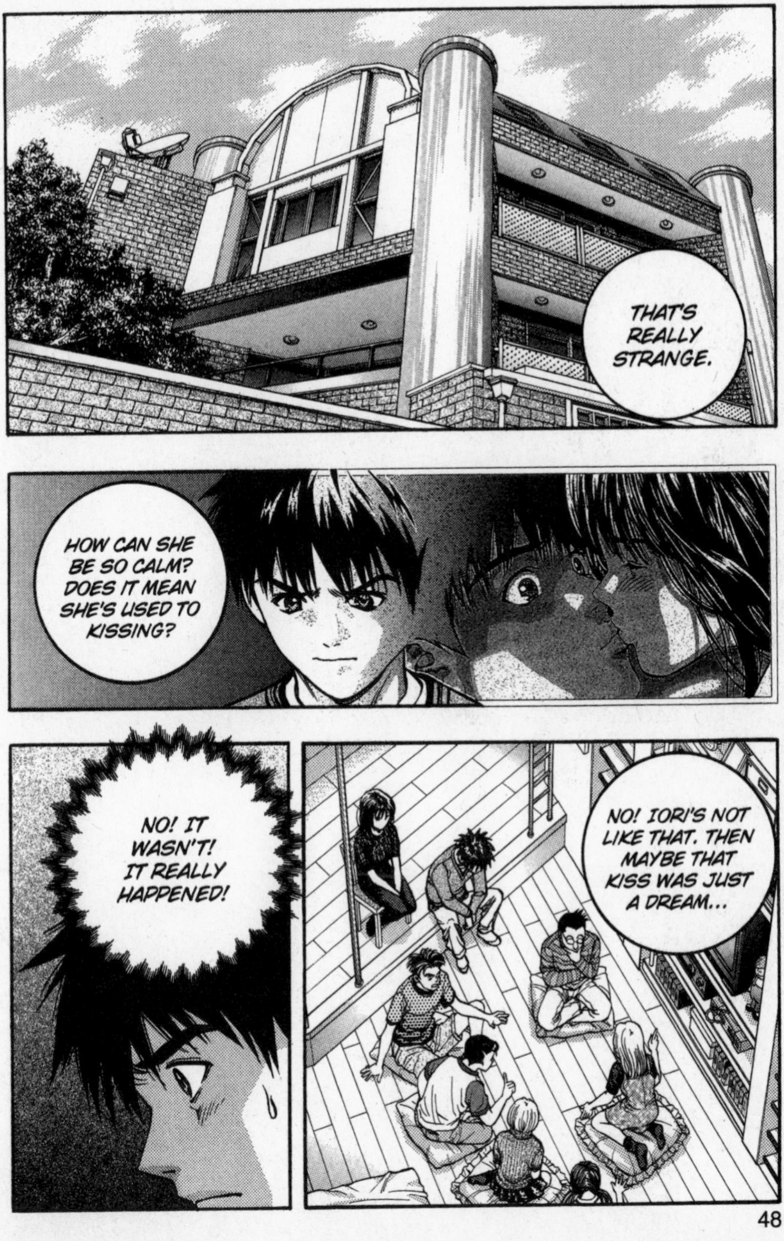
THAT'S REALLY STRANGE.
HOW CAN SHE BE SO CALM? DOES IT MEAN SHE'S USED TO KISSING?
NO! IORI'S NOT LIKE THAT. THEN MAYBE THAT KISS WAS JUST A DREAM...
NO! IT WASN'T! IT REALLY HAPPENED!

READ THIS WAY

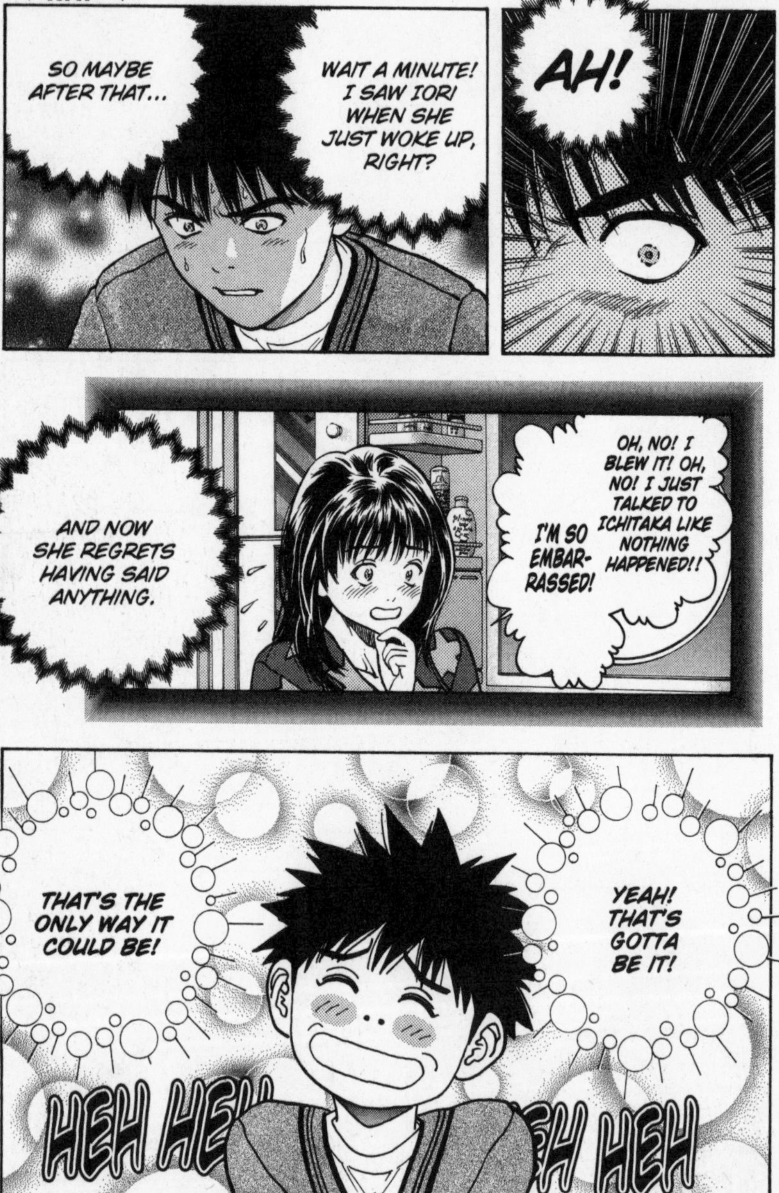
AH!
WAIT A MINUTE! I SAW IORI WHEN SHE JUST WOKE UP, RIGHT?
SO MAYBE AFTER THAT...
OH, NO! I BLEW IT! OH, NO! I JUST TALKED TO ICHITAKA LIKE NOTHING HAPPENED!!
I'M SO EMBARRASSED!
AND NOW SHE REGRETS HAVING SAID ANYTHING.
YEAH! THAT'S GOTTA BE IT!
THAT'S THE ONLY WAY IT COULD BE!
HEH HEH
HEH HEH

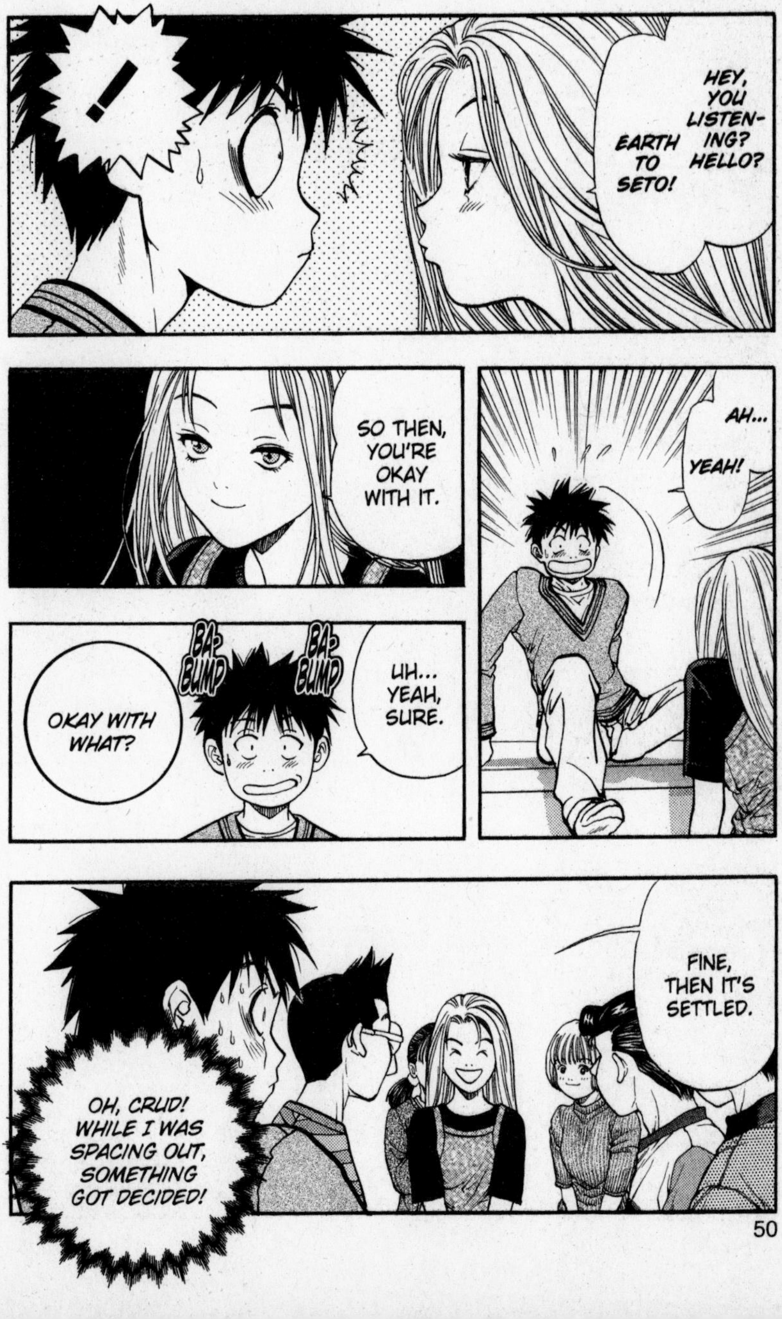
!
HEY, YOU LISTENING? HELLO?
EARTH TO SETO!
AH...
YEAH!
SO THEN, YOU'RE OKAY WITH IT.
UH... YEAH, SURE.
BA-BUMP
BA-BUMP
OKAY WITH WHAT?
FINE, THEN IT'S SETTLED.
OH, CRUD! WHILE I WAS SPACING OUT, SOMETHING GOT DECIDED!

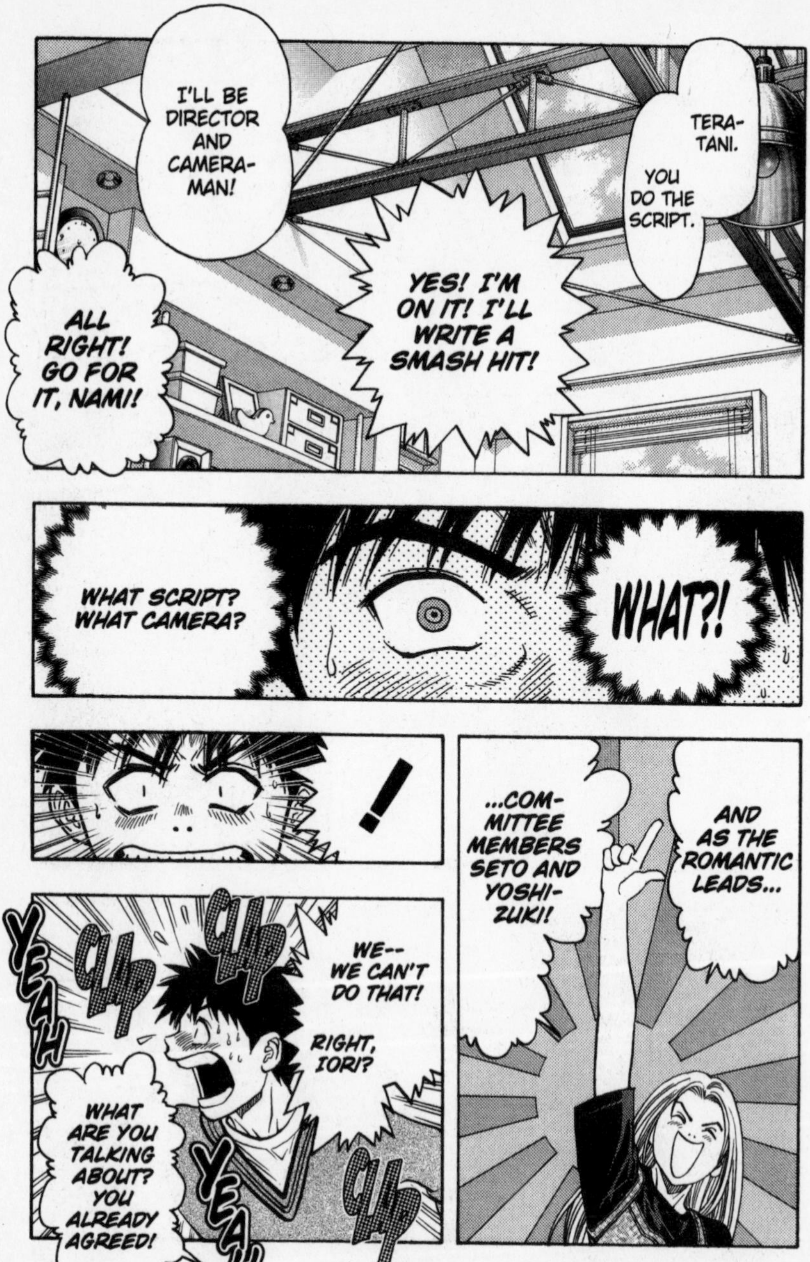
I'LL BE DIRECTOR AND CAMERA-MAN!
TERA-TANI.
YOU DO THE SCRIPT.
YES! I'M ON IT! I'LL WRITE A SMASH HIT!
ALL RIGHT! GO FOR IT, NAMI!
WHAT?!
WHAT SCRIPT? WHAT CAMERA?
AND AS THE ROMANTIC LEADS...
...COM-MITTEE MEMBERS SETO AND YOSHI-ZUKI!
!
CLAP
CLAP
YEAH
WE-- WE CAN'T DO THAT!
RIGHT, IORI?
CLAP
YEAH
WHAT ARE YOU TALKING ABOUT? YOU ALREADY AGREED!

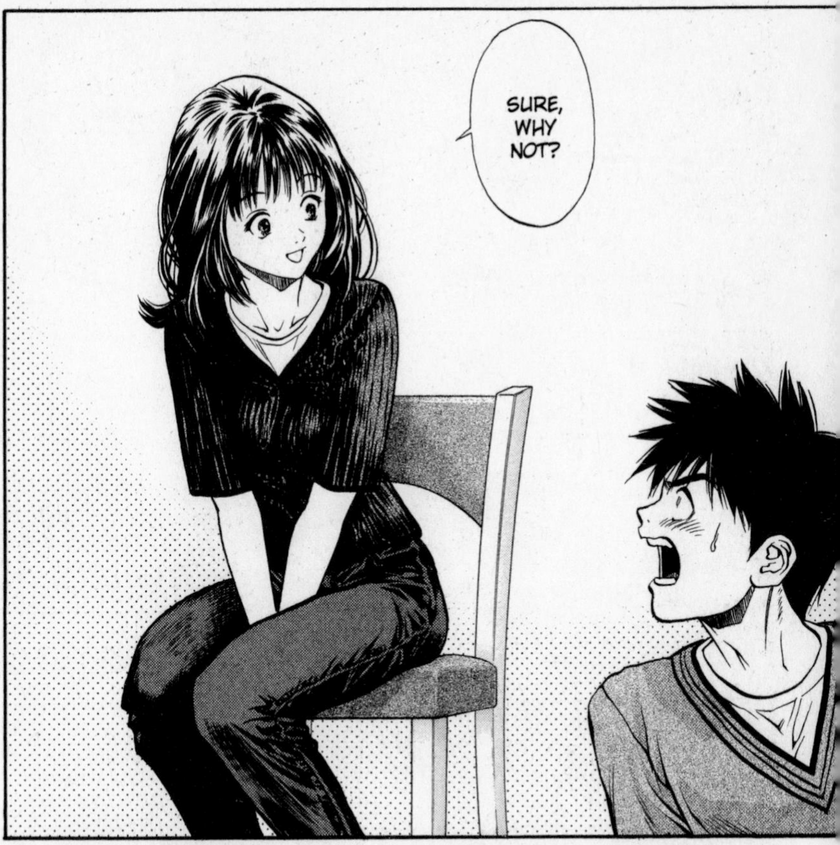
SURE, WHY NOT?
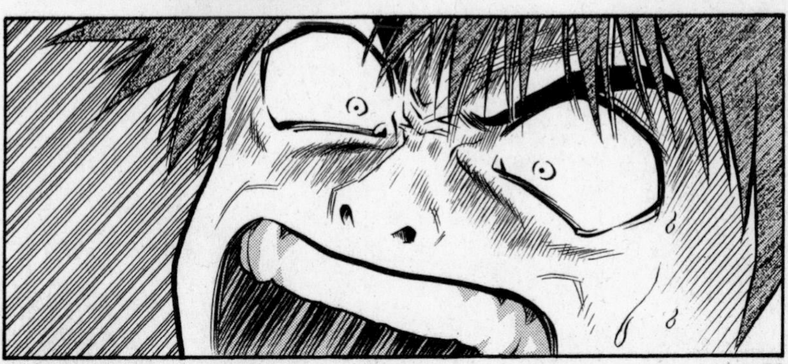

READ THIS WAY

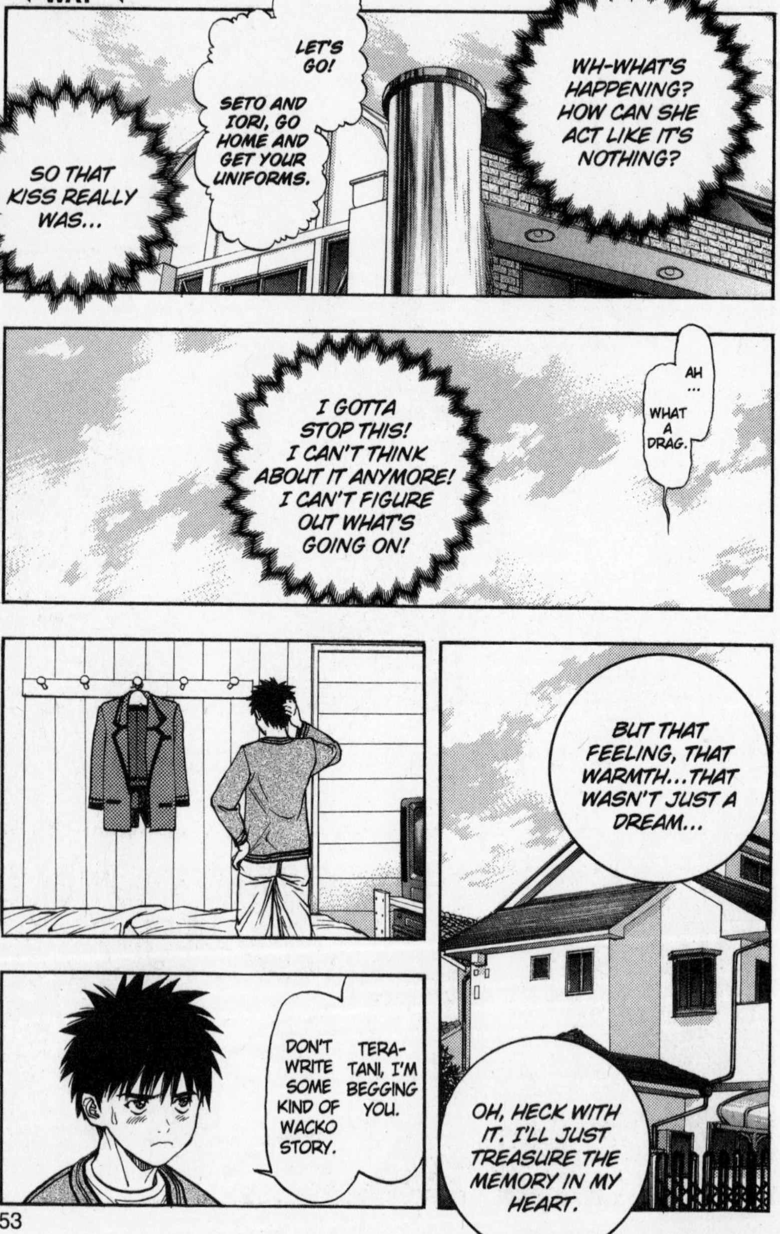
WH-WHAT'S HAPPENING? HOW CAN SHE ACT LIKE IT'S NOTHING?
LET'S GO!
SETO AND IORI, GO HOME AND GET YOUR UNIFORMS.
SO THAT KISS REALLY WAS...
AH... WHAT A DRAG.
I GOTTA STOP THIS! I CAN'T THINK ABOUT IT ANYMORE! I CAN'T FIGURE OUT WHAT'S GOING ON!
BUT THAT FEELING, THAT WARMTH...THAT WASN'T JUST A DREAM...
OH, HECK WITH IT. I'LL JUST TREASURE THE MEMORY IN MY HEART.
TERA-TANI, I'M BEGGING YOU.
DON'T WRITE SOME KIND OF WACKO STORY.

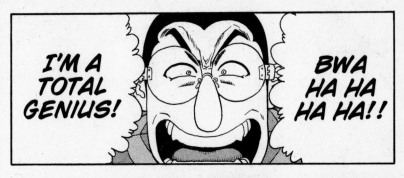

BWA HA HA HA HA!!
I'M A TOTAL GENIUS!
YOU MEAN YOU'RE ALREADY DONE? NO WAY!
OF COURSE!
BEFORE I SHOW ANYBODY ELSE, I'M GOING TO LET YOU HAVE A PEEK. BUT IT'S TOP SECRET!
WHAT'S SO TOP SECRET?
PASSION AT WANDA HIGH
BY YASUMASA TERATANI
……
I GOT A BAD FEELING ABOUT THIS.

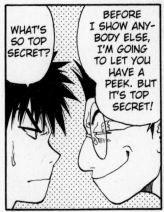

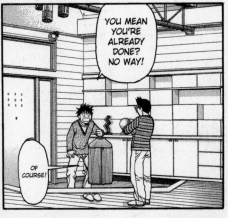

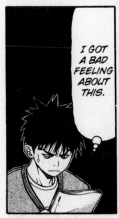

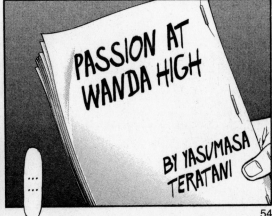

READ THIS WAY

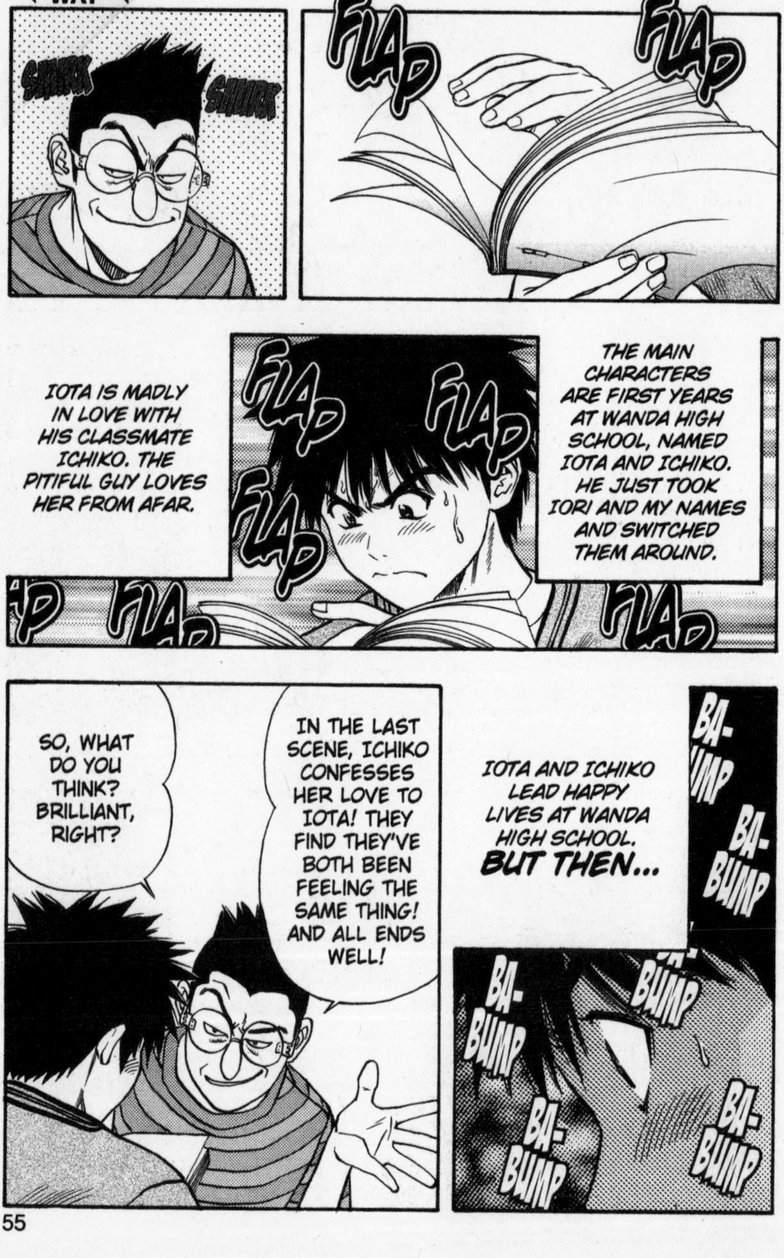
FLAP
FLAP
THE MAIN CHARACTERS ARE FIRST YEARS AT WANDA HIGH SCHOOL, NAMED IOTA AND ICHIKO. HE JUST TOOK IORI AND MY NAMES AND SWITCHED THEM AROUND.
FLAP
FLAP
FLAP
FLAP
IOTA IS MADLY IN LOVE WITH HIS CLASSMATE ICHIKO. THE PITIFUL GUY LOVES HER FROM AFAR.
BA-BUMP
BA-BUMP
IOTA AND ICHIKO LEAD HAPPY LIVES AT WANDA HIGH SCHOOL. **BUT THEN...**
IN THE LAST SCENE, ICHIKO CONFESSES HER LOVE TO IOTA! THEY FIND THEY'VE BOTH BEEN FEELING THE SAME THING! AND ALL ENDS WELL!
SO, WHAT DO YOU THINK? BRILLIANT, RIGHT?
BA-BUMP
BA-BUMP
BA-BUMP
BA-BUMP

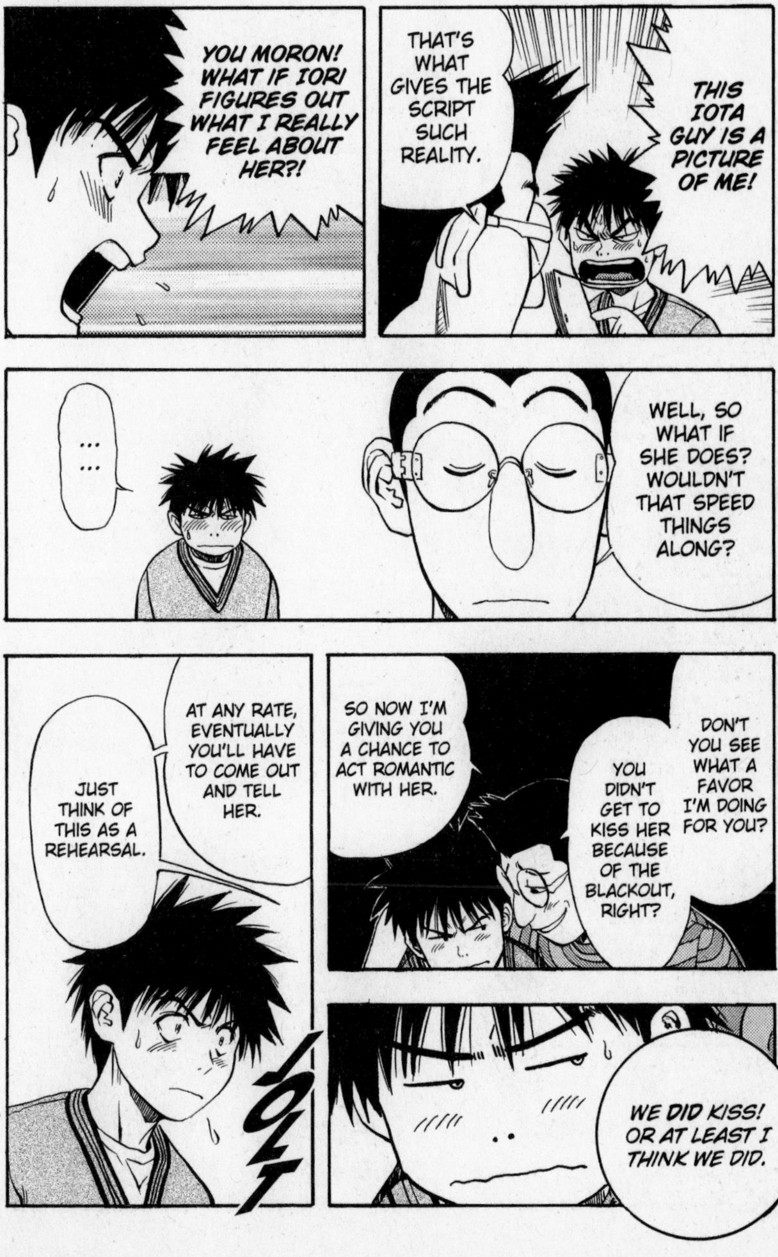
THIS IOTA GUY IS A PICTURE OF ME!
THAT'S WHAT GIVES THE SCRIPT SUCH REALITY.
YOU MORON! WHAT IF IORI FIGURES OUT WHAT I REALLY FEEL ABOUT HER?!
WELL, SO WHAT IF SHE DOES? WOULDN'T THAT SPEED THINGS ALONG?
......
DON'T YOU SEE WHAT A FAVOR I'M DOING FOR YOU?
YOU DIDN'T GET TO KISS HER BECAUSE OF THE BLACKOUT, RIGHT?
SO NOW I'M GIVING YOU A CHANCE TO ACT ROMANTIC WITH HER.
WE DID KISS! OR AT LEAST I THINK WE DID.
AT ANY RATE, EVENTUALLY YOU'LL HAVE TO COME OUT AND TELL HER.
JUST THINK OF THIS AS A REHEARSAL.
JOLT

READ THIS WAY

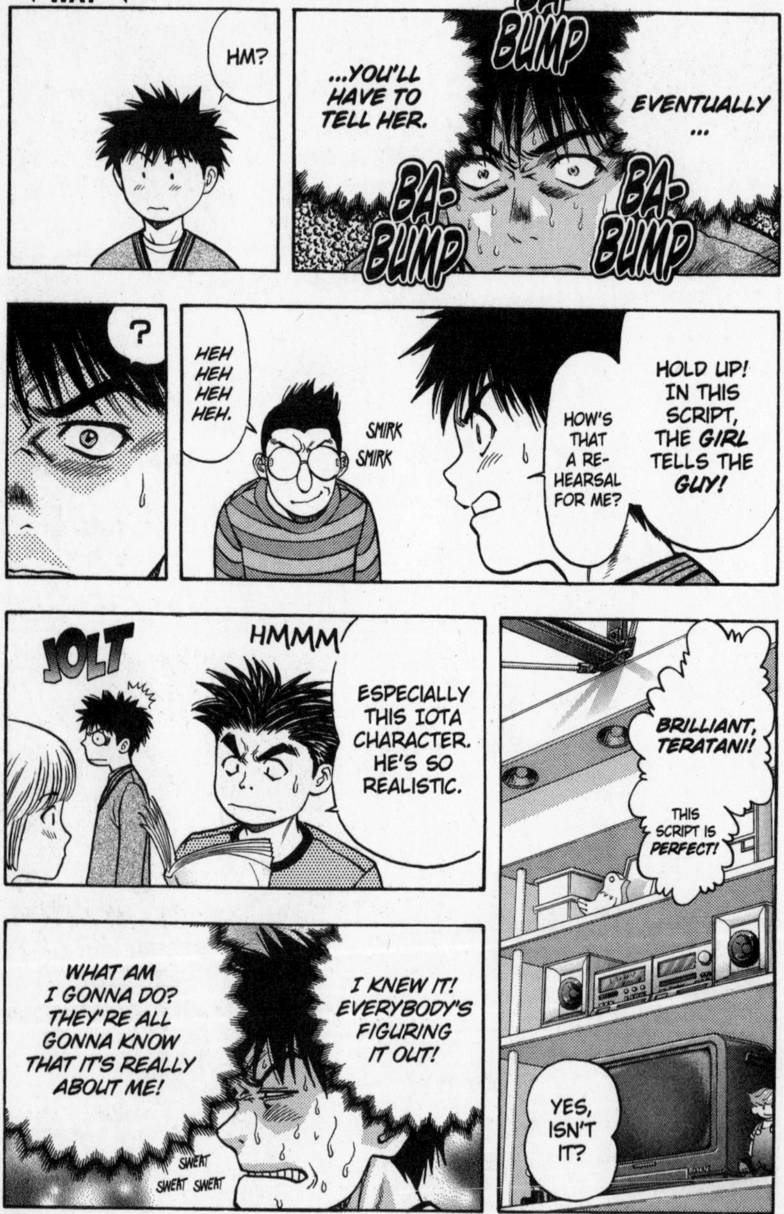
BA-BUMP
EVENTUALLY ...
...YOU'LL HAVE TO TELL HER.
BA-BUMP
BA-BUMP
HM?
HOLD UP! IN THIS SCRIPT, THE GIRL TELLS THE GUY!
HOW'S THAT A RE-HEARSAL FOR ME?
SMIRK SMIRK
HEH HEH HEH HEH.
?
BRILLIANT, TERATANI!
THIS SCRIPT IS PERFECT!
YES, ISN'T IT?
HMMM
ESPECIALLY THIS IOTA CHARACTER. HE'S SO REALISTIC.
JOLT
I KNEW IT! EVERYBODY'S FIGURING IT OUT!
WHAT AM I GONNA DO? THEY'RE ALL GONNA KNOW THAT IT'S REALLY ABOUT ME!
SWEAT SWEAT SWEAT

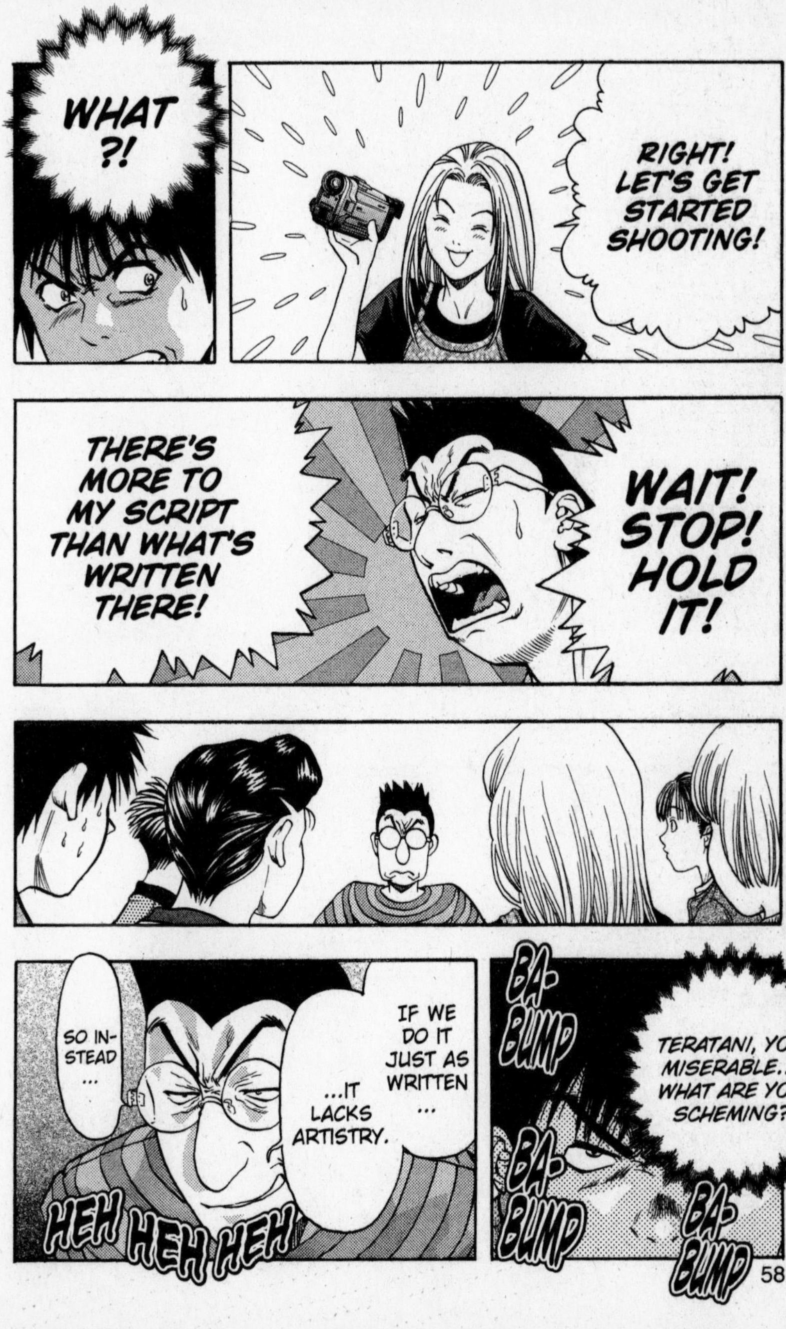
RIGHT! LET'S GET STARTED SHOOTING!
WHAT ?!
WAIT! STOP! HOLD IT!
THERE'S MORE TO MY SCRIPT THAN WHAT'S WRITTEN THERE!
BA-BUMP
BA-BUMP
BA-BUMP
TERATANI, YOU MISERABLE... WHAT ARE YOU SCHEMING?
IF WE DO IT JUST AS WRITTEN ...
...IT LACKS ARTISTRY.
SO IN-STEAD ...
HEH HEH HEH

READ THIS WAY

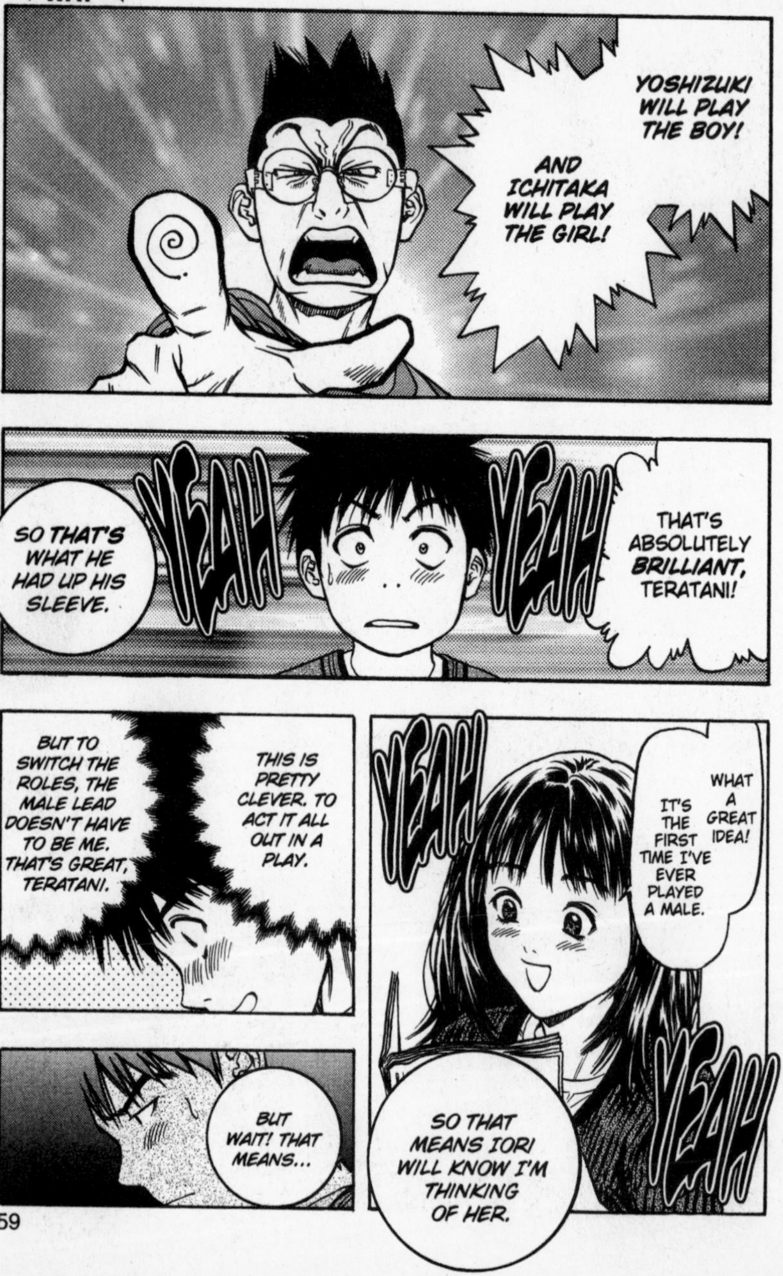

YOSHIZUKI WILL PLAY THE BOY!
AND ICHITAKA WILL PLAY THE GIRL!
THAT'S ABSOLUTELY BRILLIANT, TERATANI!
YEAH
YEAH
SO THAT'S WHAT HE HAD UP HIS SLEEVE.
YEAH
WHAT A GREAT IDEA!
IT'S THE FIRST TIME I'VE EVER PLAYED A MALE.
YEAH
THIS IS PRETTY CLEVER. TO ACT IT ALL OUT IN A PLAY.
BUT TO SWITCH THE ROLES, THE MALE LEAD DOESN'T HAVE TO BE ME. THAT'S GREAT, TERATANI.
BUT WAIT! THAT MEANS...
SO THAT MEANS IORI WILL KNOW I'M THINKING OF HER.

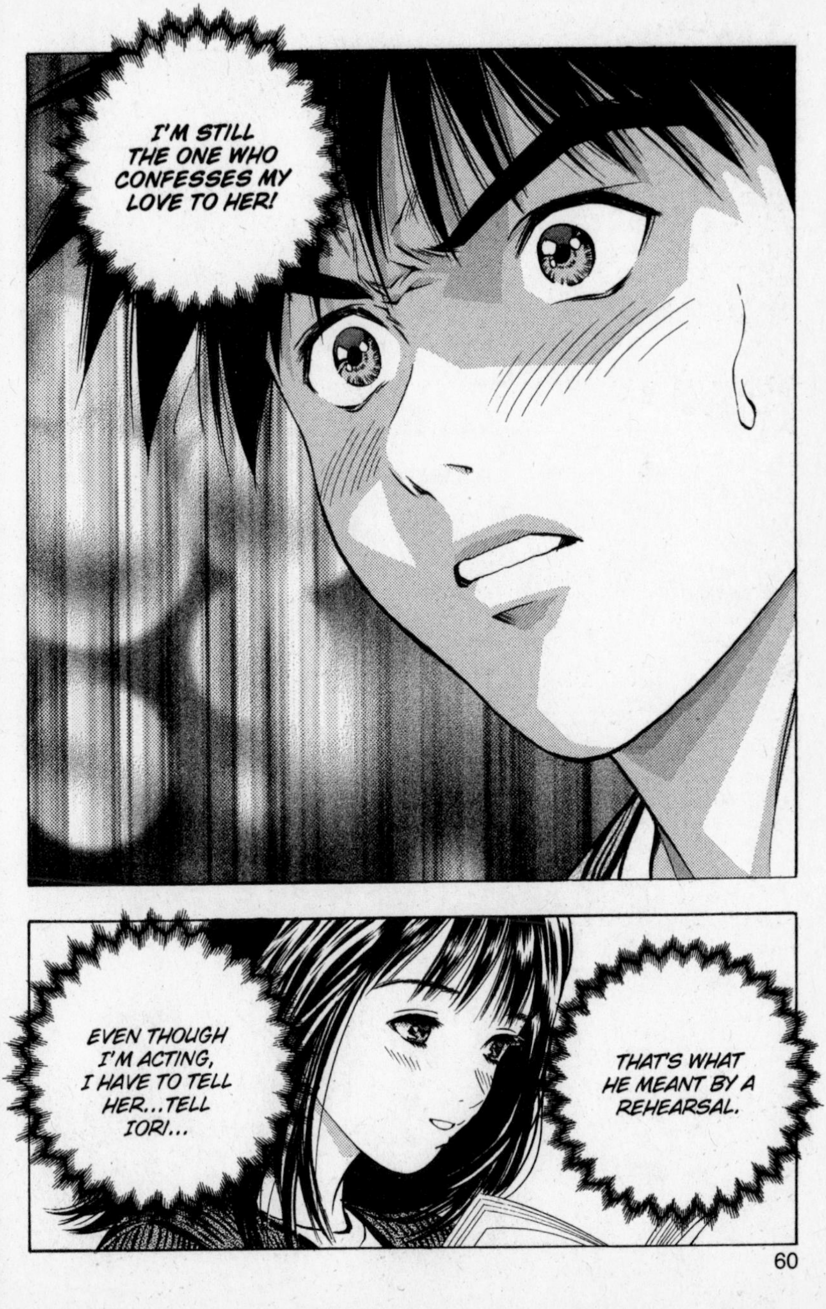
I'M STILL THE ONE WHO CONFESSES MY LOVE TO HER!
THAT'S WHAT HE MEANT BY A REHEARSAL.
EVEN THOUGH I'M ACTING, I HAVE TO TELL HER...TELL IORI...

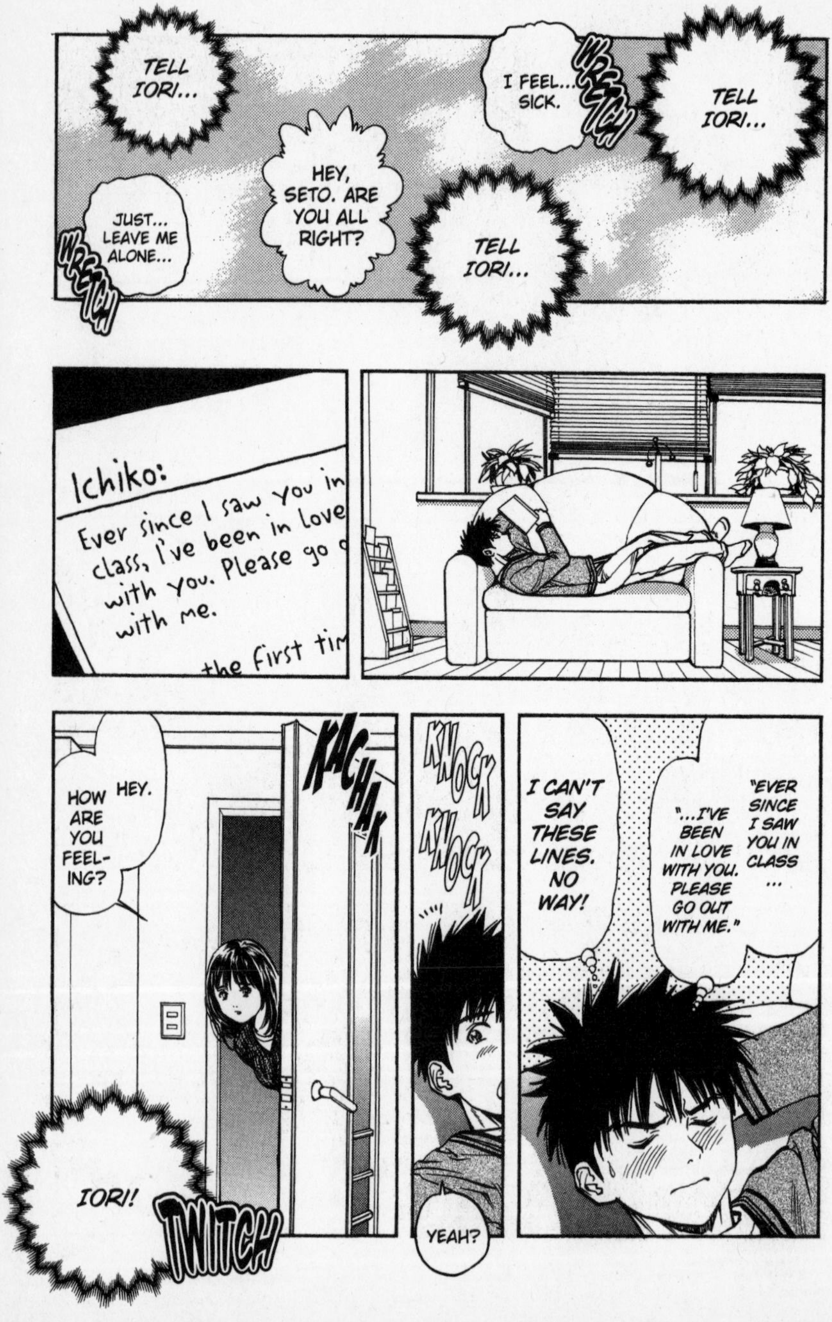
TELL IORI...
WRETCH
I FEEL... SICK.
TELL IORI...
HEY, SETO. ARE YOU ALL RIGHT?
TELL IORI...
JUST... LEAVE ME ALONE...
WRETCH
Ichiko:
Ever since I saw you in
class, I've been in love
with you. Please go o
with me.
the first tim
"EVER SINCE I SAW YOU IN CLASS ...
"...I'VE BEEN IN LOVE WITH YOU. PLEASE GO OUT WITH ME."
I CAN'T SAY THESE LINES. NO WAY!
KNOCK
KNOCK
YEAH?
KACHAK
HEY.
HOW ARE YOU FEELING?
IORI!
TWITCH

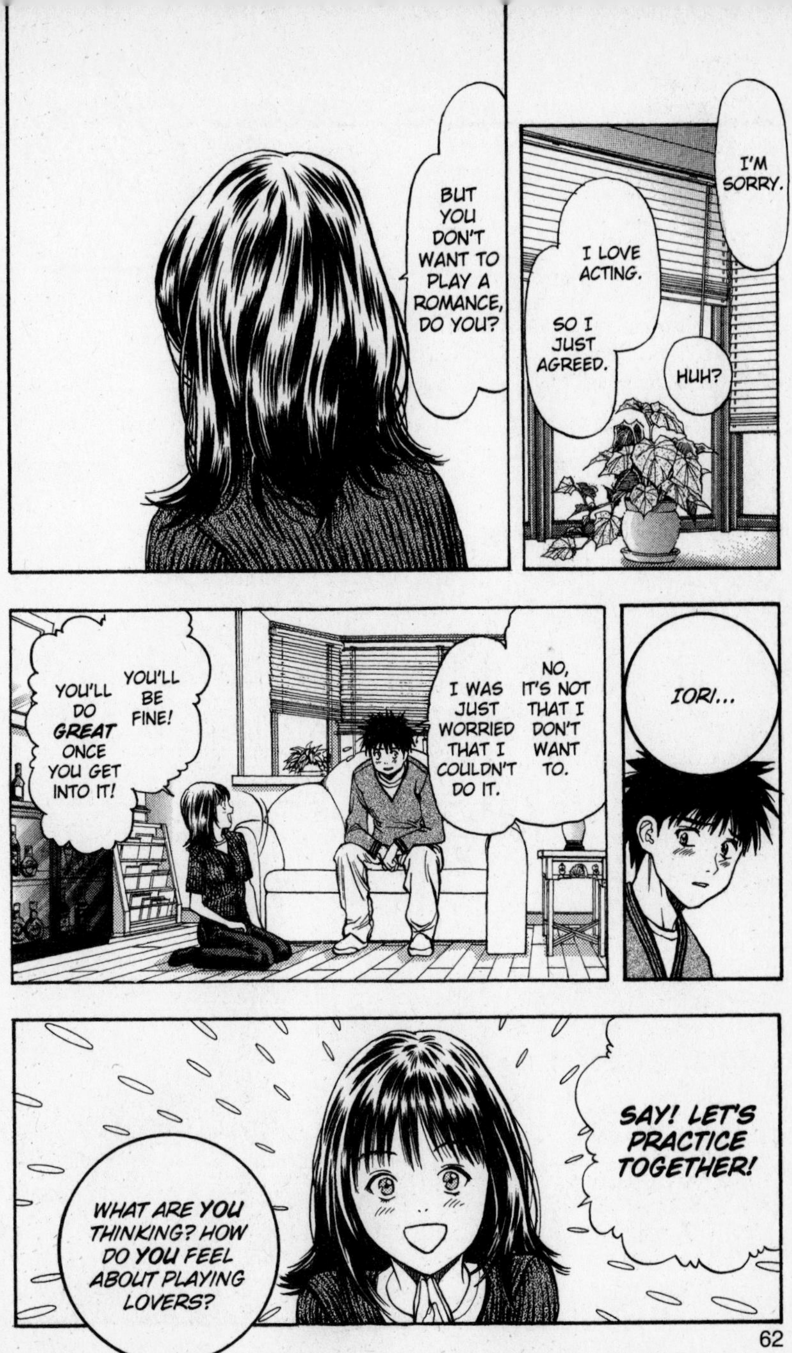
I'M SORRY.
HUH?
I LOVE ACTING.
SO I JUST AGREED.
BUT YOU DON'T WANT TO PLAY A ROMANCE, DO YOU?
IORI...
NO, IT'S NOT THAT I DON'T WANT TO.
I WAS JUST WORRIED THAT I COULDN'T DO IT.
YOU'LL BE FINE!
YOU'LL DO GREAT ONCE YOU GET INTO IT!
SAY! LET'S PRACTICE TOGETHER!
WHAT ARE YOU THINKING? HOW DO YOU FEEL ABOUT PLAYING LOVERS?

READ THIS WAY

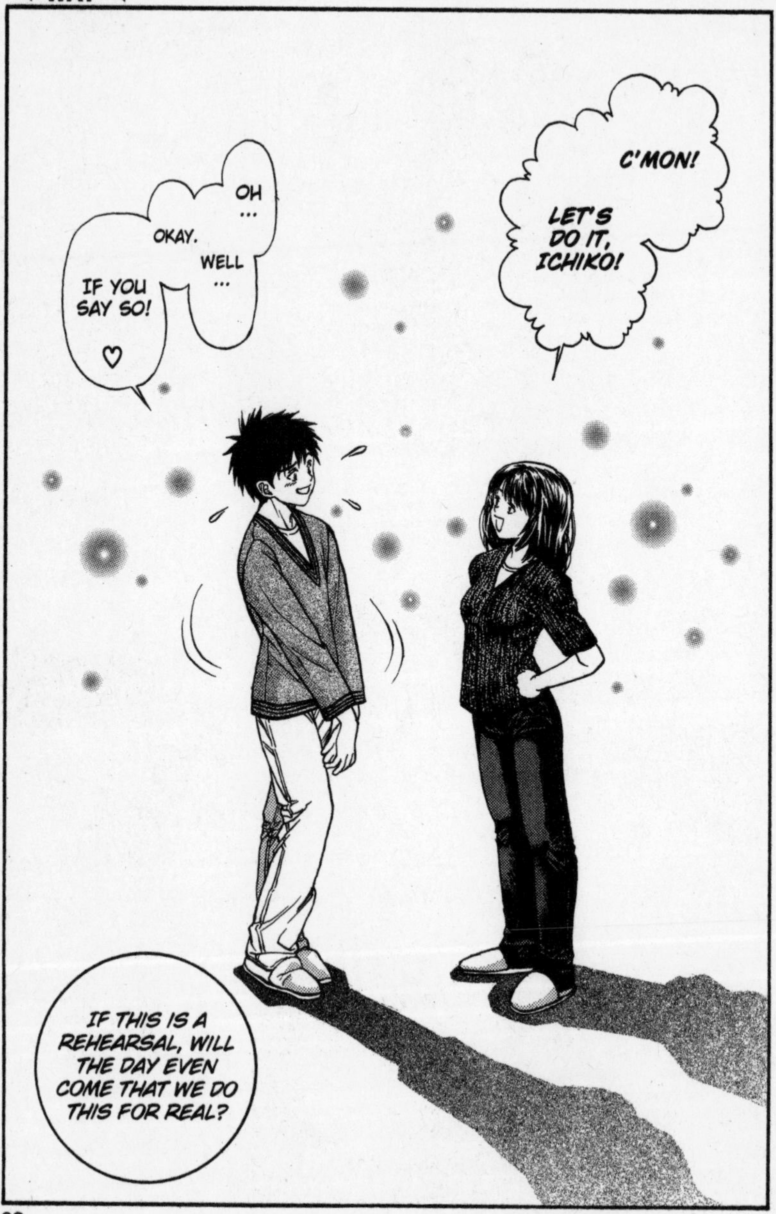
C'MON!
LET'S DO IT, ICHIKO!
OH ...
WELL ...
OKAY.
IF YOU SAY SO! ♡
IF THIS IS A REHEARSAL, WILL THE DAY EVEN COME THAT WE DO THIS FOR REAL?

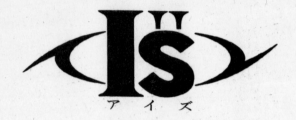

Chapter 58:
Ichiko's Feelings

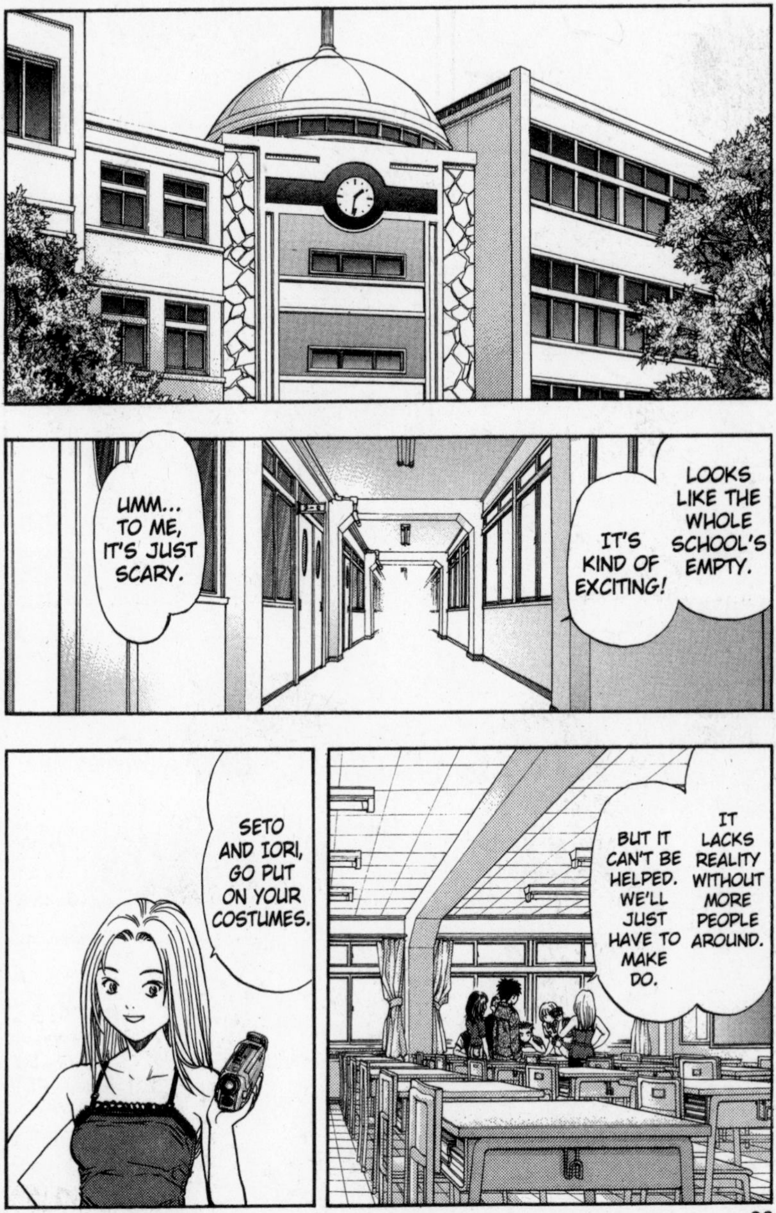
LOOKS LIKE THE WHOLE SCHOOL'S EMPTY.
IT'S KIND OF EXCITING!
UMM... TO ME, IT'S JUST SCARY.
IT LACKS REALITY WITHOUT MORE PEOPLE AROUND.
BUT IT CAN'T BE HELPED. WE'LL JUST HAVE TO MAKE DO.
SETO AND IORI, GO PUT ON YOUR COSTUMES.

READ THIS WAY

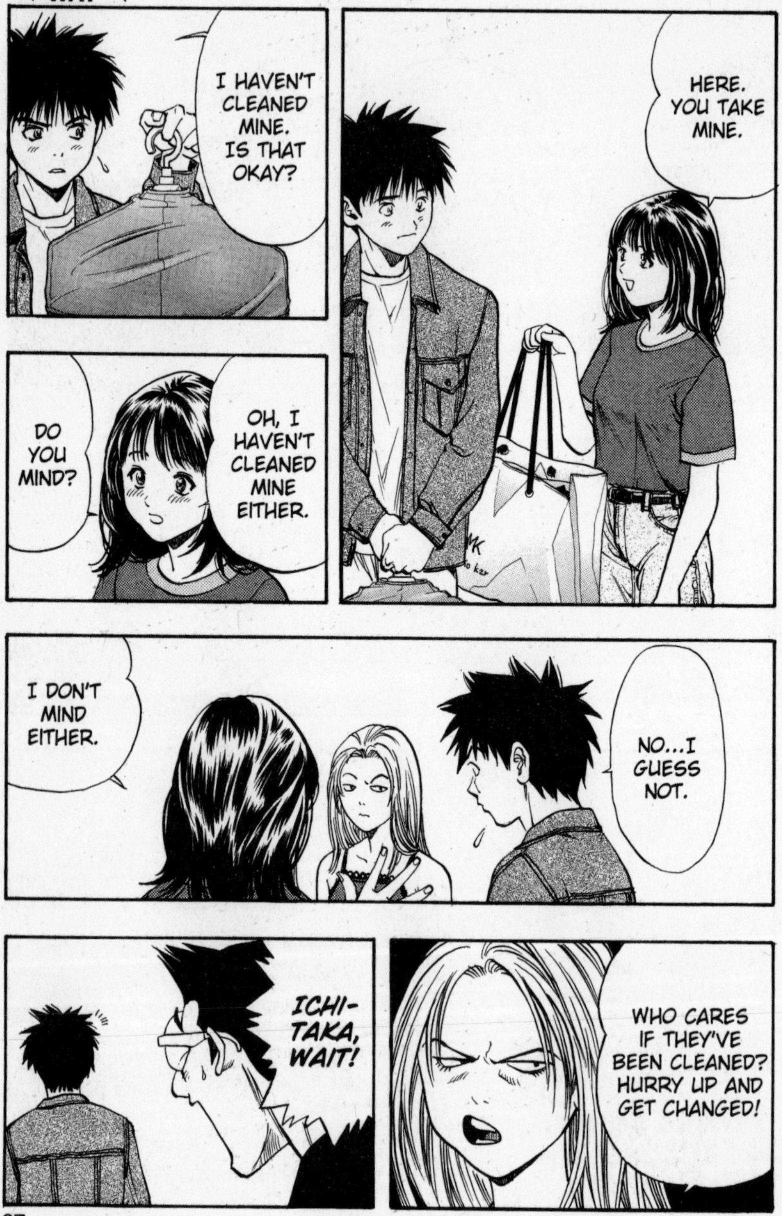
HERE. YOU TAKE MINE.
I HAVEN'T CLEANED MINE. IS THAT OKAY?
OH, I HAVEN'T CLEANED MINE EITHER.
DO YOU MIND?
NO...I GUESS NOT.
I DON'T MIND EITHER.
WHO CARES IF THEY'VE BEEN CLEANED? HURRY UP AND GET CHANGED!
ICHI-TAKA, WAIT!

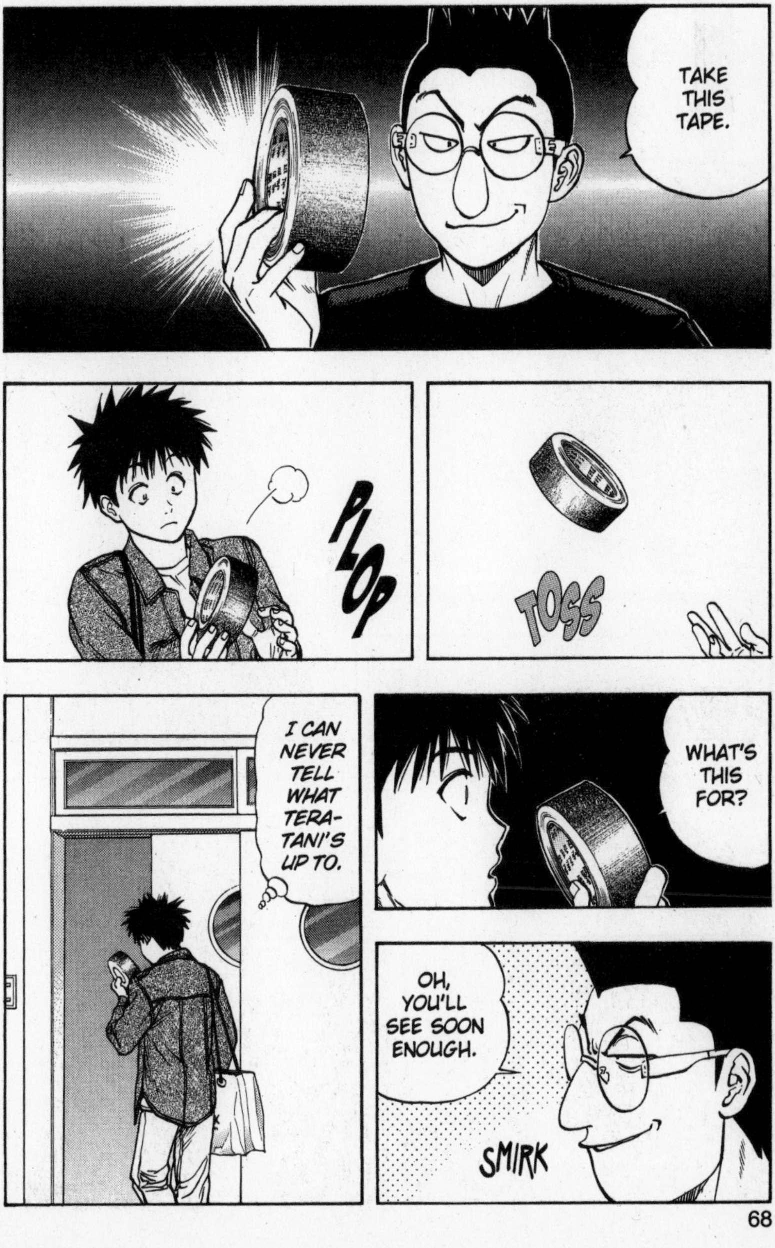
TAKE THIS TAPE.
TOSS
PLOP
WHAT'S THIS FOR?
OH, YOU'LL SEE SOON ENOUGH.
SMIRK
I CAN NEVER TELL WHAT TERA-TANI'S UP TO.

READ THIS WAY

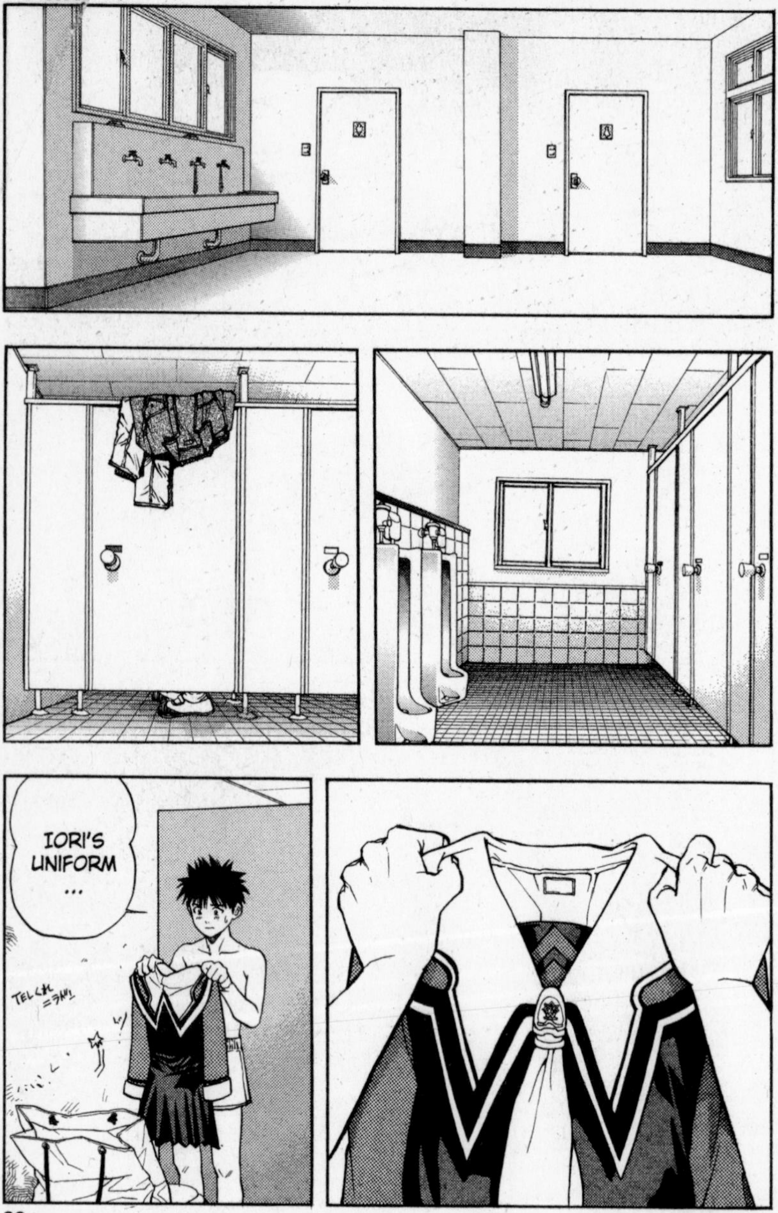
IORI'S UNIFORM ...

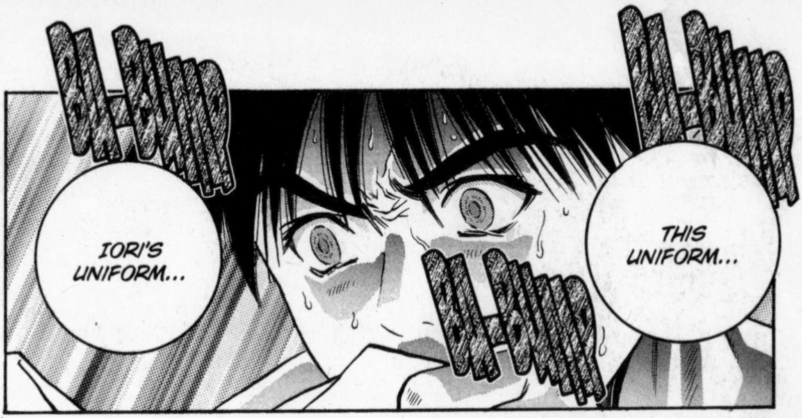
BA-BUMP
THIS UNIFORM...
BA-BUMP
IORI'S UNIFORM...
BA-BUMP
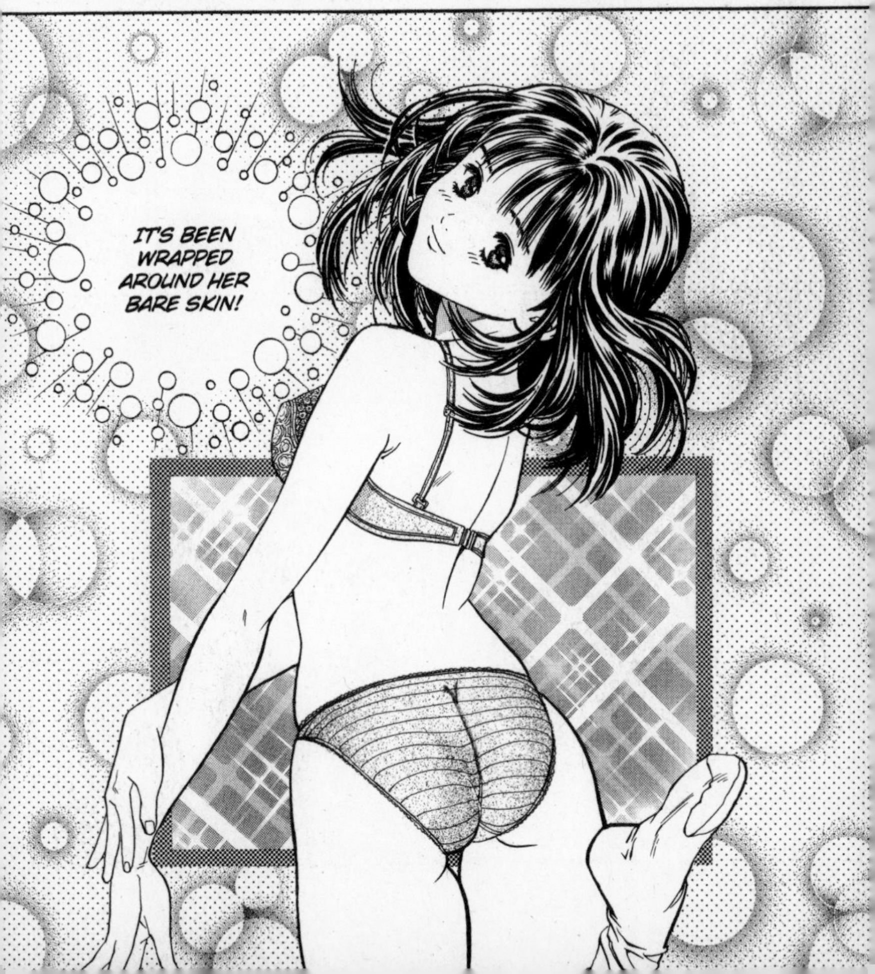
IT'S BEEN WRAPPED AROUND HER BARE SKIN!

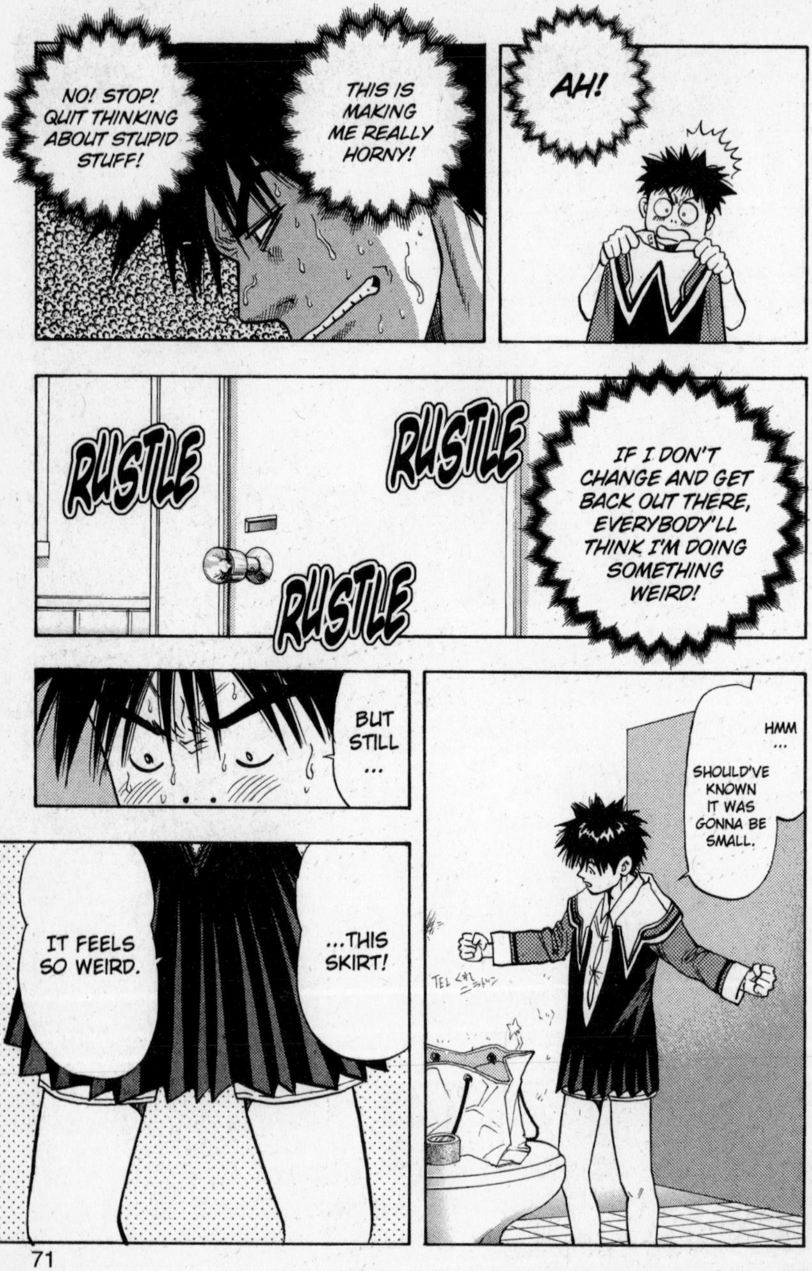
AH!
THIS IS MAKING ME REALLY HORNY!
NO! STOP! QUIT THINKING ABOUT STUPID STUFF!
IF I DON'T CHANGE AND GET BACK OUT THERE, EVERYBODY'LL THINK I'M DOING SOMETHING WEIRD!
RUSTLE
RUSTLE
RUSTLE
HMM ...
SHOULD'VE KNOWN IT WAS GONNA BE SMALL.
BUT STILL ...
...THIS SKIRT!
IT FEELS SO WEIRD.

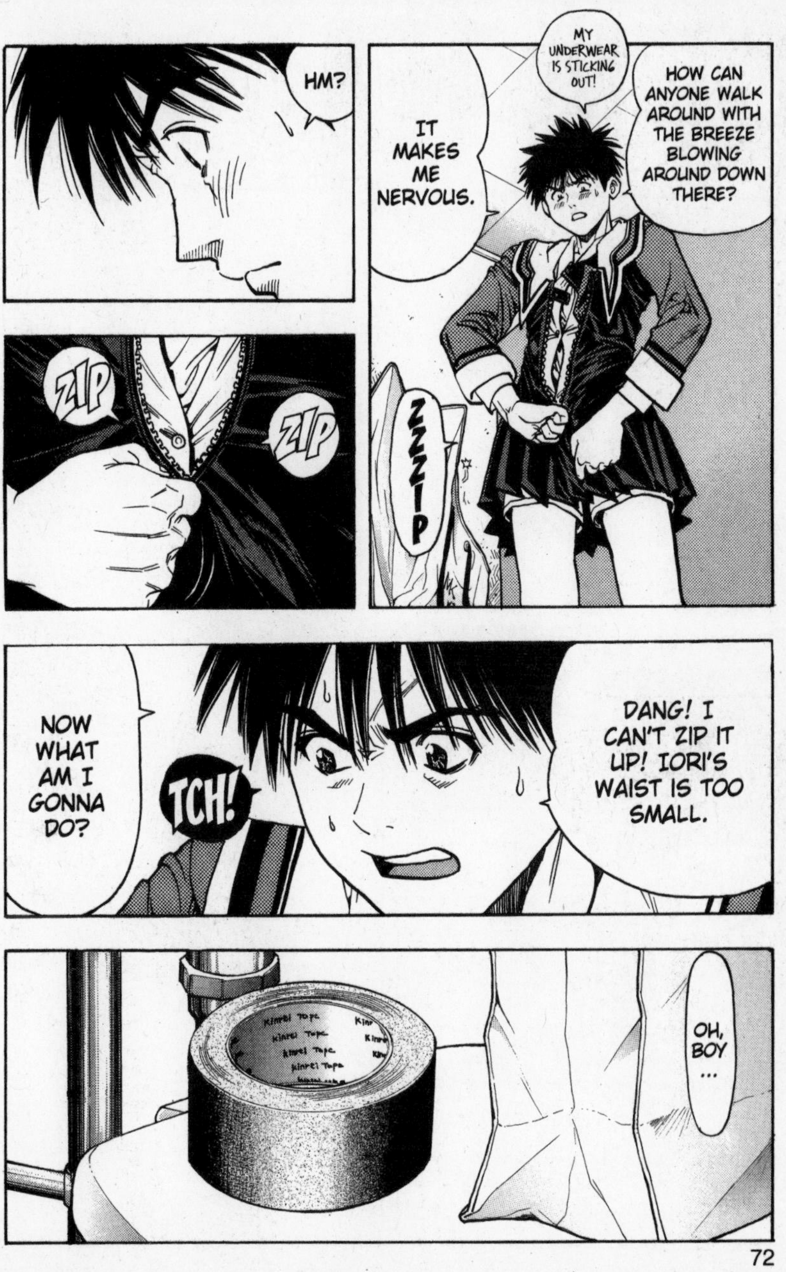
HOW CAN ANYONE WALK AROUND WITH THE BREEZE BLOWING AROUND DOWN THERE?
MY UNDERWEAR IS STICKING OUT!
IT MAKES ME NERVOUS.
ZZZZIP
HM?
ZIP
ZIP
DANG! I CAN'T ZIP IT UP! IORI'S WAIST IS TOO SMALL.
TCH!
NOW WHAT AM I GONNA DO?
OH, BOY...

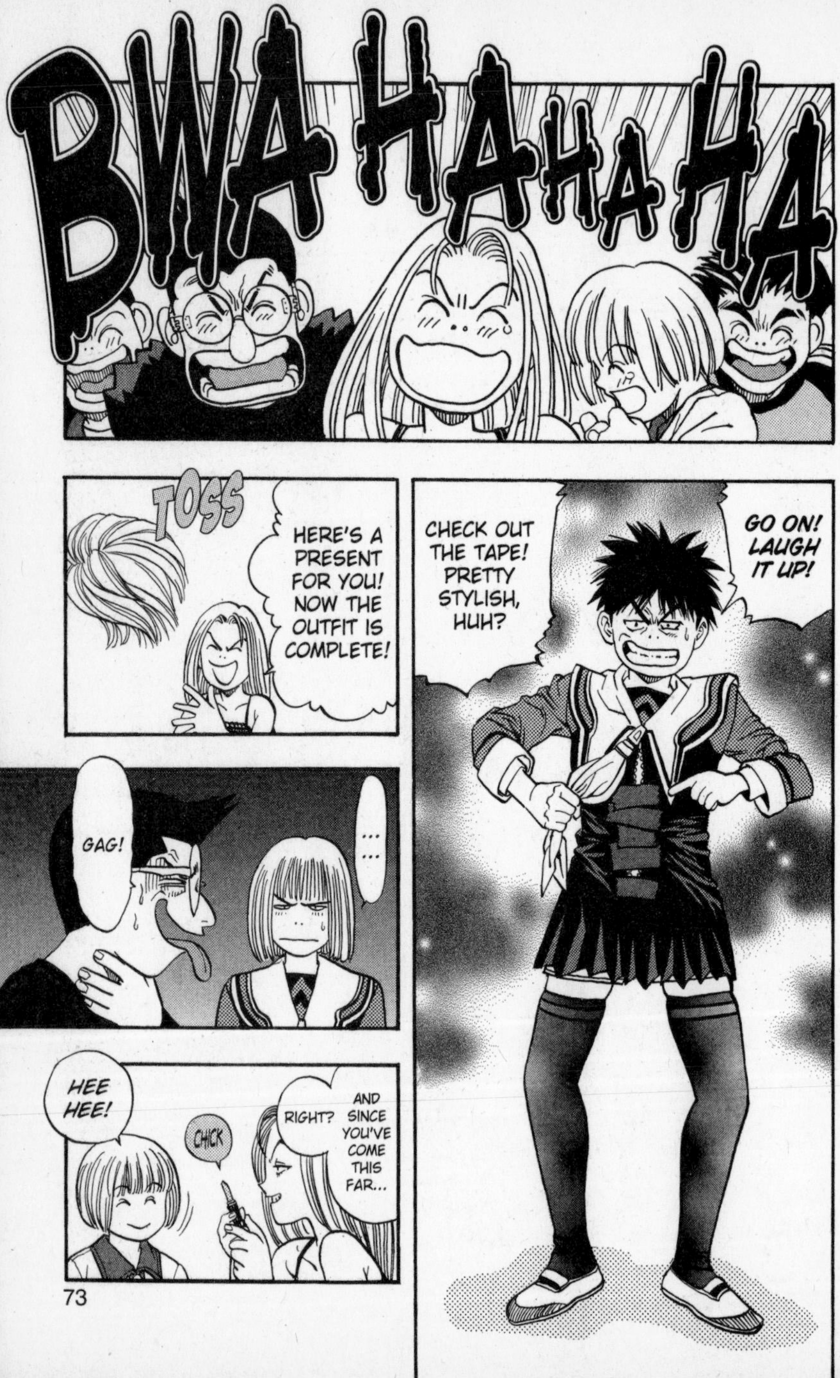
BWAHAHAHA
GO ON! LAUGH IT UP!
CHECK OUT THE TAPE! PRETTY STYLISH, HUH?
HERE'S A PRESENT FOR YOU! NOW THE OUTFIT IS COMPLETE!
TOSS
... ...
GAG!
AND SINCE YOU'VE COME THIS FAR...
RIGHT?
CHICK
HEE HEE!

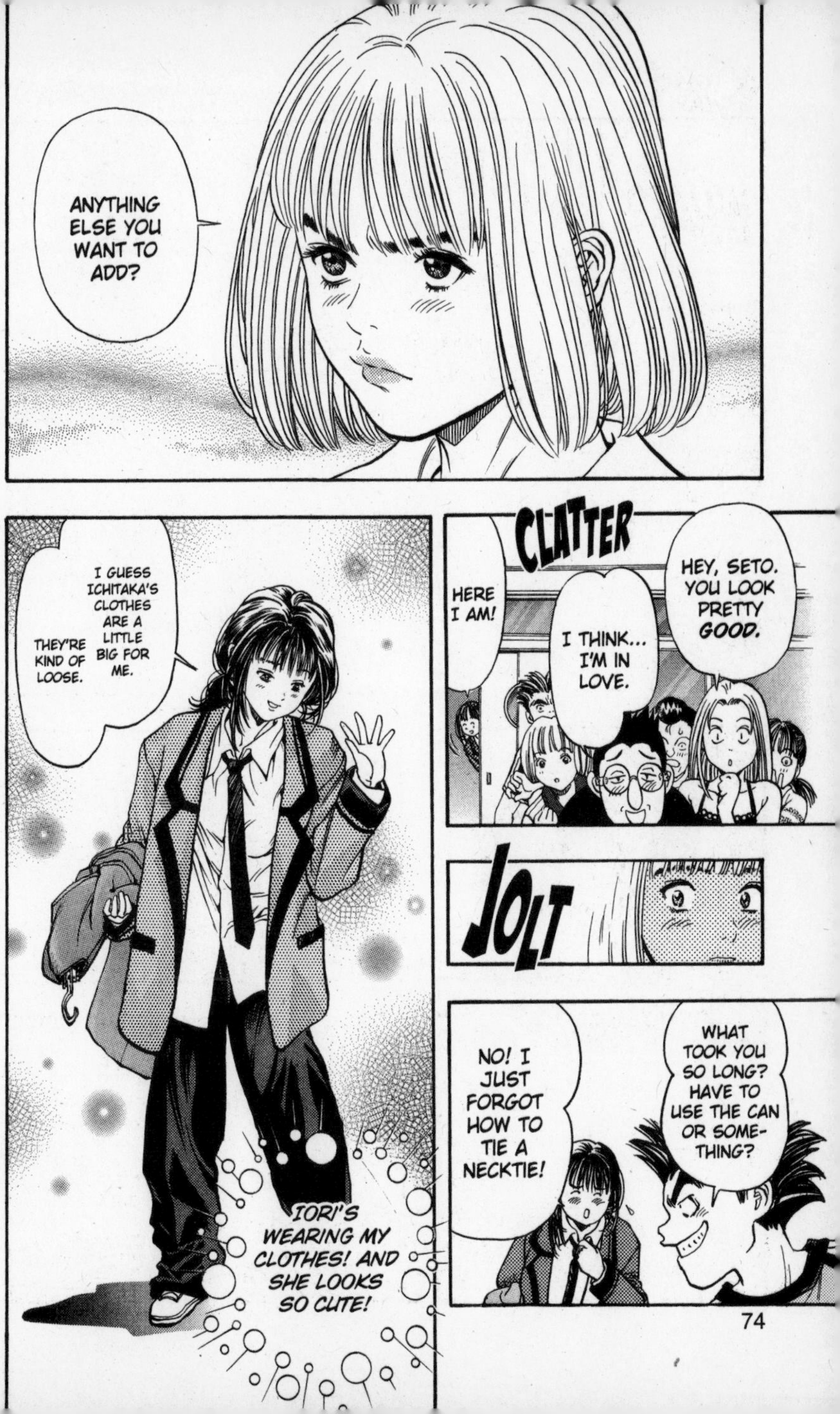
ANYTHING ELSE YOU WANT TO ADD?
HEY, SETO. YOU LOOK PRETTY GOOD.
CLATTER
I THINK... I'M IN LOVE.
HERE I AM!
JOLT
WHAT TOOK YOU SO LONG? HAVE TO USE THE CAN OR SOME-THING?
NO! I JUST FORGOT HOW TO TIE A NECKTIE!
I GUESS ICHITAKA'S CLOTHES ARE A LITTLE BIG FOR ME.
THEY'RE KIND OF LOOSE.
IORI'S WEARING MY CLOTHES! AND SHE LOOKS SO CUTE!

READ THIS WAY

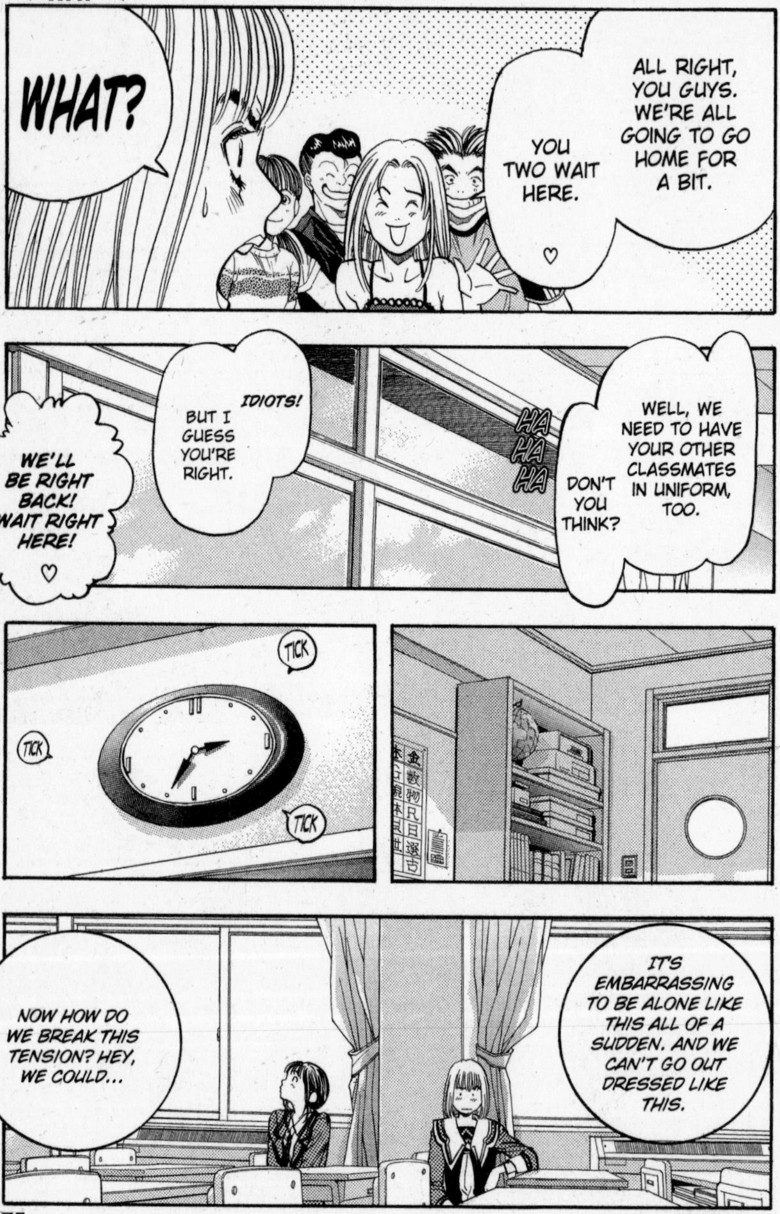
ALL RIGHT, YOU GUYS. WE'RE ALL GOING TO GO HOME FOR A BIT.
YOU TWO WAIT HERE. ♡
WHAT?
WELL, WE NEED TO HAVE YOUR OTHER CLASSMATES IN UNIFORM, TOO.
DON'T YOU THINK?
HA HA HA
IDIOTS!
BUT I GUESS YOU'RE RIGHT.
WE'LL BE RIGHT BACK! WAIT RIGHT HERE! ♡
TICK
TICK
TICK
IT'S EMBARRASSING TO BE ALONE LIKE THIS ALL OF A SUDDEN. AND WE CAN'T GO OUT DRESSED LIKE THIS.
NOW HOW DO WE BREAK THIS TENSION? HEY, WE COULD...

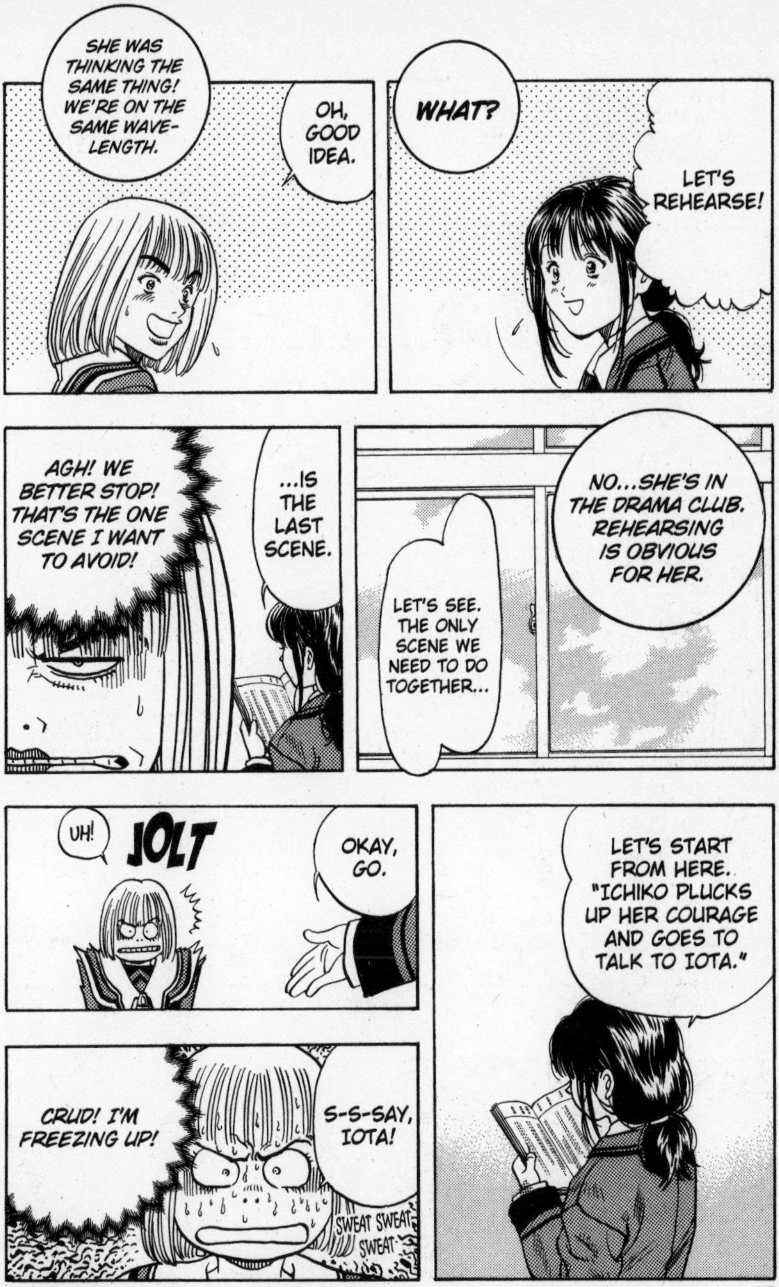
LET'S REHEARSE!
WHAT?
OH, GOOD IDEA.
SHE WAS THINKING THE SAME THING! WE'RE ON THE SAME WAVE-LENGTH.
NO...SHE'S IN THE DRAMA CLUB. REHEARSING IS OBVIOUS FOR HER.
LET'S SEE. THE ONLY SCENE WE NEED TO DO TOGETHER...
...IS THE LAST SCENE.
AGH! WE BETTER STOP! THAT'S THE ONE SCENE I WANT TO AVOID!
LET'S START FROM HERE. "ICHIKO PLUCKS UP HER COURAGE AND GOES TO TALK TO IOTA."
OKAY, GO.
JOLT
UH!
S-S-SAY, IOTA!
CRUD! I'M FREEZING UP!
SWEAT SWEAT SWEAT

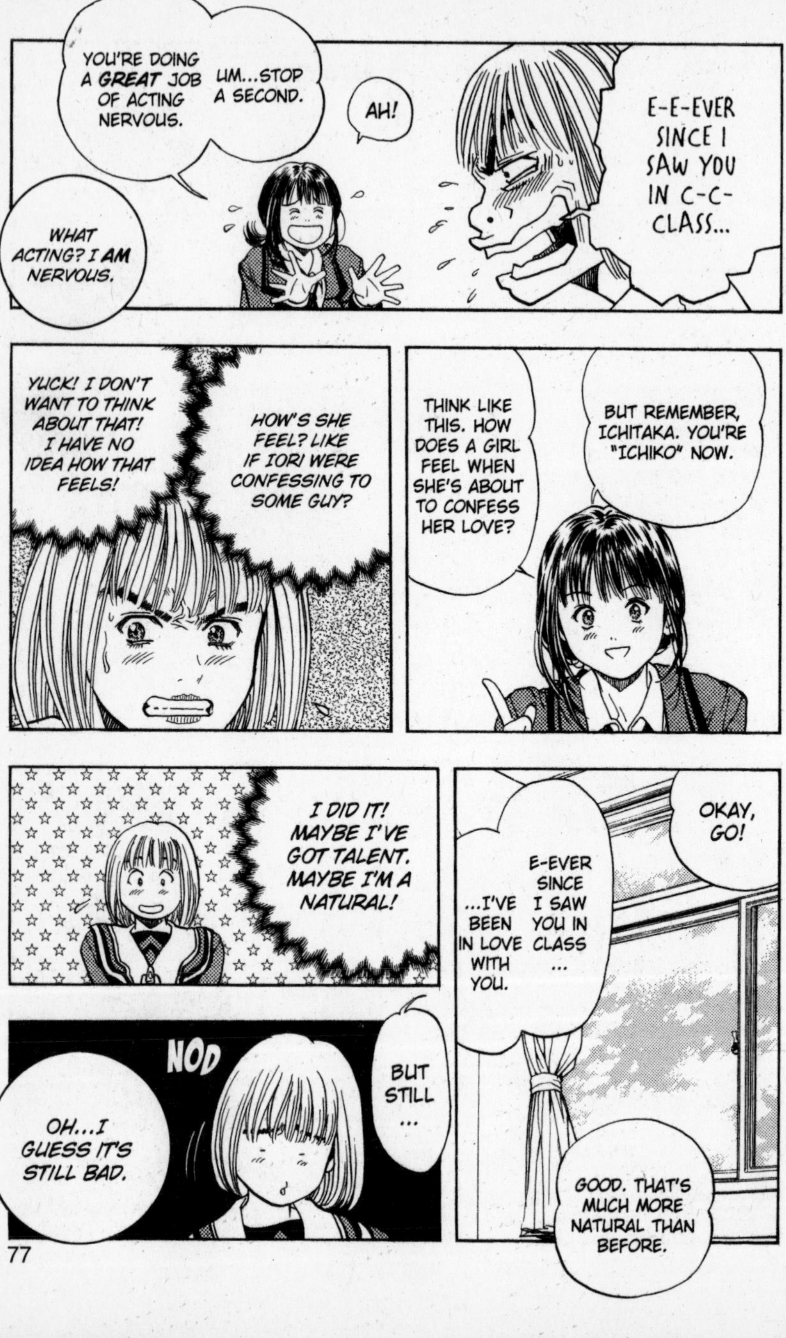
E-E-EVER SINCE I SAW YOU IN C-C-CLASS...
AH!
UM...STOP A SECOND.
YOU'RE DOING A GREAT JOB OF ACTING NERVOUS.
WHAT ACTING? I AM NERVOUS.
BUT REMEMBER, ICHITAKA. YOU'RE "ICHIKO" NOW.
THINK LIKE THIS. HOW DOES A GIRL FEEL WHEN SHE'S ABOUT TO CONFESS HER LOVE?
HOW'S SHE FEEL? LIKE IF IORI WERE CONFESSING TO SOME GUY?
YUCK! I DON'T WANT TO THINK ABOUT THAT! I HAVE NO IDEA HOW THAT FEELS!
OKAY, GO!
E-EVER SINCE I SAW YOU IN CLASS ...
...I'VE BEEN IN LOVE WITH YOU.
GOOD. THAT'S MUCH MORE NATURAL THAN BEFORE.
I DID IT! MAYBE I'VE GOT TALENT. MAYBE I'M A NATURAL!
BUT STILL ...
NOD
OH...I GUESS IT'S STILL BAD.

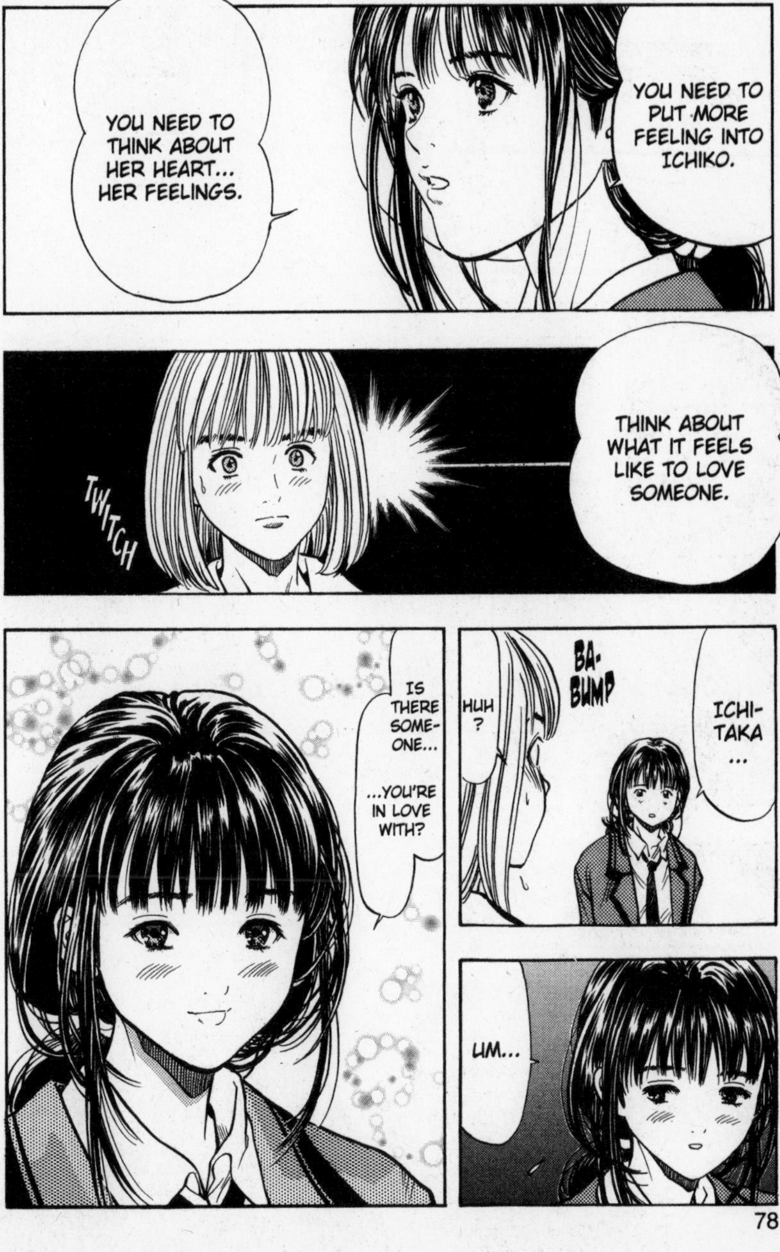
YOU NEED TO PUT MORE FEELING INTO ICHIKO.
YOU NEED TO THINK ABOUT HER HEART... HER FEELINGS.
THINK ABOUT WHAT IT FEELS LIKE TO LOVE SOMEONE.
TWITCH
ICHI-TAKA...
BA-BUMP
HUH?
UM...
IS THERE SOMEONE...
...YOU'RE IN LOVE WITH?

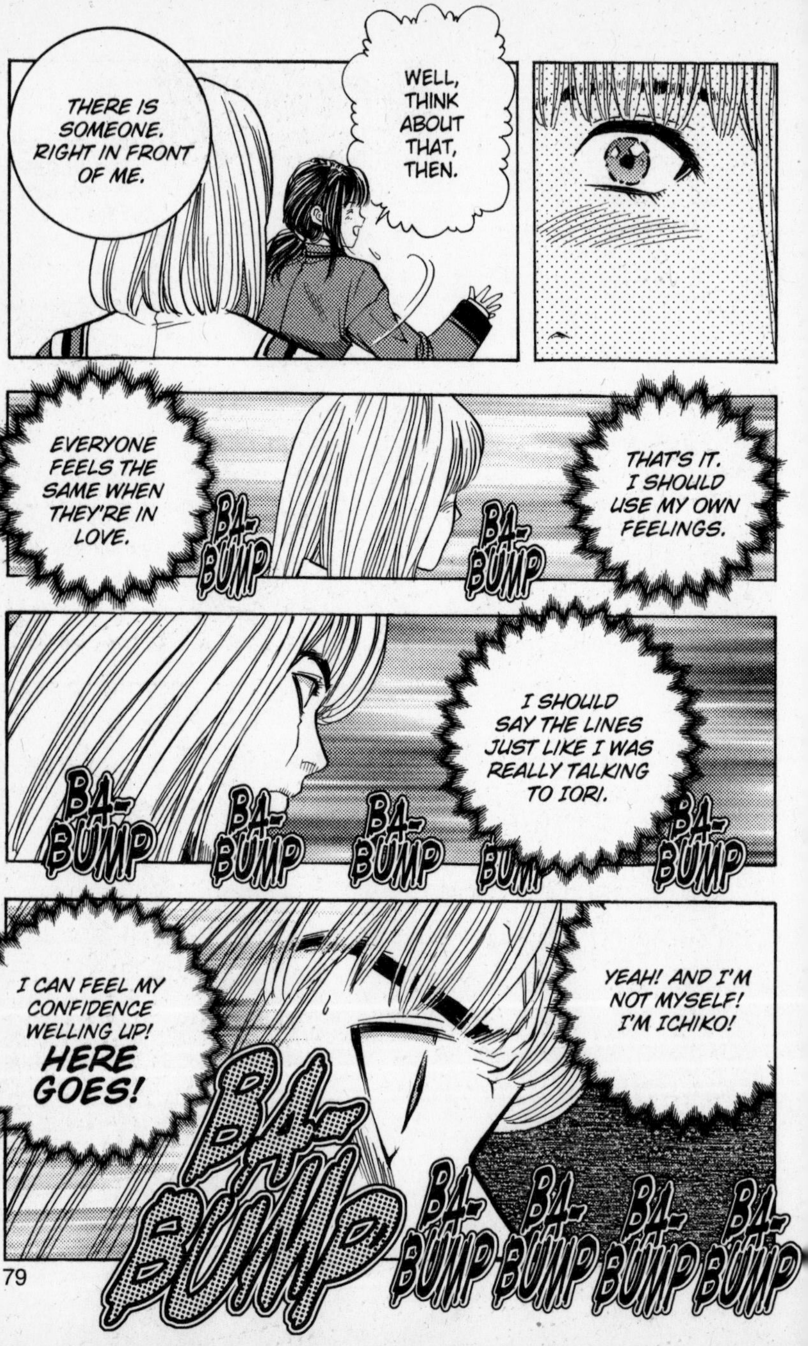
WELL, THINK ABOUT THAT, THEN.
THERE IS SOMEONE. RIGHT IN FRONT OF ME.
THAT'S IT. I SHOULD USE MY OWN FEELINGS.
BA-BUMP
BA-BUMP
EVERYONE FEELS THE SAME WHEN THEY'RE IN LOVE.
BA-BUMP
I SHOULD SAY THE LINES JUST LIKE I WAS REALLY TALKING TO IORI.
BA-BUMP
BA-BUMP
BA-BUMP
YEAH! AND I'M NOT MYSELF! I'M ICHIKO!
I CAN FEEL MY CONFIDENCE WELLING UP! **HERE GOES!**
BA-BUMP
BA-BUMP
BA-BUMP
BA-BUMP
BA-BUMP

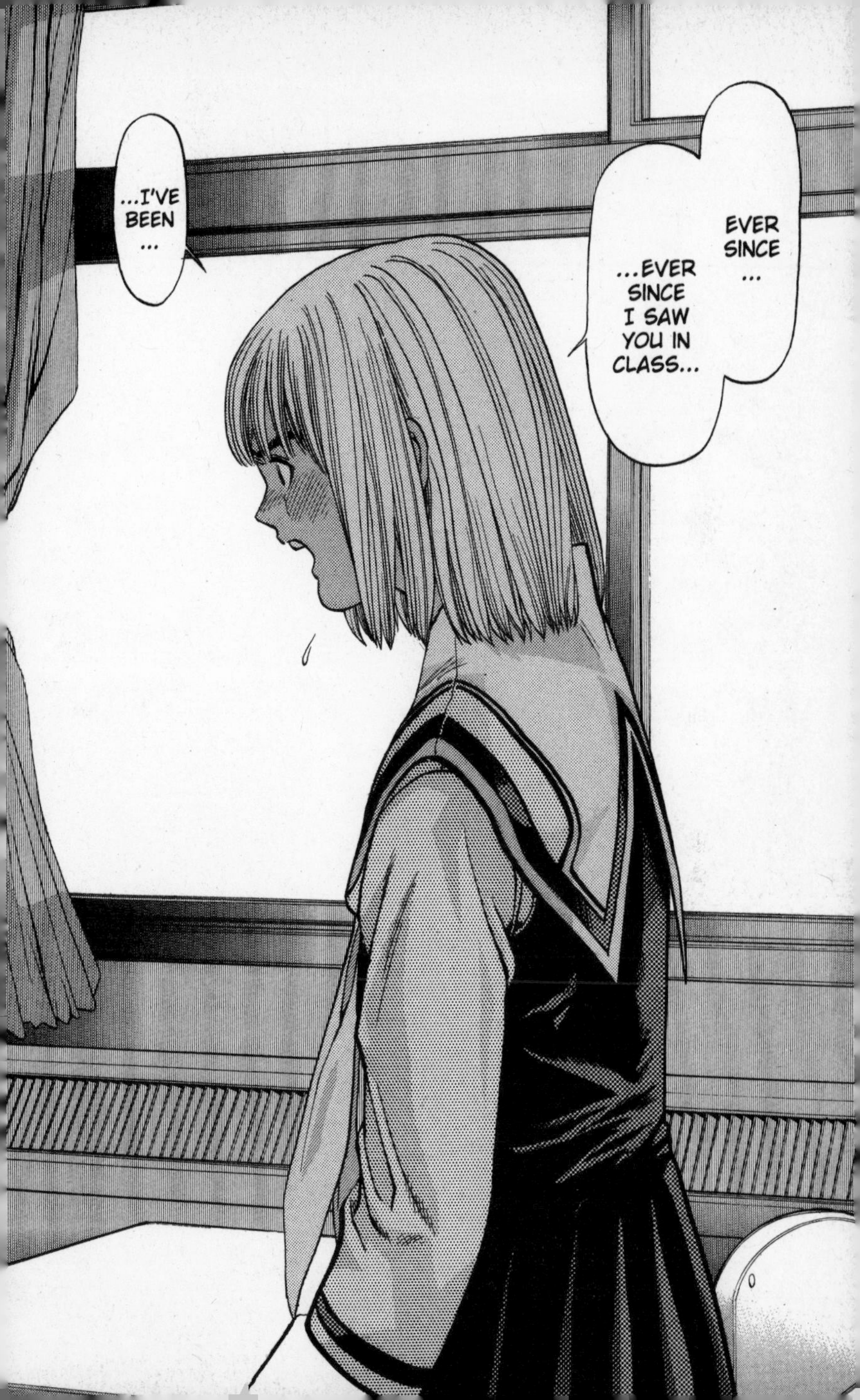
EVER SINCE ...
...EVER SINCE I SAW YOU IN CLASS...
...I'VE BEEN ...

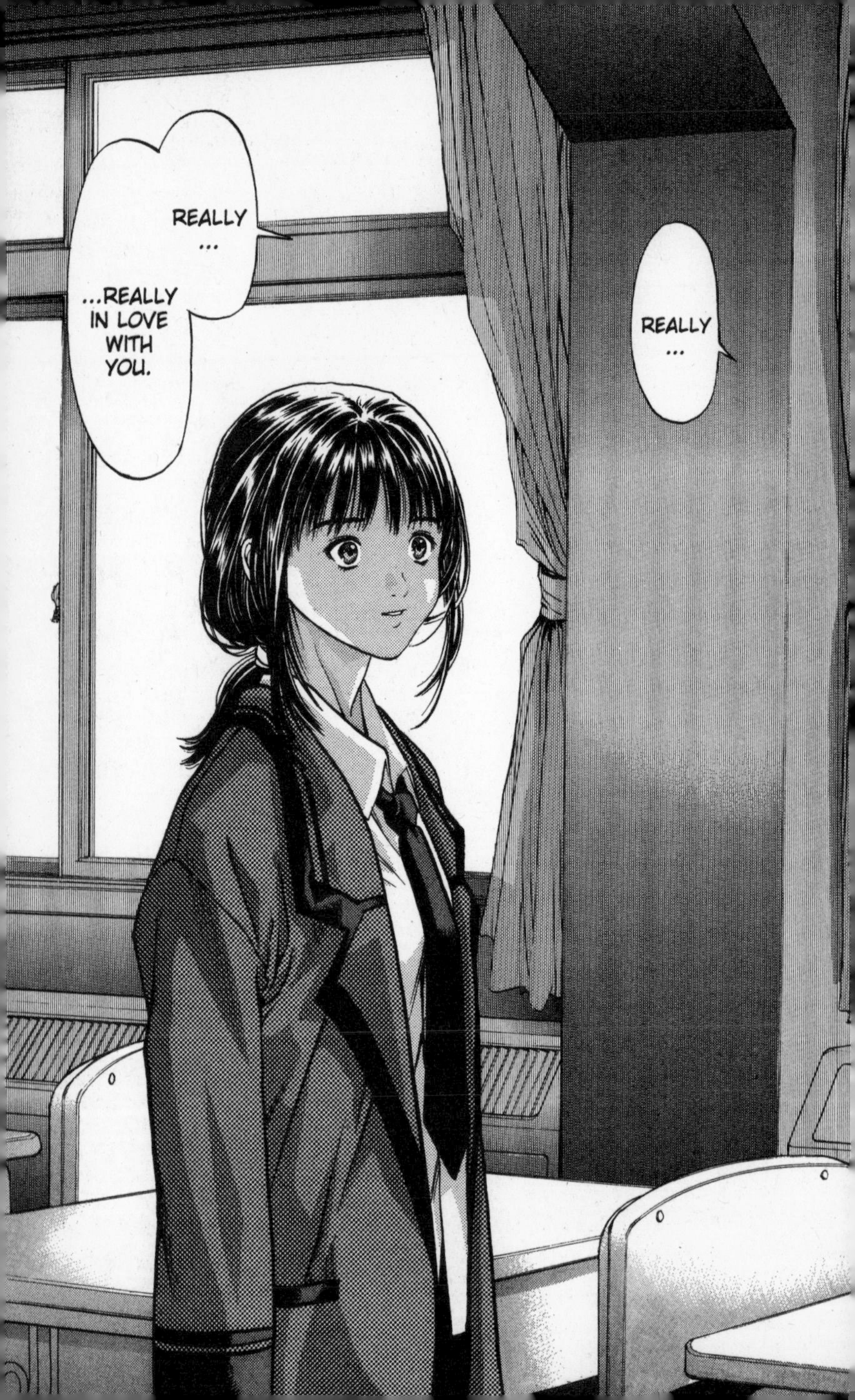
REALLY ...
REALLY ... ...REALLY IN LOVE WITH YOU.

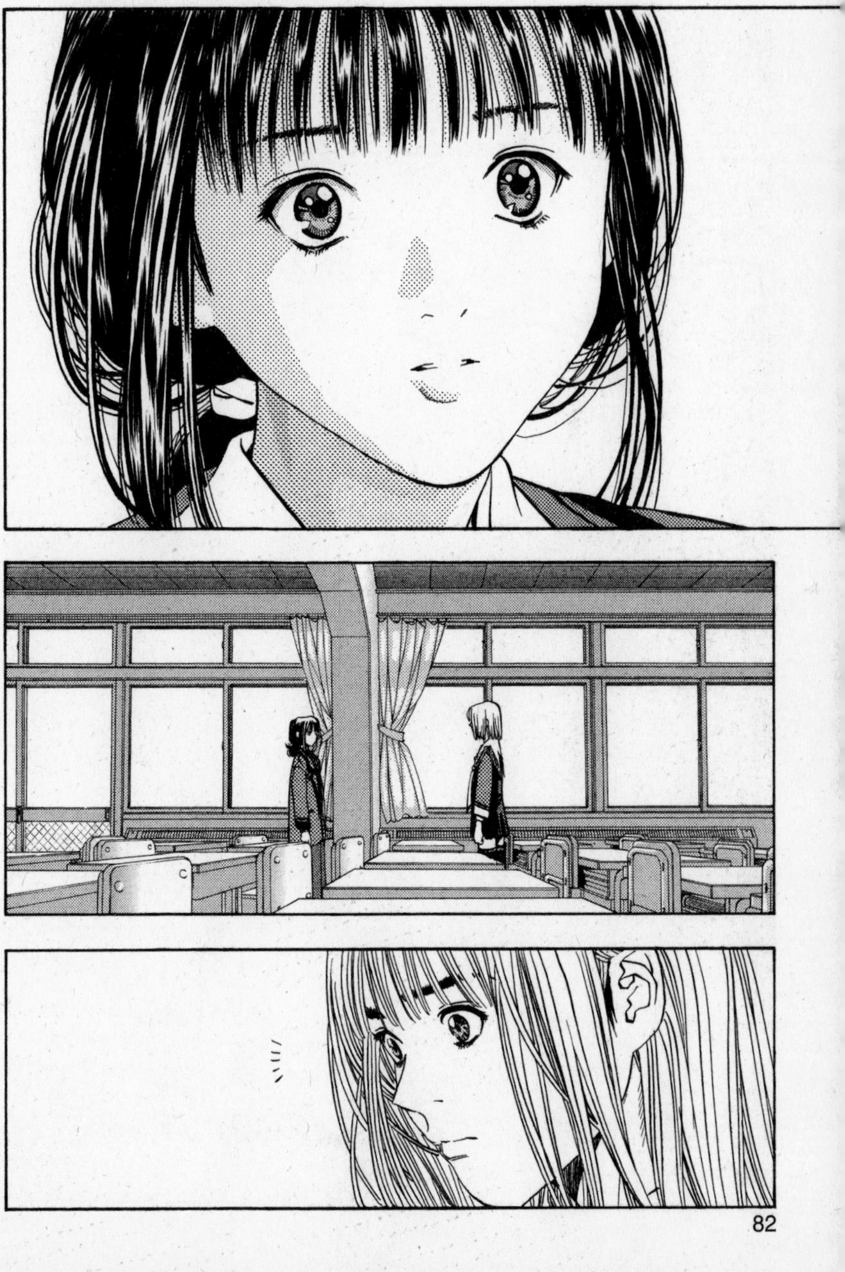

READ THIS WAY

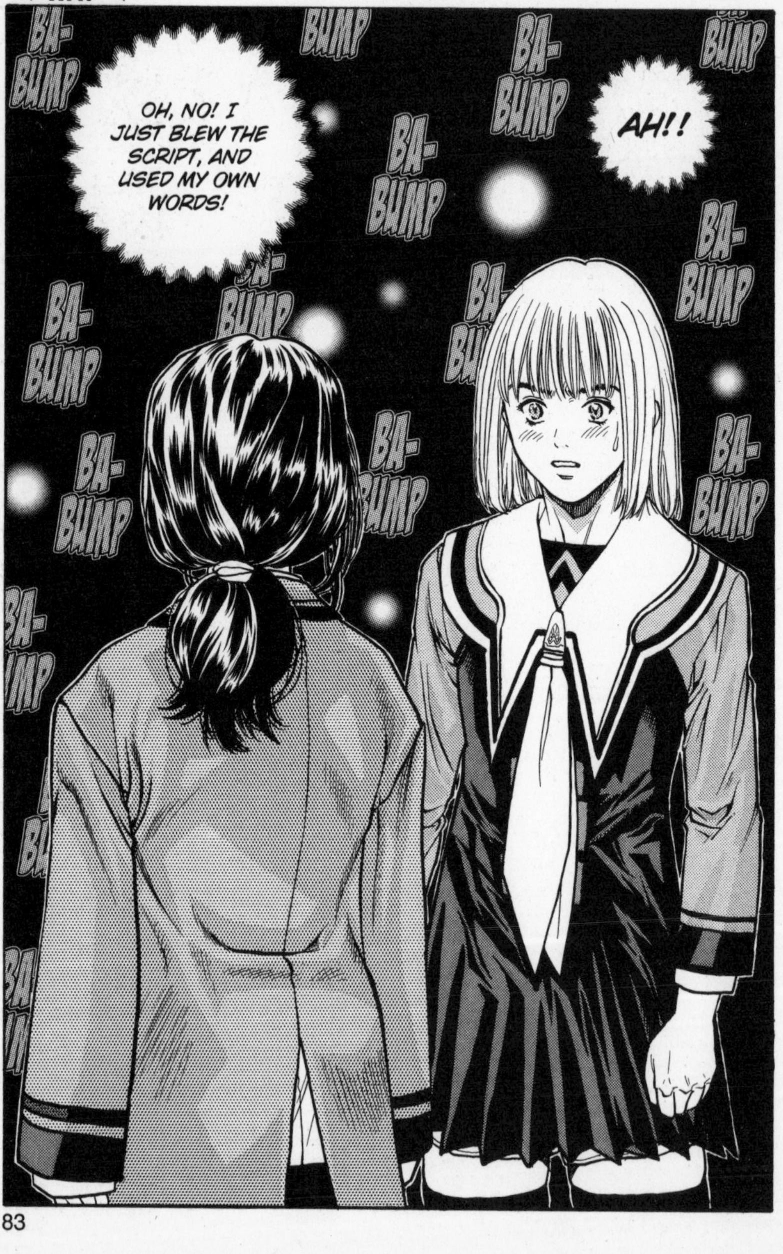
BA-BUMP
BA-BUMP
AH!!
BUMP
BA-BUMP
OH, NO! I JUST BLEW THE SCRIPT, AND USED MY OWN WORDS!
BA-BUMP
BA-BUMP
BA-BUMP
BA-BUMP
BA-BUMP
BA-BUMP

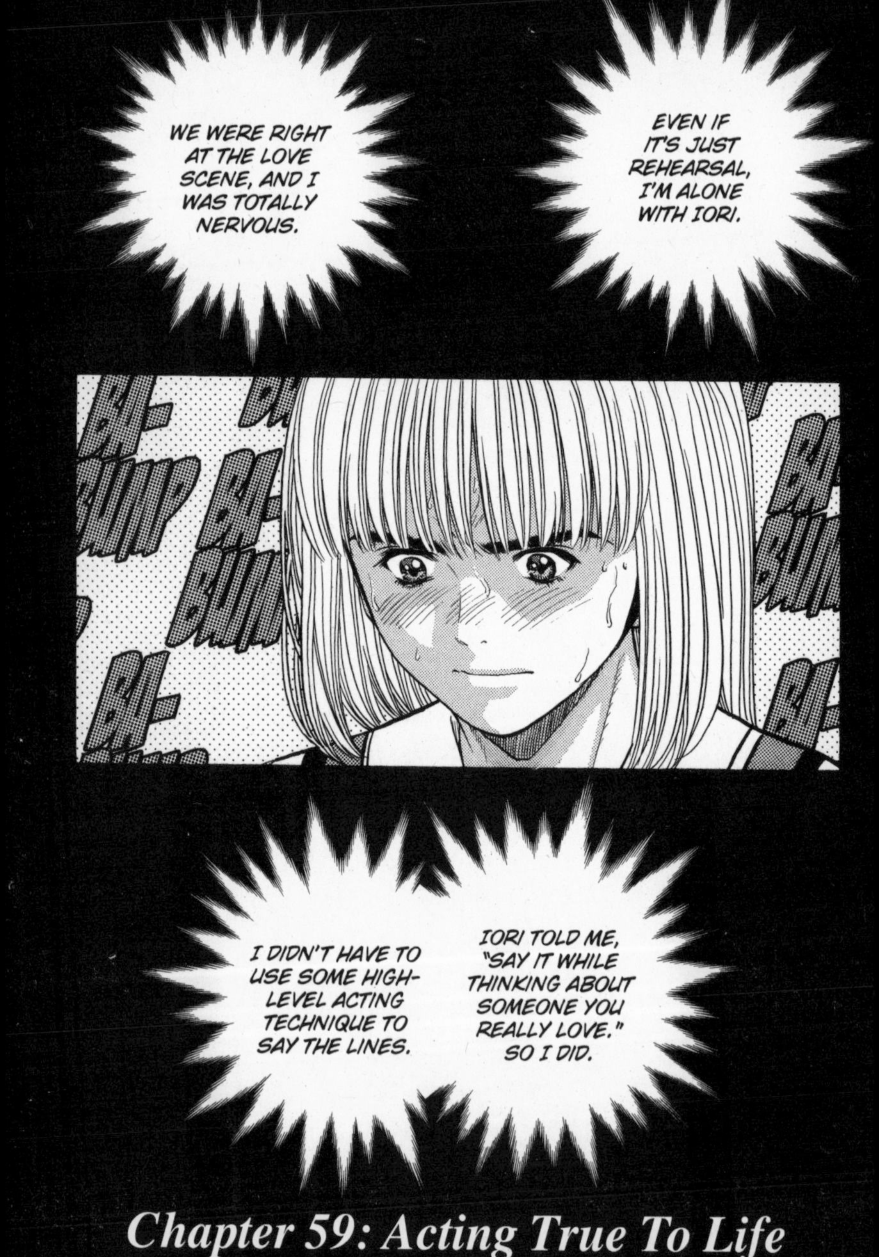
EVEN IF IT'S JUST REHEARSAL, I'M ALONE WITH IORI.
WE WERE RIGHT AT THE LOVE SCENE, AND I WAS TOTALLY NERVOUS.
BA-BUMP
IORI TOLD ME, "SAY IT WHILE THINKING ABOUT SOMEONE YOU REALLY LOVE." SO I DID.
I DIDN'T HAVE TO USE SOME HIGH-LEVEL ACTING TECHNIQUE TO SAY THE LINES.

Chapter 59: Acting True To Life

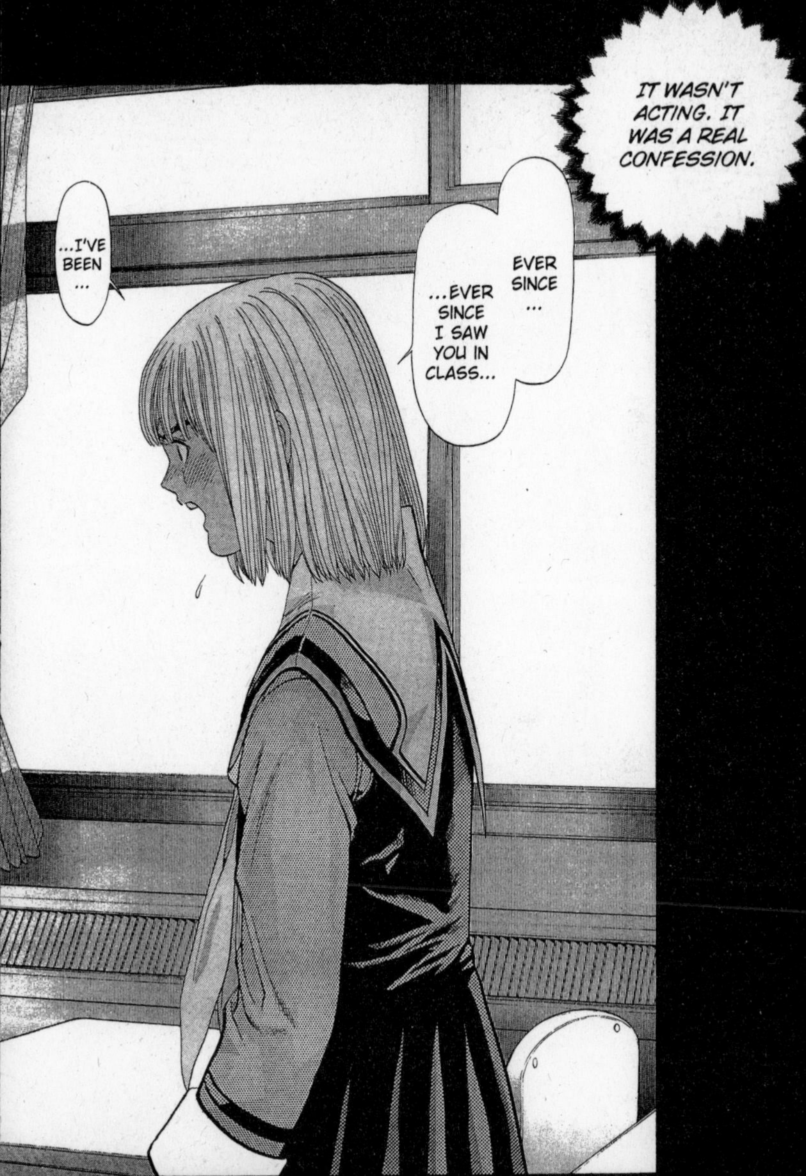
IT WASN'T ACTING. IT WAS A REAL CONFESSION.
EVER SINCE ...
...EVER SINCE I SAW YOU IN CLASS...
...I'VE BEEN ...

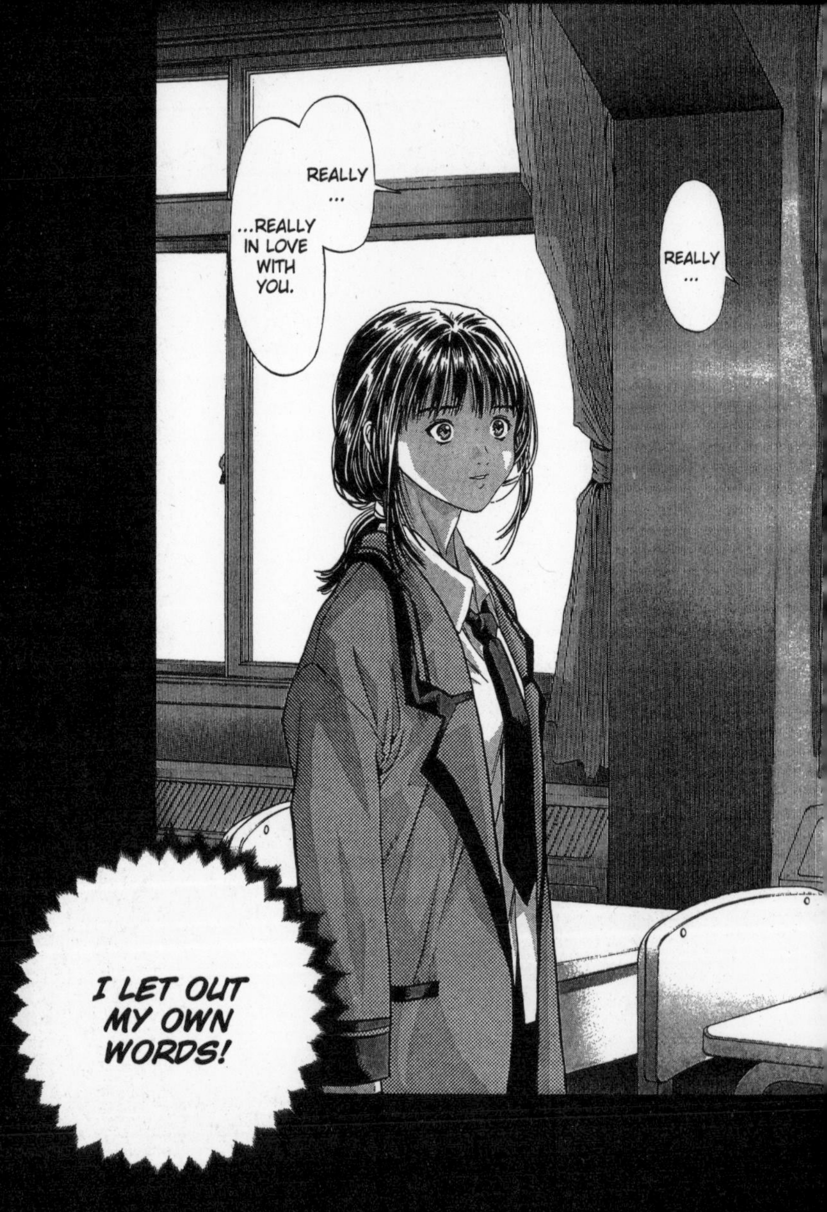
REALLY ...
REALLY ... ...REALLY IN LOVE WITH YOU.
I LET OUT MY OWN WORDS!

Chapter 59:
Acting True To Life

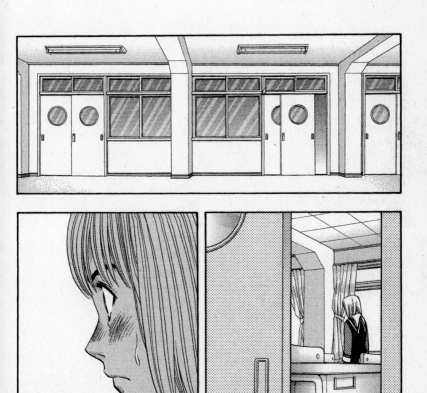

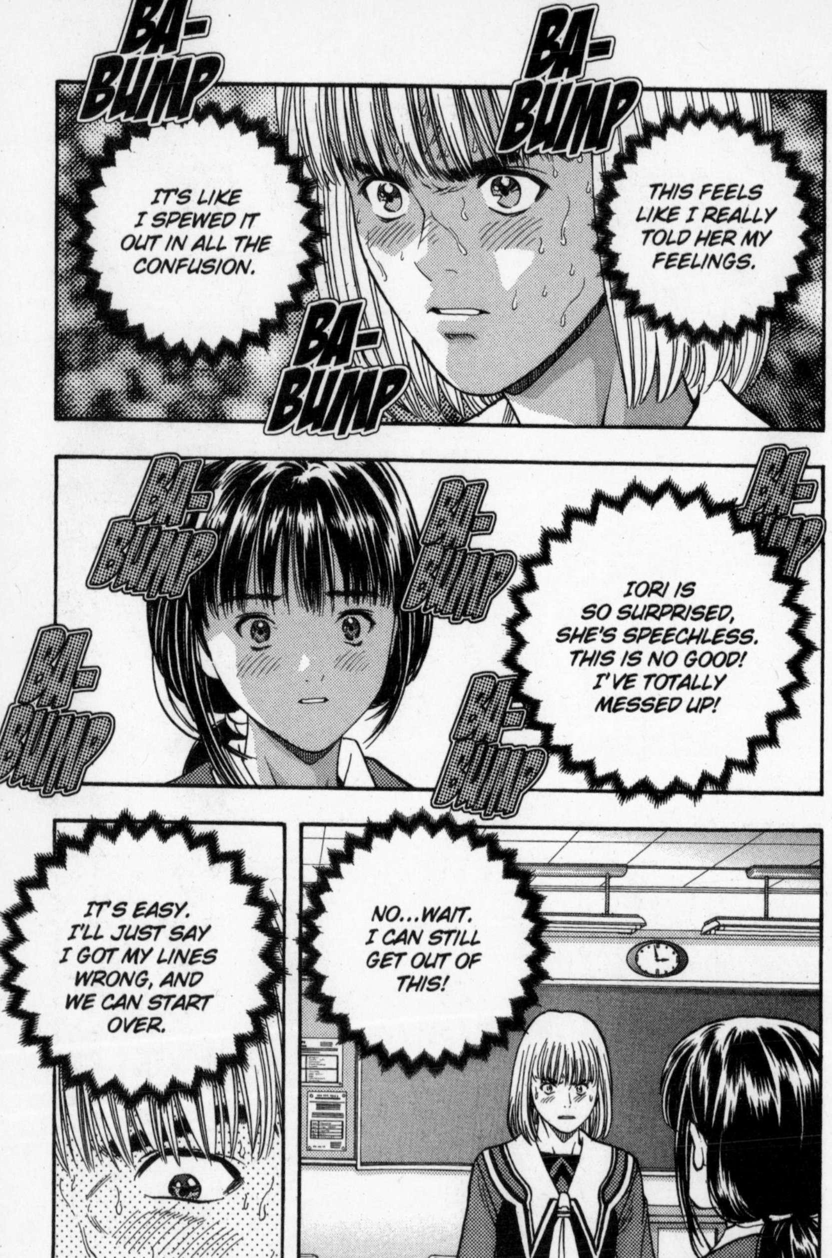
BA-BUMP
THIS FEELS LIKE I REALLY TOLD HER MY FEELINGS.
BA-BUMP
IT'S LIKE I SPEWED IT OUT IN ALL THE CONFUSION.
BA-BUMP
BA-BUMP
IORI IS SO SURPRISED, SHE'S SPEECHLESS. THIS IS NO GOOD! I'VE TOTALLY MESSED UP!
BA-BUMP
BA-BUMP
BA-BUMP
BA-BUMP
NO...WAIT. I CAN STILL GET OUT OF THIS!
IT'S EASY. I'LL JUST SAY I GOT MY LINES WRONG, AND WE CAN START OVER.

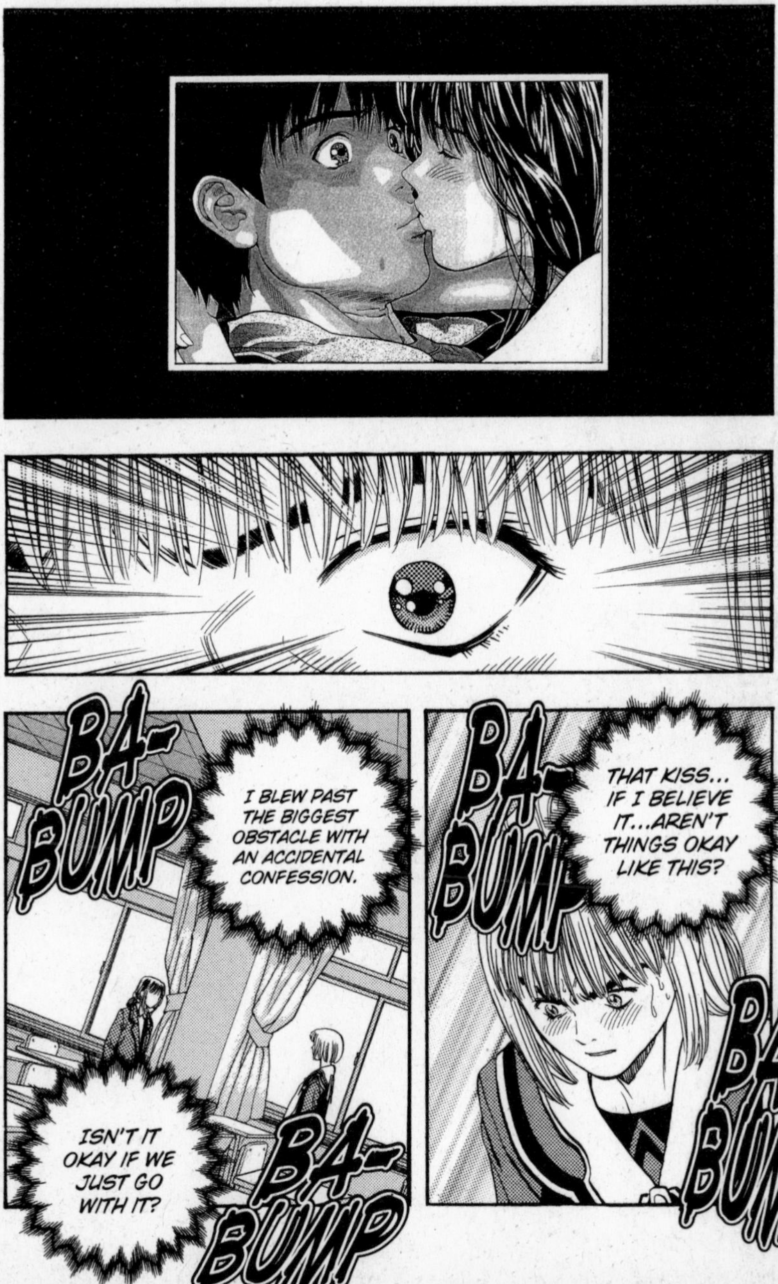
BA-BUMP
THAT KISS... IF I BELIEVE IT...AREN'T THINGS OKAY LIKE THIS?
BA-BUMP
BA-BUMP
I BLEW PAST THE BIGGEST OBSTACLE WITH AN ACCIDENTAL CONFESSION.
ISN'T IT OKAY IF WE JUST GO WITH IT?
BA-BUMP

READ THIS WAY

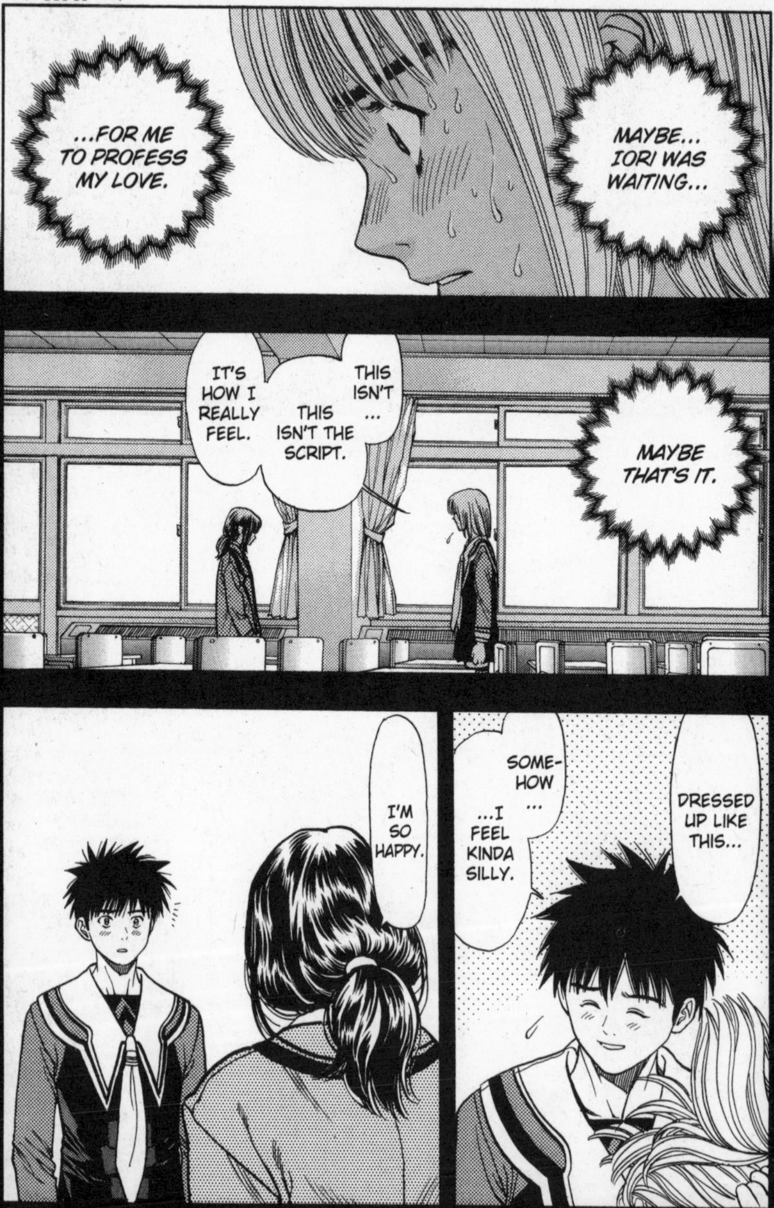
MAYBE... IORI WAS WAITING...
...FOR ME TO PROFESS MY LOVE.
MAYBE THAT'S IT.
THIS ISN'T ...
THIS ISN'T THE SCRIPT.
IT'S HOW I REALLY FEEL.
DRESSED UP LIKE THIS...
SOME-HOW ...
...I FEEL KINDA SILLY.
I'M SO HAPPY.

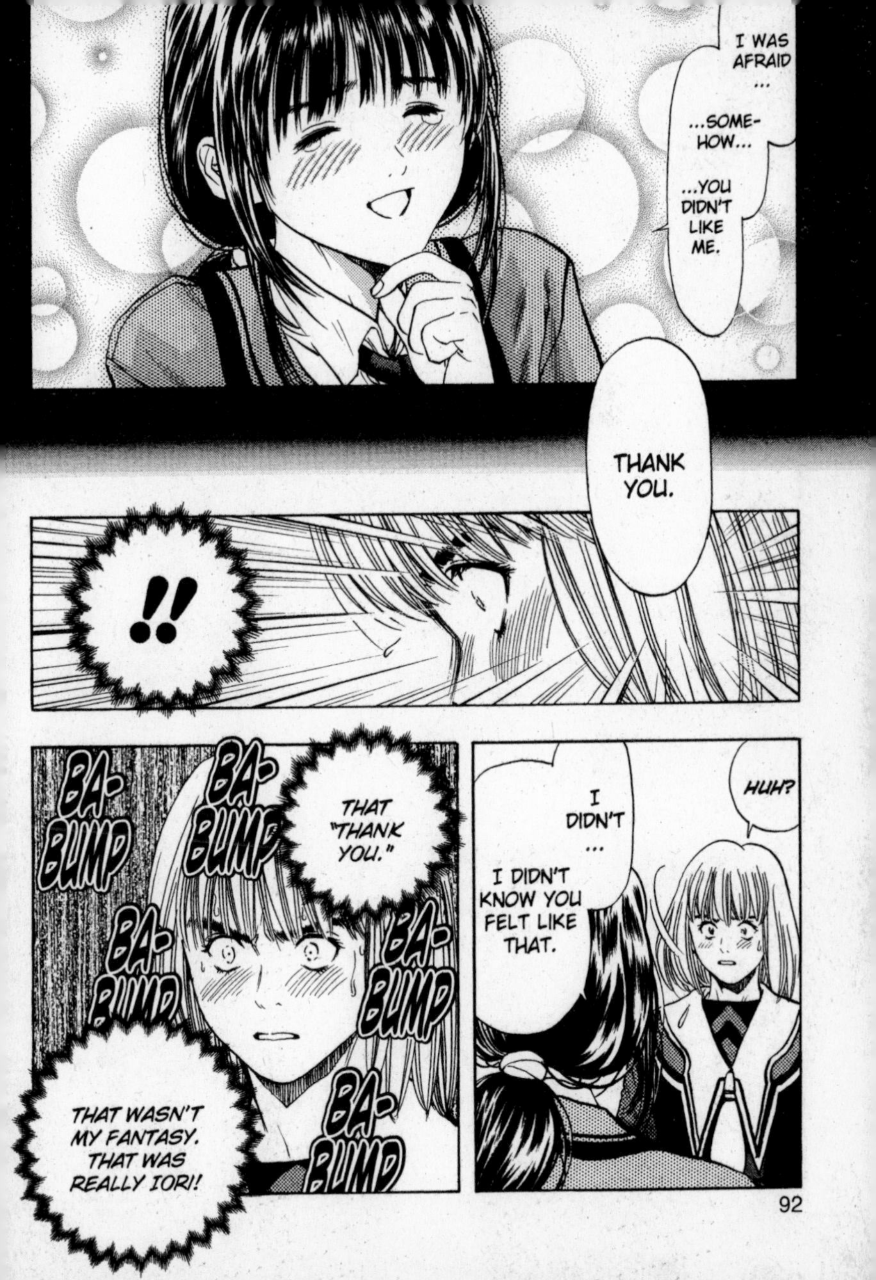
I WAS AFRAID ...
...SOME-HOW...
...YOU DIDN'T LIKE ME.
THANK YOU.
!!
HUH?
I DIDN'T ...
I DIDN'T KNOW YOU FELT LIKE THAT.
BA-BUMP
THAT "THANK YOU."
BA-BUMP
BA-BUMP
BA-BUMP
BA-BUMP
THAT WASN'T MY FANTASY. THAT WAS REALLY IORI!

READ THIS WAY

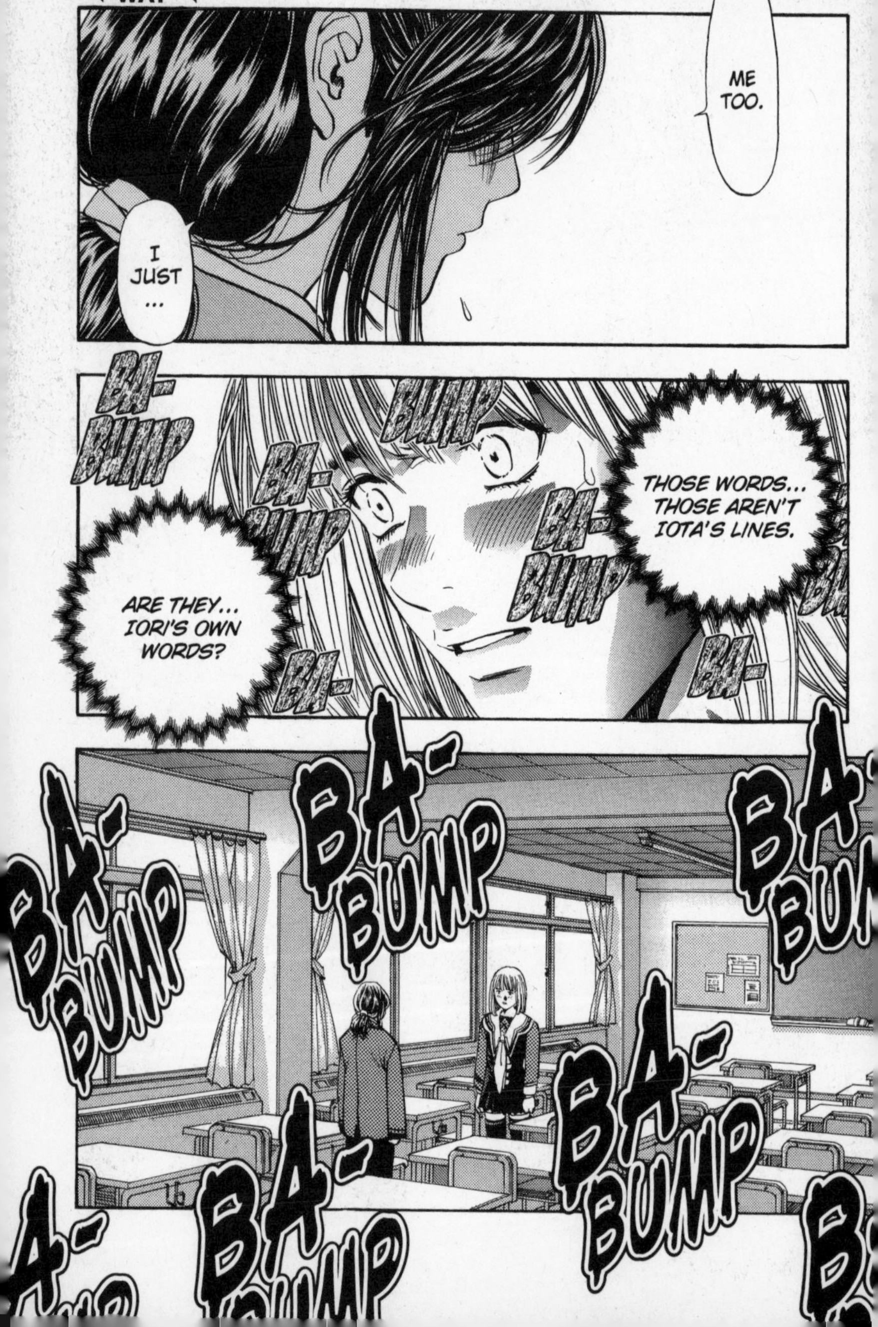
ME TOO.
I JUST ...
BUMP
BA-BUMP
BA-BUMP
THOSE WORDS... THOSE AREN'T IOTA'S LINES.
BA-BUMP
ARE THEY... IORI'S OWN WORDS?
BA-
BA-
BA-BUMP
BA-BUMP
BA-BUMP
BA-BUMP

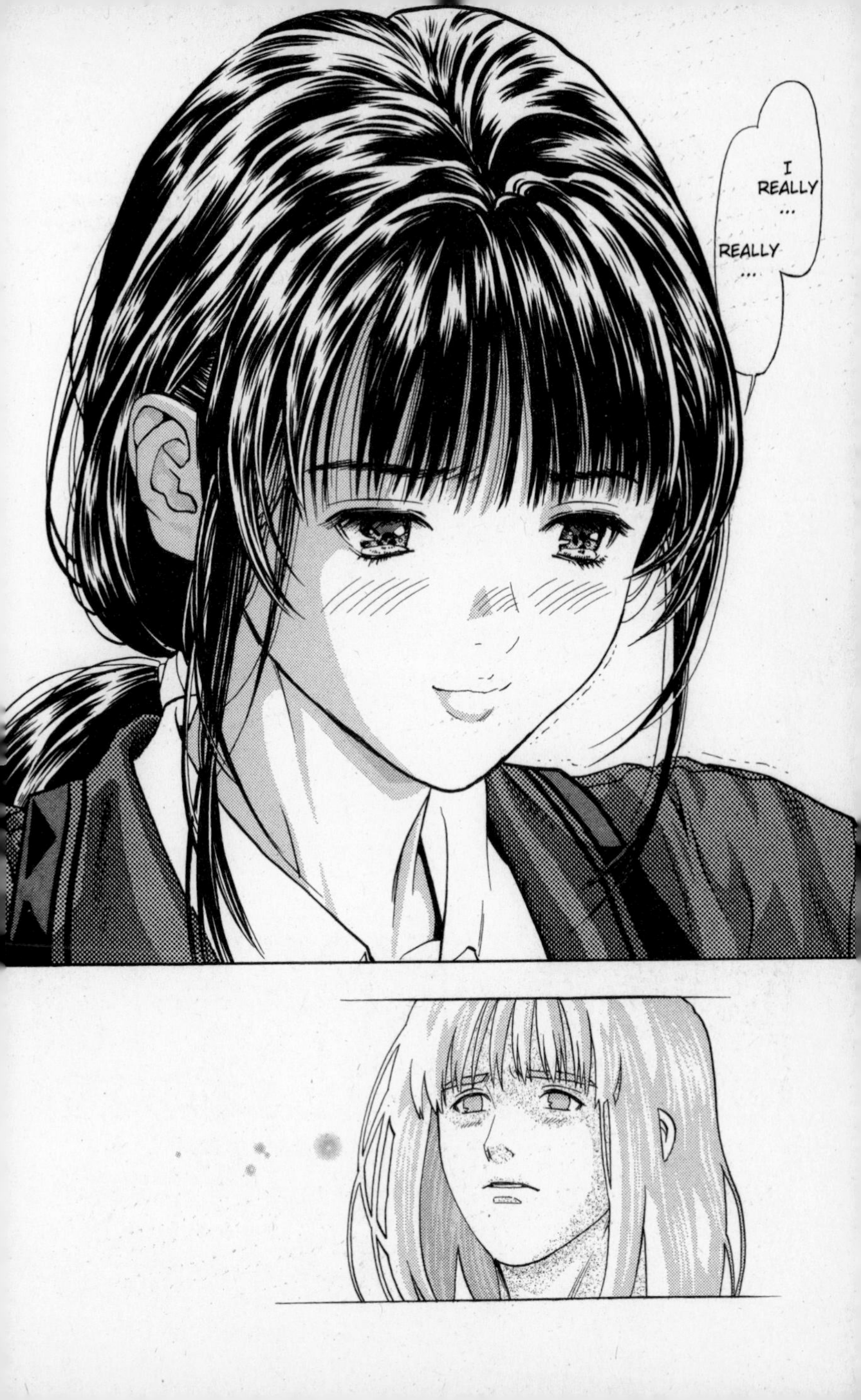
I REALLY ... REALLY ...

I ALWAYS THOUGHT THIS WOULD PROBABLY TAKE GREAT COURAGE AND DETERMINATION.

BUT REALITY IS MORE LIKE THIS. JUST A FEW WORDS, AND IT'S DONE.

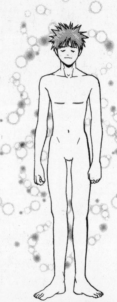

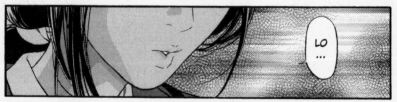

LO...

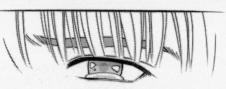

...UNREQUITED LOVE...

THE TIME OF...

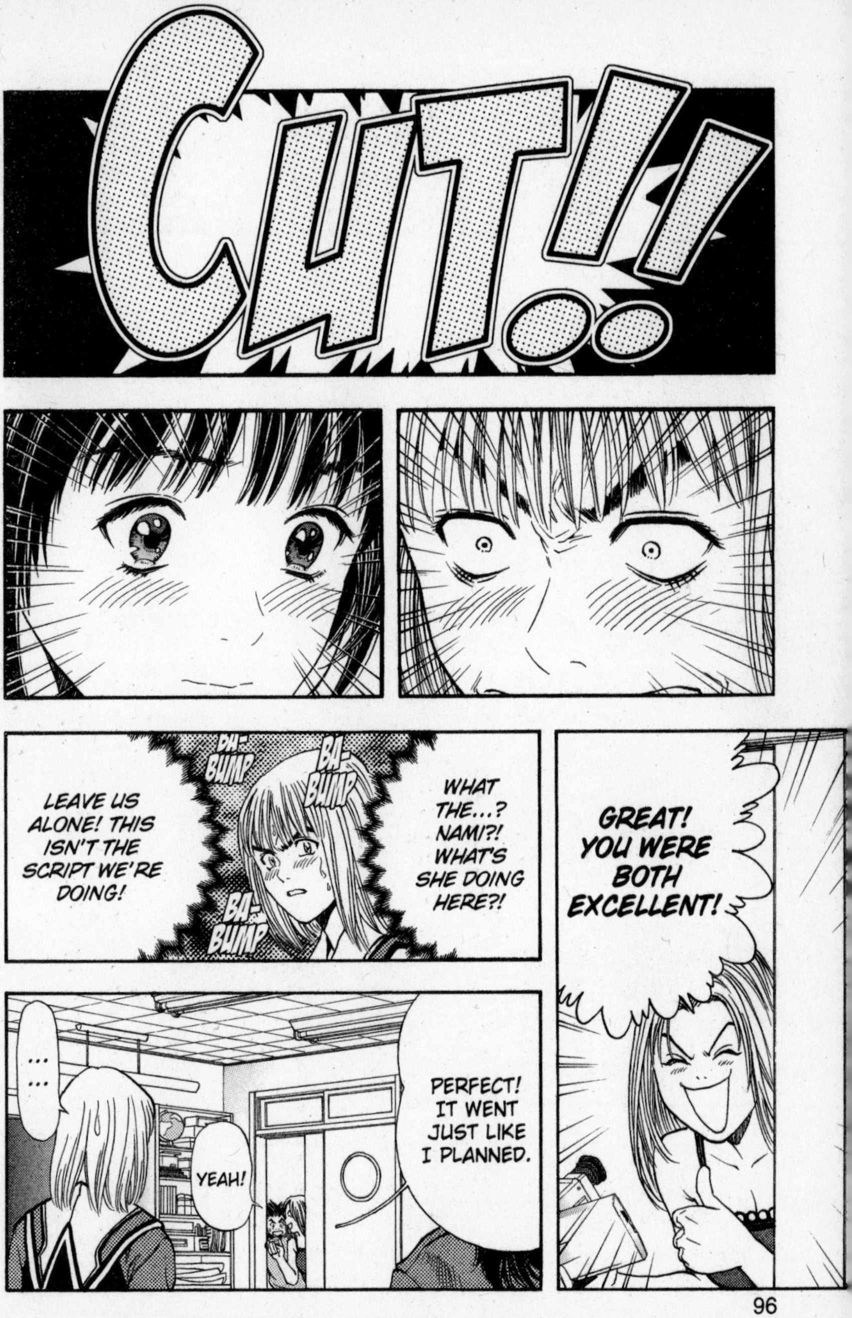
CUT!!
GREAT! YOU WERE BOTH EXCELLENT!
BA-BUMP
BA-BUMP
WHAT THE...? NAMI?! WHAT'S SHE DOING HERE?!
BA-BUMP
LEAVE US ALONE! THIS ISN'T THE SCRIPT WE'RE DOING!
PERFECT! IT WENT JUST LIKE I PLANNED.
YEAH!
... ...

READ THIS WAY

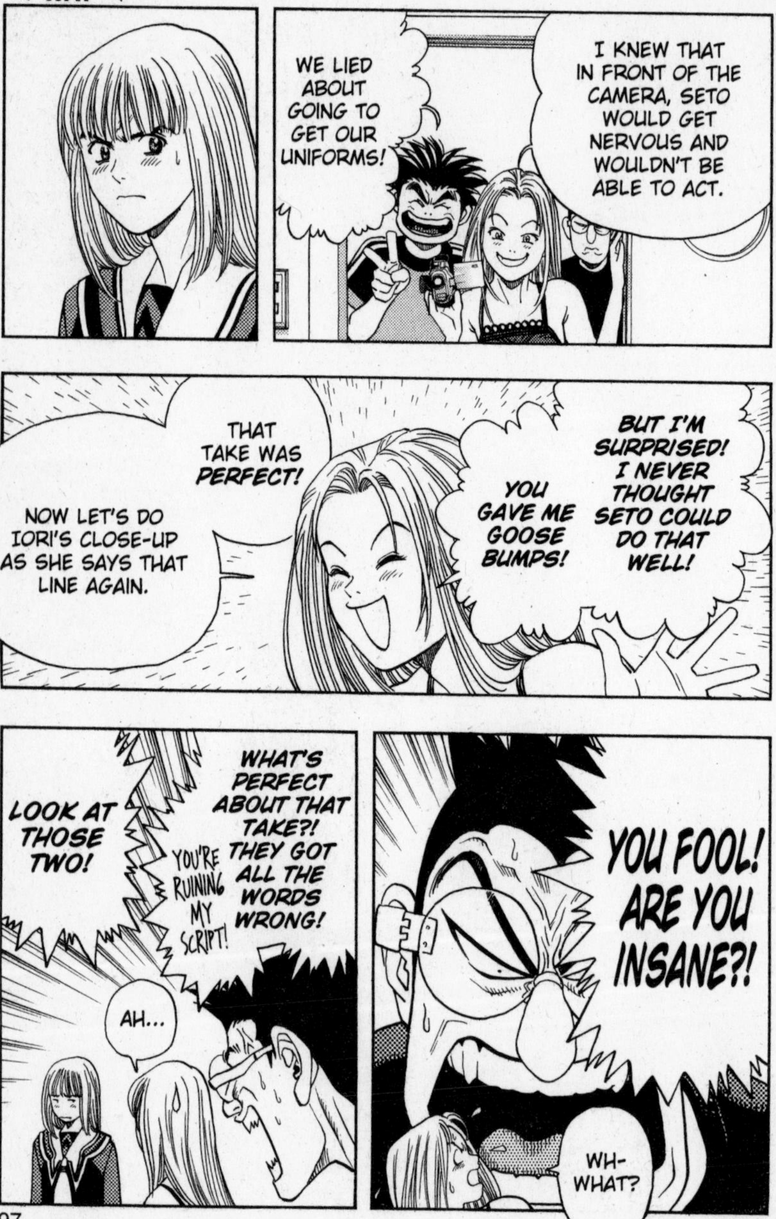
I KNEW THAT IN FRONT OF THE CAMERA, SETO WOULD GET NERVOUS AND WOULDN'T BE ABLE TO ACT.
WE LIED ABOUT GOING TO GET OUR UNIFORMS!
BUT I'M SURPRISED! I NEVER THOUGHT SETO COULD DO THAT WELL!
YOU GAVE ME GOOSE BUMPS!
THAT TAKE WAS PERFECT!
NOW LET'S DO IORI'S CLOSE-UP AS SHE SAYS THAT LINE AGAIN.
YOU FOOL! ARE YOU INSANE?!
WH- WHAT?
WHAT'S PERFECT ABOUT THAT TAKE?! THEY GOT ALL THE WORDS WRONG!
YOU'RE RUINING MY SCRIPT!
LOOK AT THOSE TWO!
AH...

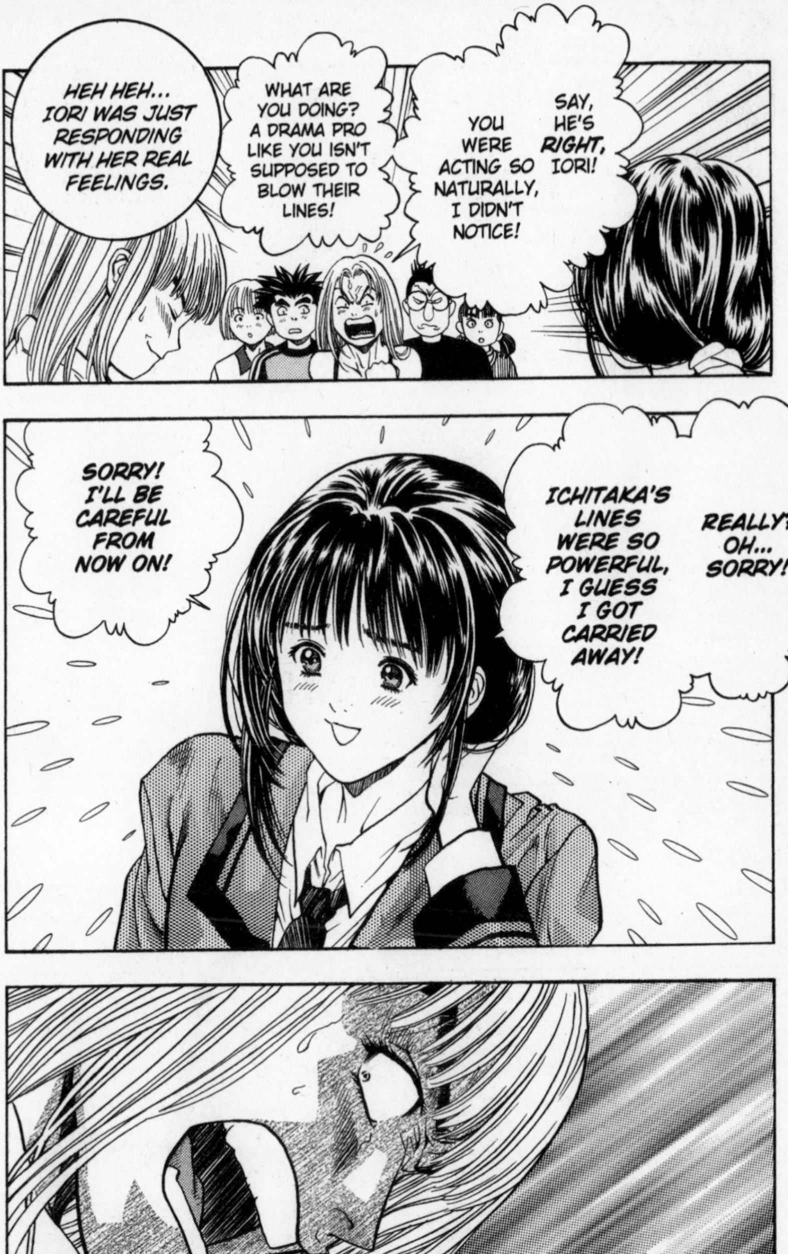
SAY, HE'S RIGHT, IORI!
YOU WERE ACTING SO NATURALLY, I DIDN'T NOTICE!
WHAT ARE YOU DOING? A DRAMA PRO LIKE YOU ISN'T SUPPOSED TO BLOW THEIR LINES!
HEH HEH... IORI WAS JUST RESPONDING WITH HER REAL FEELINGS.
REALLY? OH... SORRY!
ICHITAKA'S LINES WERE SO POWERFUL, I GUESS I GOT CARRIED AWAY!
SORRY! I'LL BE CAREFUL FROM NOW ON!

READ THIS WAY

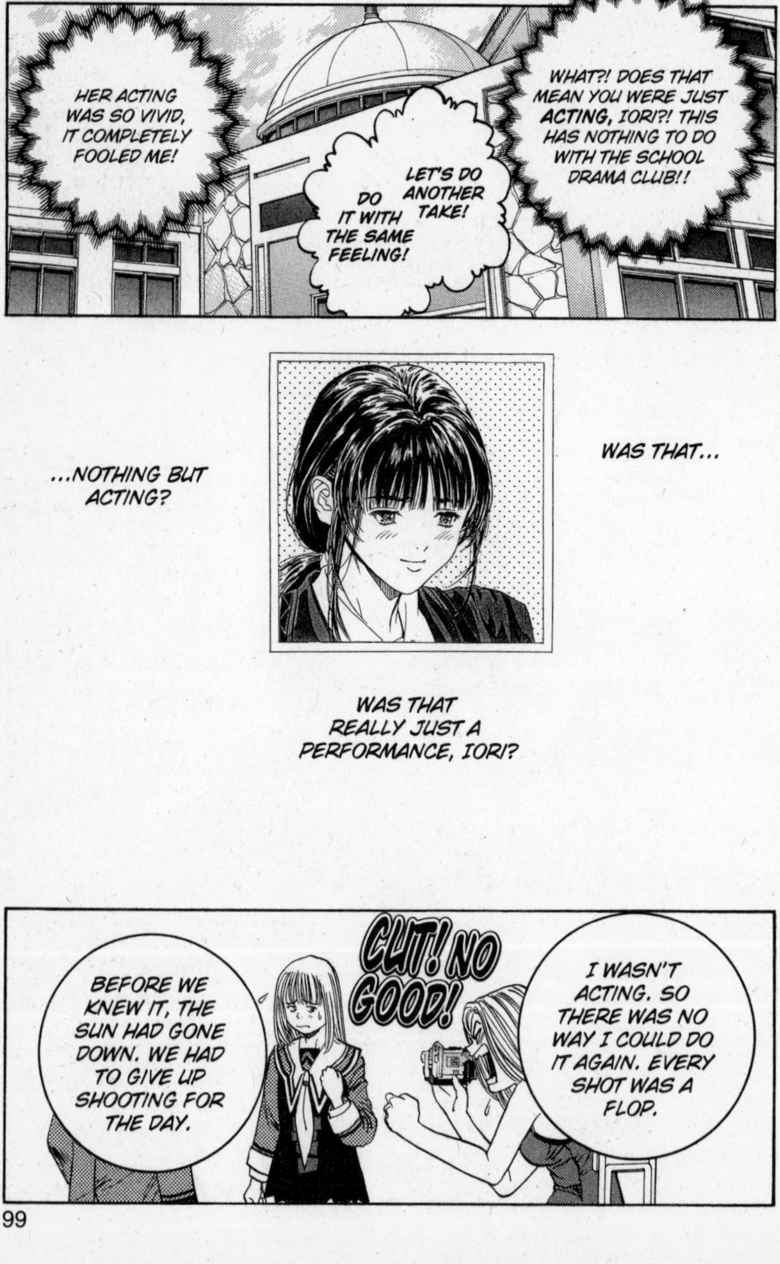
WHAT?! DOES THAT MEAN YOU WERE JUST **ACTING,** IORI?! THIS HAS NOTHING TO DO WITH THE SCHOOL DRAMA CLUB!!
LET'S DO ANOTHER TAKE!
DO IT WITH THE SAME FEELING!
HER ACTING WAS SO VIVID, IT COMPLETELY FOOLED ME!
WAS THAT...
...NOTHING BUT ACTING?
WAS THAT REALLY JUST A PERFORMANCE, IORI?
I WASN'T ACTING. SO THERE WAS NO WAY I COULD DO IT AGAIN. EVERY SHOT WAS A FLOP.
CUT! NO GOOD!
BEFORE WE KNEW IT, THE SUN HAD GONE DOWN. WE HAD TO GIVE UP SHOOTING FOR THE DAY.

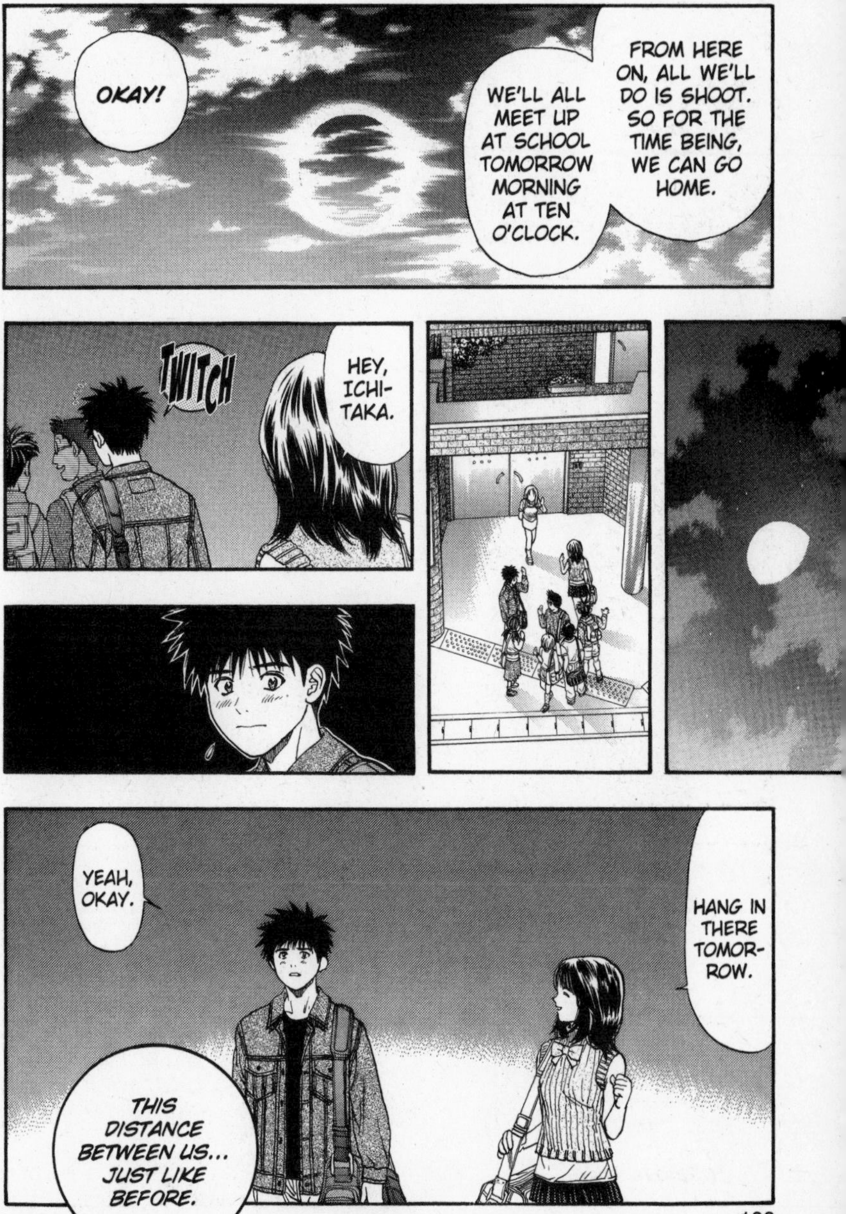
FROM HERE ON, ALL WE'LL DO IS SHOOT. SO FOR THE TIME BEING, WE CAN GO HOME.
WE'LL ALL MEET UP AT SCHOOL TOMORROW MORNING AT TEN O'CLOCK.
OKAY!
HEY, ICHI-TAKA.
TWITCH
HANG IN THERE TOMOR-ROW.
YEAH, OKAY.
THIS DISTANCE BETWEEN US... JUST LIKE BEFORE.

READ THIS WAY

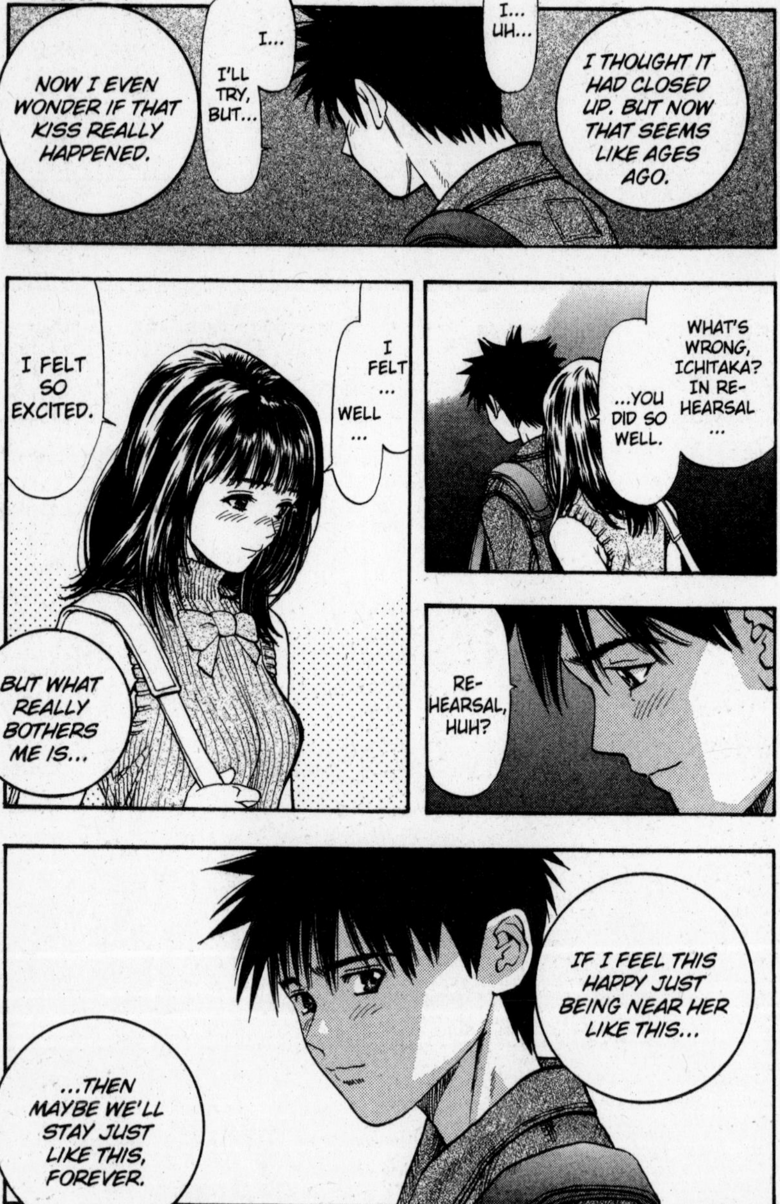
I THOUGHT IT HAD CLOSED UP. BUT NOW THAT SEEMS LIKE AGES AGO.
I... UH...
I...
I'LL TRY, BUT...
NOW I EVEN WONDER IF THAT KISS REALLY HAPPENED.
WHAT'S WRONG, ICHITAKA? IN RE-HEARSAL...
...YOU DID SO WELL.
RE-HEARSAL, HUH?
I FELT... WELL...
I FELT SO EXCITED.
BUT WHAT REALLY BOTHERS ME IS...
IF I FEEL THIS HAPPY JUST BEING NEAR HER LIKE THIS...
...THEN MAYBE WE'LL STAY JUST LIKE THIS, FOREVER.

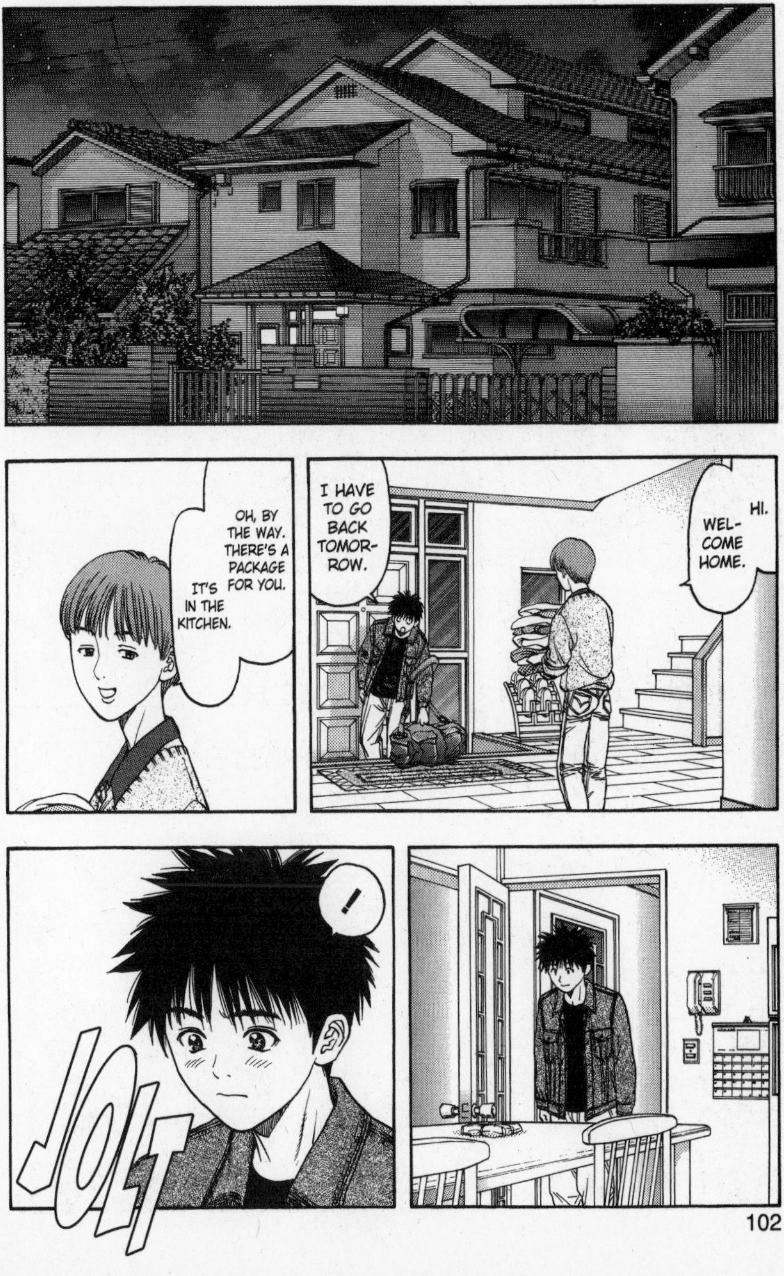
HI. WEL-COME HOME.
I HAVE TO GO BACK TOMOR-ROW.
OH, BY THE WAY. THERE'S A PACKAGE FOR YOU.
IT'S IN THE KITCHEN.
!
JOLT

READ THIS WAY

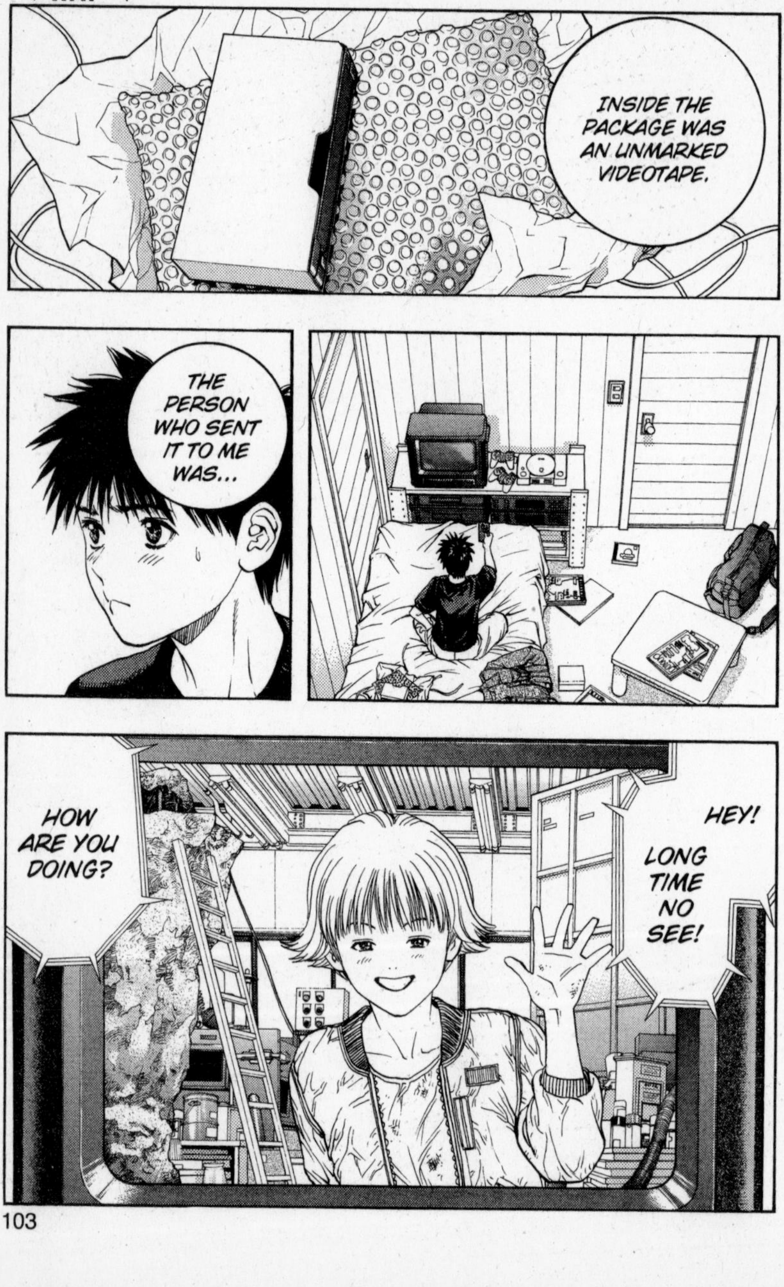
INSIDE THE PACKAGE WAS AN UNMARKED VIDEOTAPE.
THE PERSON WHO SENT IT TO ME WAS...
HEY!
LONG TIME NO SEE!
HOW ARE YOU DOING?

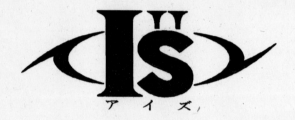

Chapter 60:
Falling Together

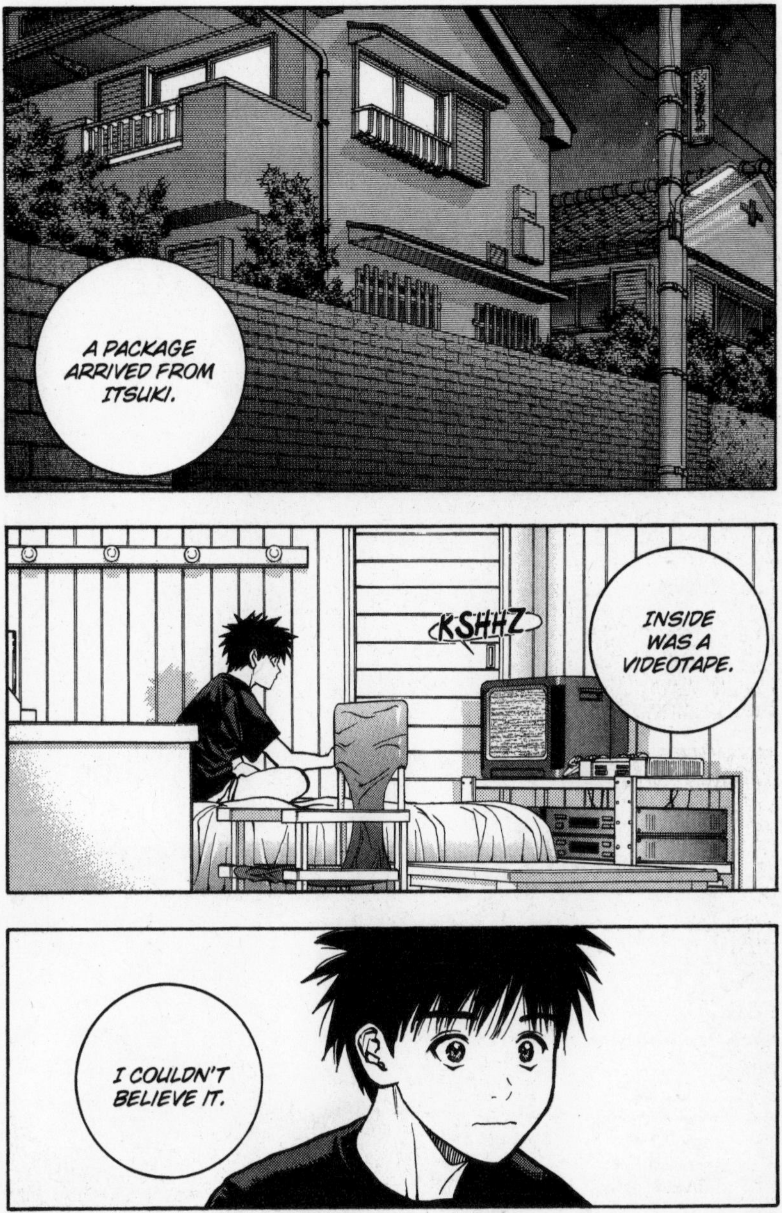
A PACKAGE ARRIVED FROM ITSUKI.
INSIDE WAS A VIDEOTAPE.
KSHHZ
I COULDN'T BELIEVE IT.

READ THIS WAY

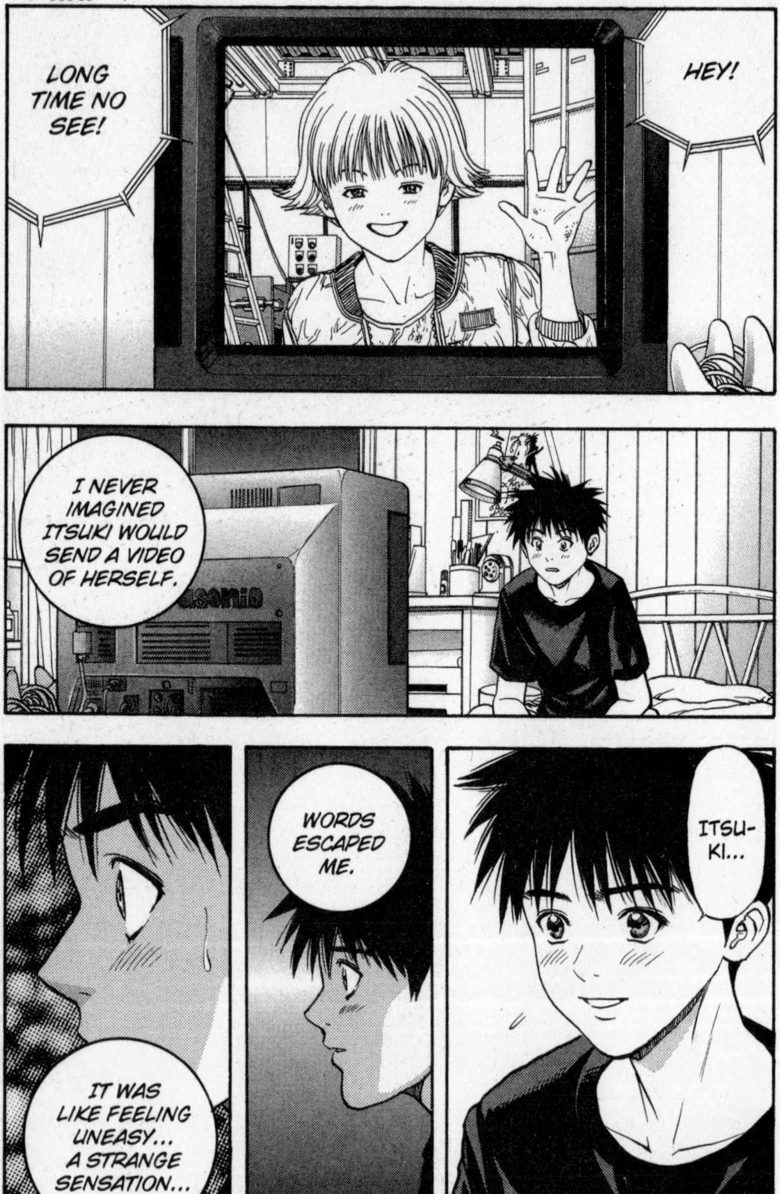
HEY!
LONG TIME NO SEE!
I NEVER IMAGINED ITSUKI WOULD SEND A VIDEO OF HERSELF.
ITSU-KI...
WORDS ESCAPED ME.
IT WAS LIKE FEELING UNEASY... A STRANGE SENSATION...

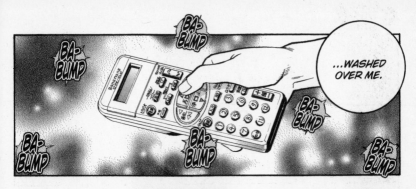

...WASHED OVER ME.
BA-BUMP
BA-BUMP
BA-BUMP
BA-BUMP
BA-BUMP
BA-BUMP
I FIGURE BY NOW...
...YOU'VE PROBABLY FORGOTTEN ABOUT ME.
EH?
TWITCH
NAH, I KNEW YOU WOULDN'T.
ITSUKI... WHY ARE YOU DOING THIS?

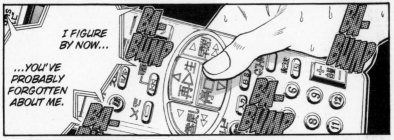

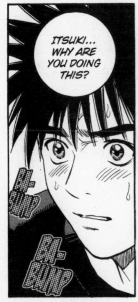

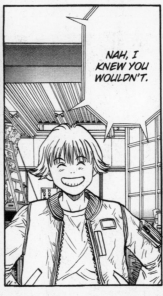

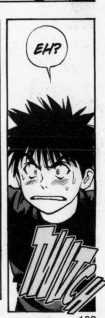

READ THIS WAY

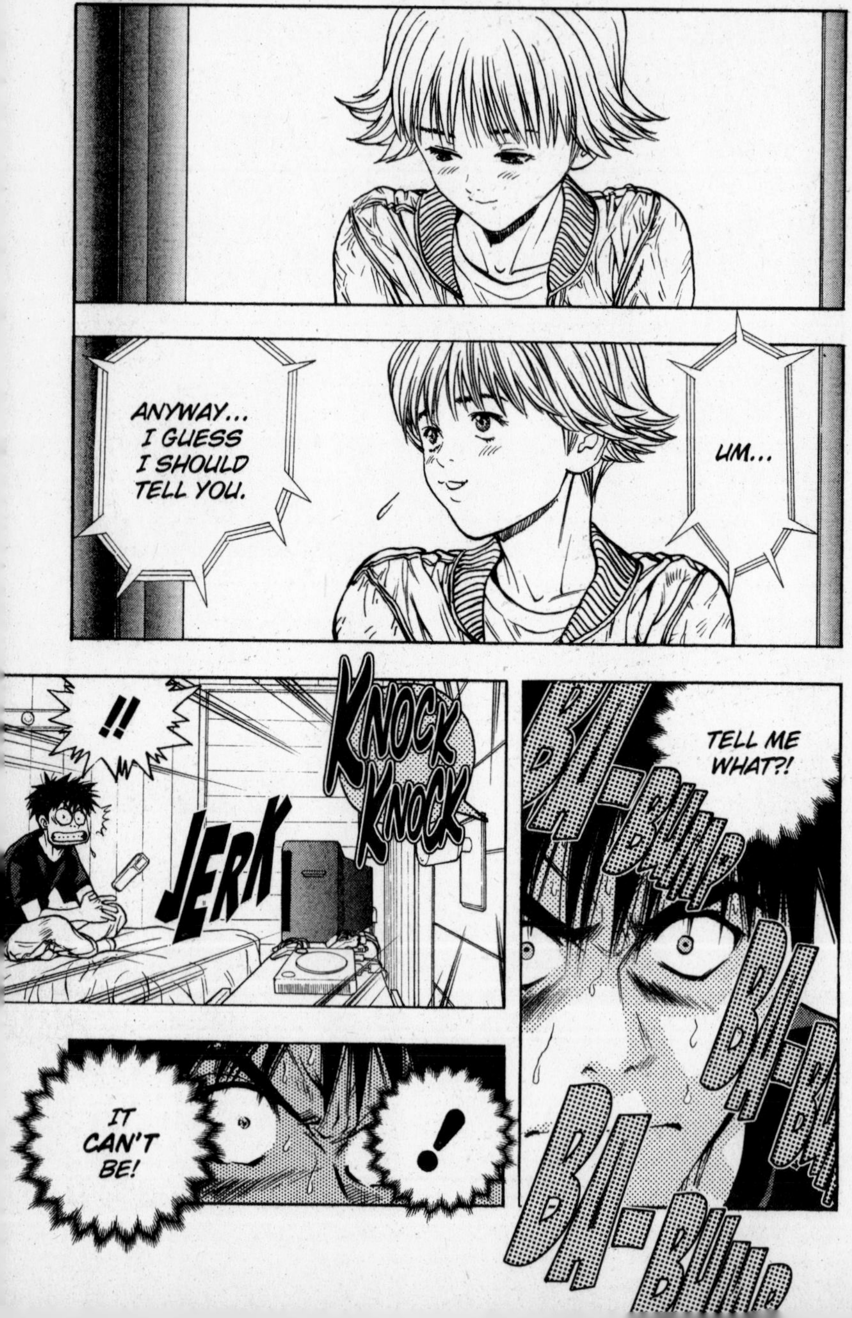
UM...
ANYWAY... I GUESS I SHOULD TELL YOU.
TELL ME WHAT?!
BA-BUMP
KNOCK KNOCK
!!
JERK
!
IT CAN'T BE!

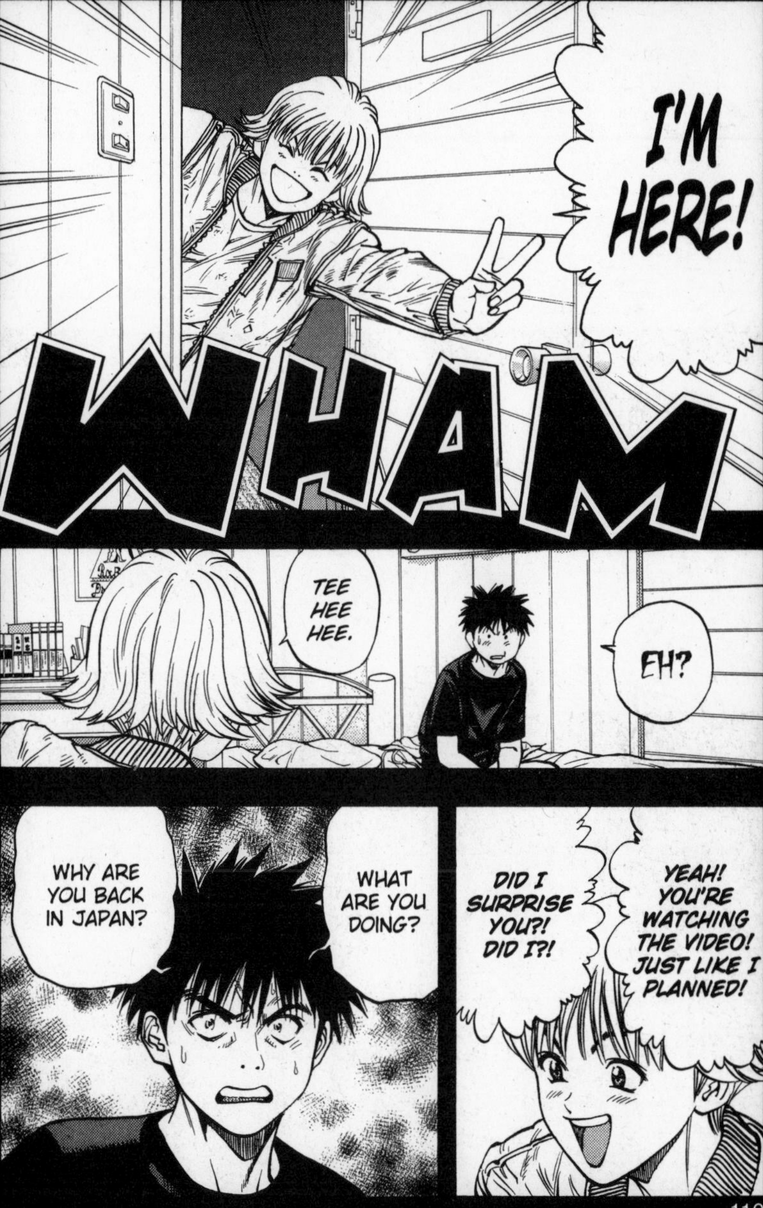
I'M HERE!
WHAM
TEE HEE HEE.
EH?
DID I SURPRISE YOU?! DID I?!
YEAH! YOU'RE WATCHING THE VIDEO! JUST LIKE I PLANNED!
WHAT ARE YOU DOING?
WHY ARE YOU BACK IN JAPAN?

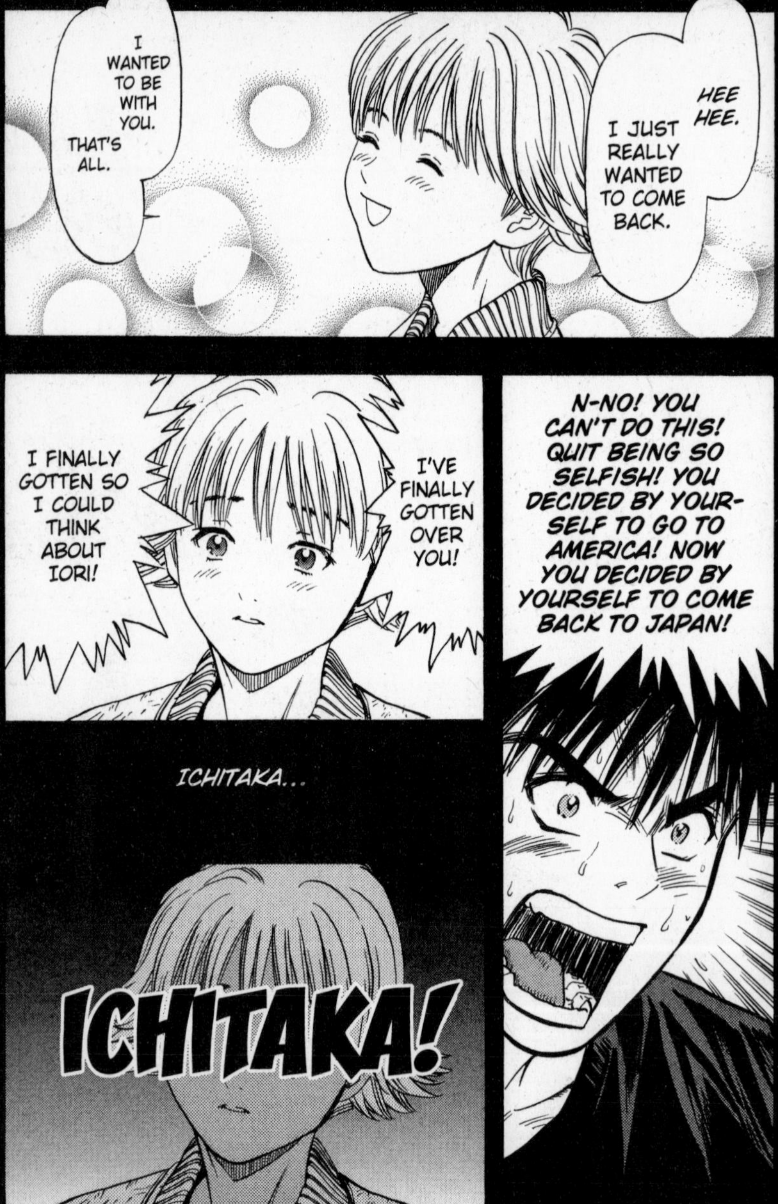
HEE HEE.
I JUST REALLY WANTED TO COME BACK.
I WANTED TO BE WITH YOU.
THAT'S ALL.
N-NO! YOU CAN'T DO THIS! QUIT BEING SO SELFISH! YOU DECIDED BY YOURSELF TO GO TO AMERICA! NOW YOU DECIDED BY YOURSELF TO COME BACK TO JAPAN!
I'VE FINALLY GOTTEN OVER YOU!
I FINALLY GOTTEN SO I COULD THINK ABOUT IORI!
ICHITAKA...
ICHITAKA!

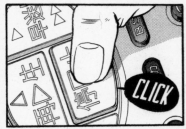

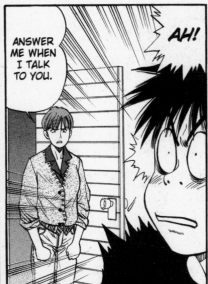

CLICK

ANSWER ME WHEN I TALK TO YOU.

AH!

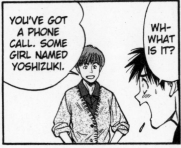

YOU'VE GOT A PHONE CALL. SOME GIRL NAMED YOSHIZUKI.

WH-WHAT IS IT?

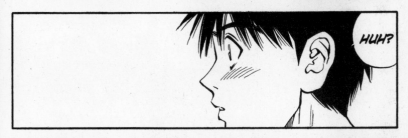

HUH?

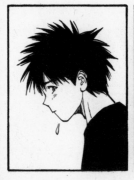

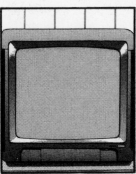

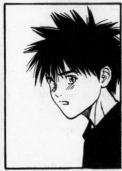

READ THIS WAY

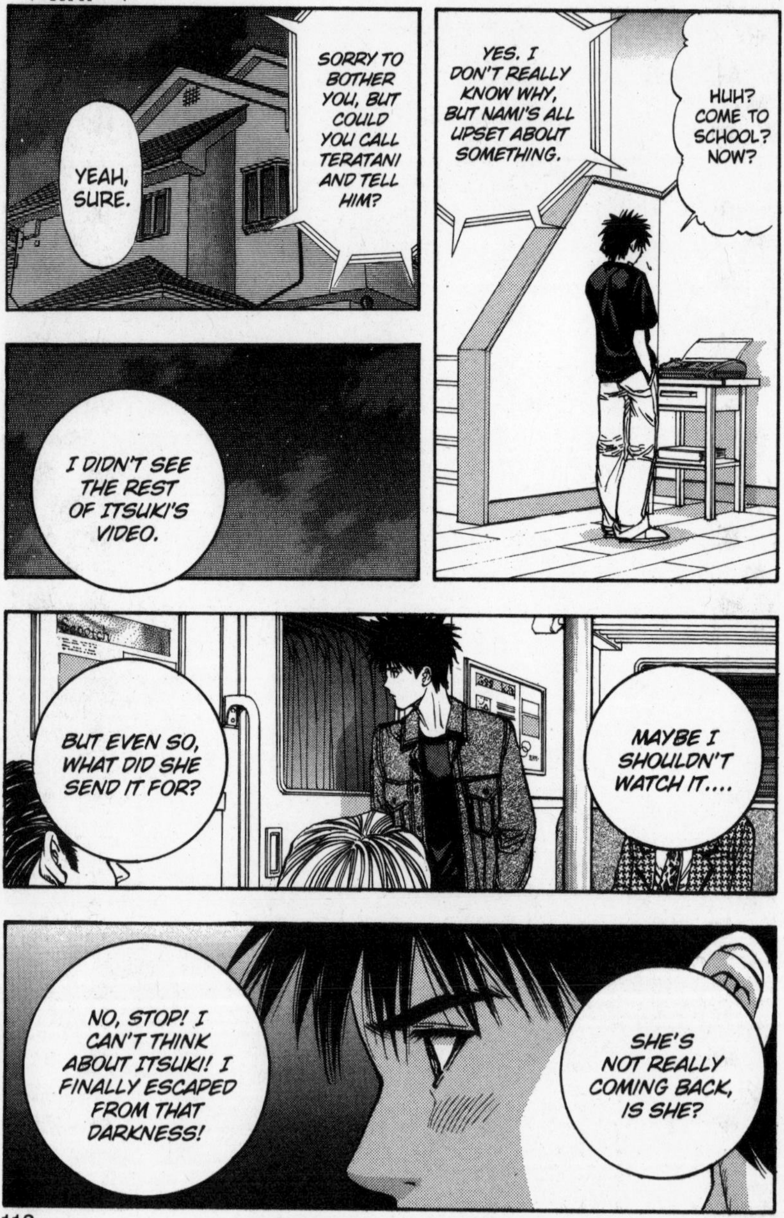
HUH? COME TO SCHOOL? NOW?
YES. I DON'T REALLY KNOW WHY, BUT NAMI'S ALL UPSET ABOUT SOMETHING.
SORRY TO BOTHER YOU, BUT COULD YOU CALL TERATANI AND TELL HIM?
YEAH, SURE.
I DIDN'T SEE THE REST OF ITSUKI'S VIDEO.
MAYBE I SHOULDN'T WATCH IT....
BUT EVEN SO, WHAT DID SHE SEND IT FOR?
SHE'S NOT REALLY COMING BACK, IS SHE?
NO, STOP! I CAN'T THINK ABOUT ITSUKI! I FINALLY ESCAPED FROM THAT DARKNESS!

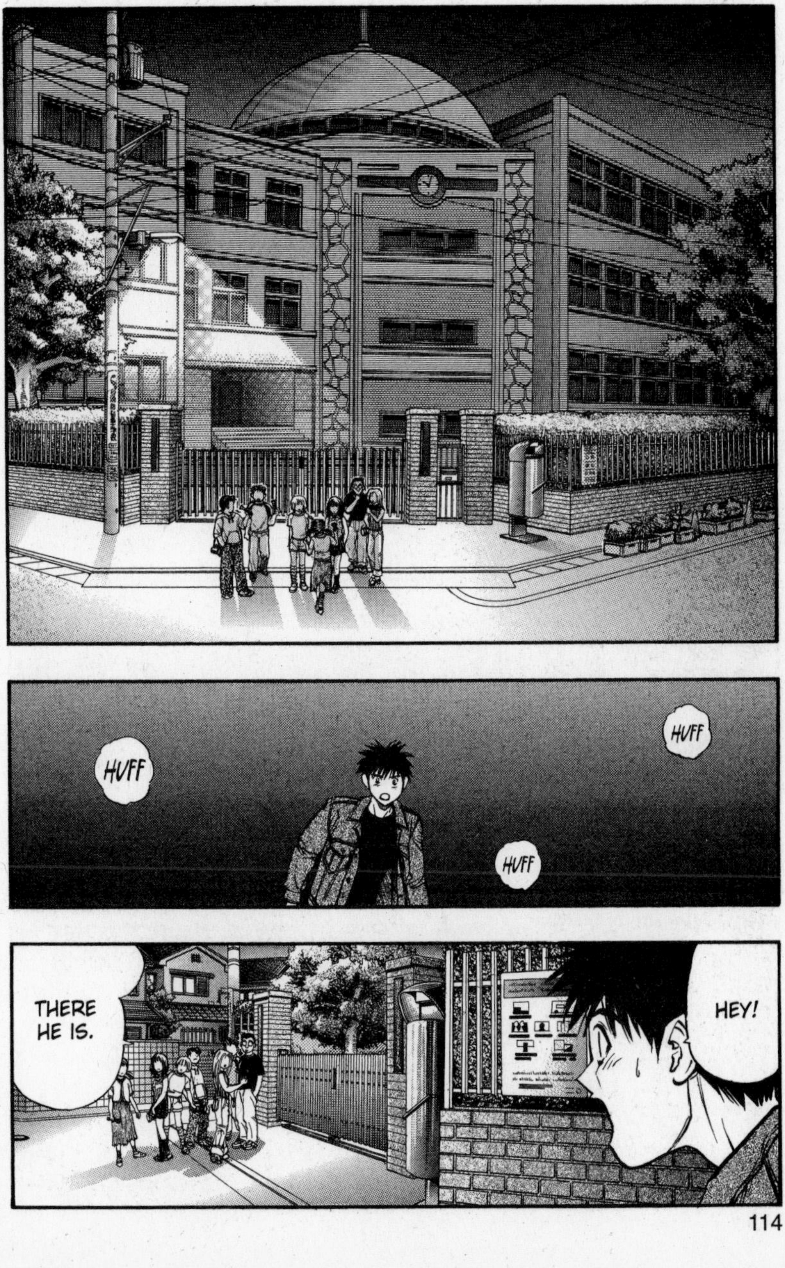
HUFF
HUFF
HUFF
HEY!
THERE HE IS.

READ THIS WAY

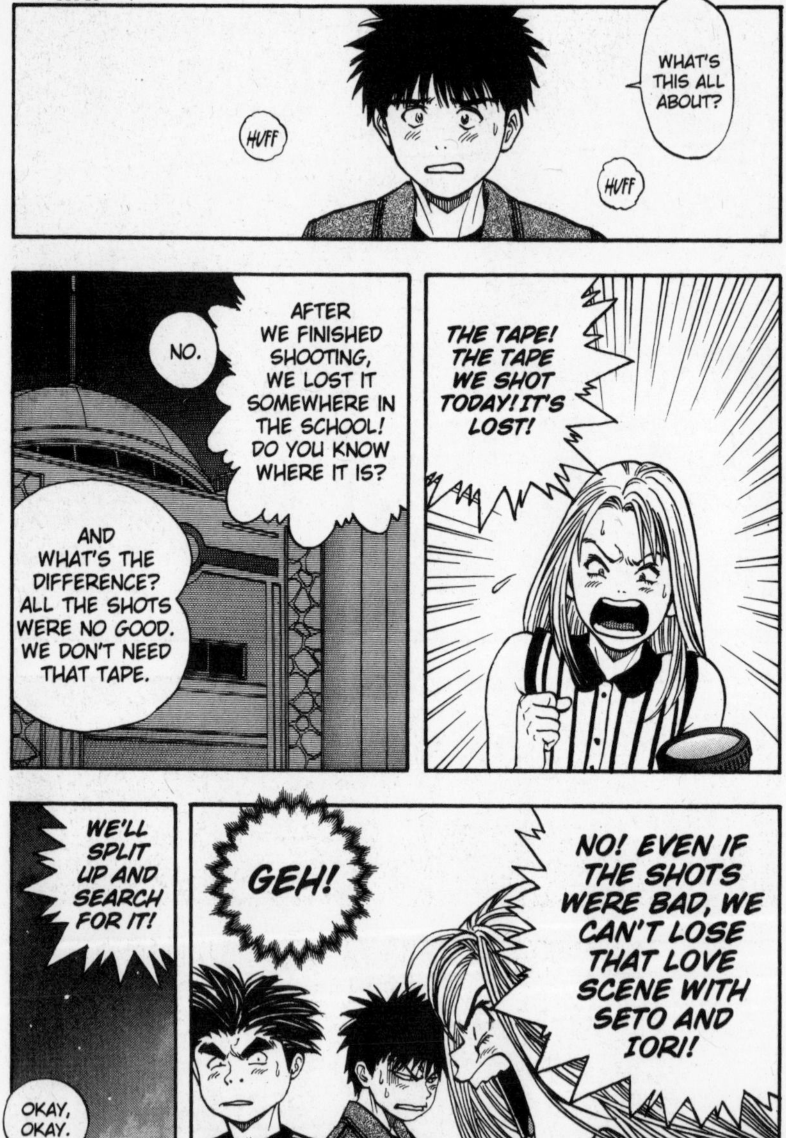
WHAT'S THIS ALL ABOUT?
HUFF
HUFF
THE TAPE! THE TAPE WE SHOT TODAY! IT'S LOST!
AFTER WE FINISHED SHOOTING, WE LOST IT SOMEWHERE IN THE SCHOOL! DO YOU KNOW WHERE IT IS?
NO.
AND WHAT'S THE DIFFERENCE? ALL THE SHOTS WERE NO GOOD. WE DON'T NEED THAT TAPE.
NO! EVEN IF THE SHOTS WERE BAD, WE CAN'T LOSE THAT LOVE SCENE WITH SETO AND IORI!
GEH!
WE'LL SPLIT UP AND SEARCH FOR IT!
OKAY, OKAY.

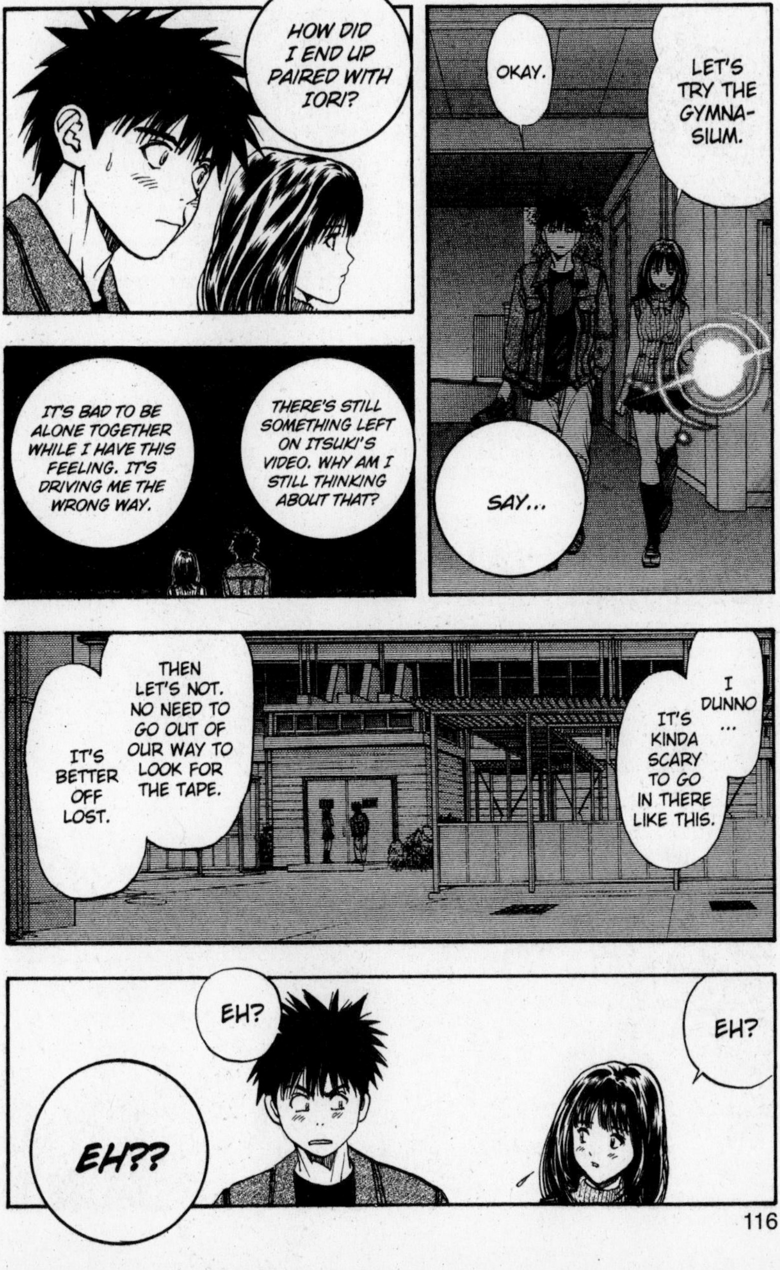

LET'S TRY THE GYMNASIUM.
OKAY.
SAY...
HOW DID I END UP PAIRED WITH IORI?
THERE'S STILL SOMETHING LEFT ON ITSUKI'S VIDEO. WHY AM I STILL THINKING ABOUT THAT?
IT'S BAD TO BE ALONE TOGETHER WHILE I HAVE THIS FEELING. IT'S DRIVING ME THE WRONG WAY.
I DUNNO...
IT'S KINDA SCARY TO GO IN THERE LIKE THIS.
THEN LET'S NOT. NO NEED TO GO OUT OF OUR WAY TO LOOK FOR THE TAPE.
IT'S BETTER OFF LOST.
EH?
EH?
EH??

READ THIS WAY

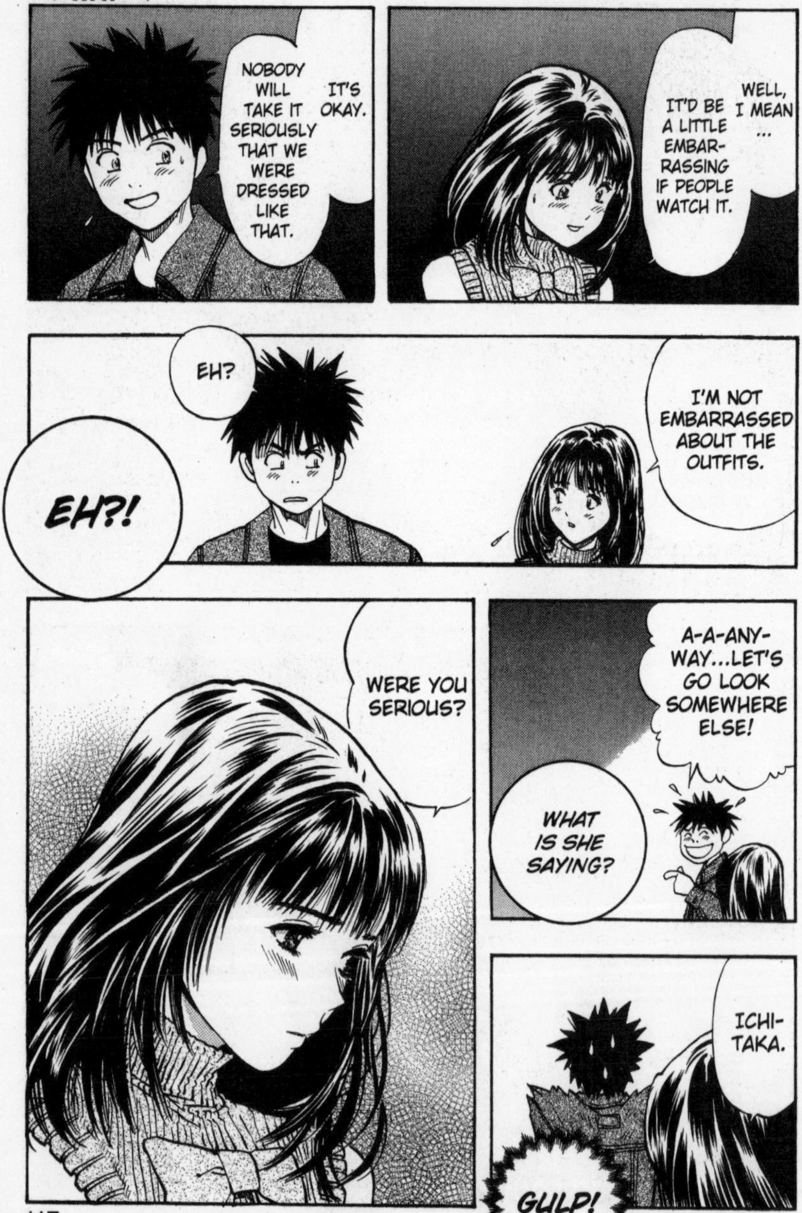
WELL, I MEAN ...
IT'D BE A LITTLE EMBARRASSING IF PEOPLE WATCH IT.
IT'S OKAY.
NOBODY WILL TAKE IT SERIOUSLY THAT WE WERE DRESSED LIKE THAT.
I'M NOT EMBARRASSED ABOUT THE OUTFITS.
EH?
EH?!
A-A-ANYWAY...LET'S GO LOOK SOMEWHERE ELSE!
WHAT IS SHE SAYING?
ICHITAKA.
GULP!
WERE YOU SERIOUS?

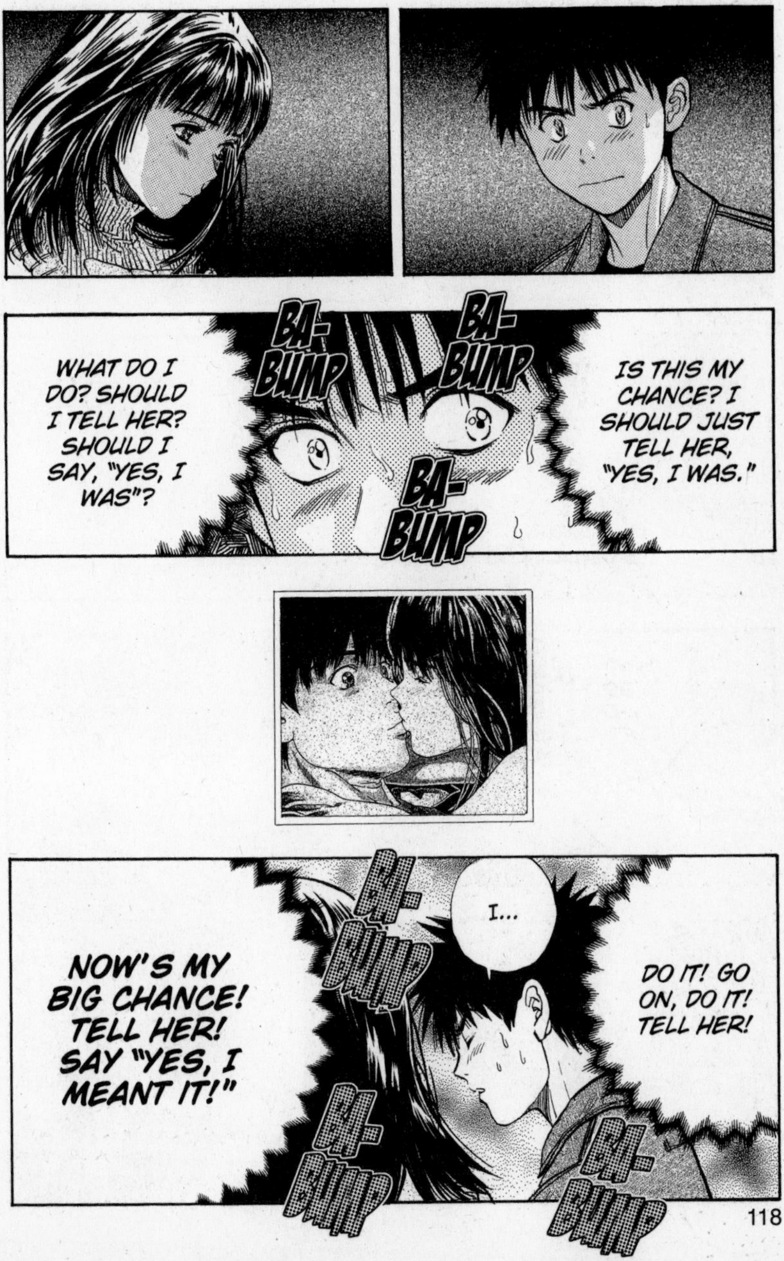
IS THIS MY CHANCE? I SHOULD JUST TELL HER, "YES, I WAS."
BA-BUMP
BA-BUMP
BA-BUMP
WHAT DO I DO? SHOULD I TELL HER? SHOULD I SAY, "YES, I WAS"?
I...
DO IT! GO ON, DO IT! TELL HER!
NOW'S MY BIG CHANCE! TELL HER! SAY "YES, I MEANT IT!"

READ THIS WAY

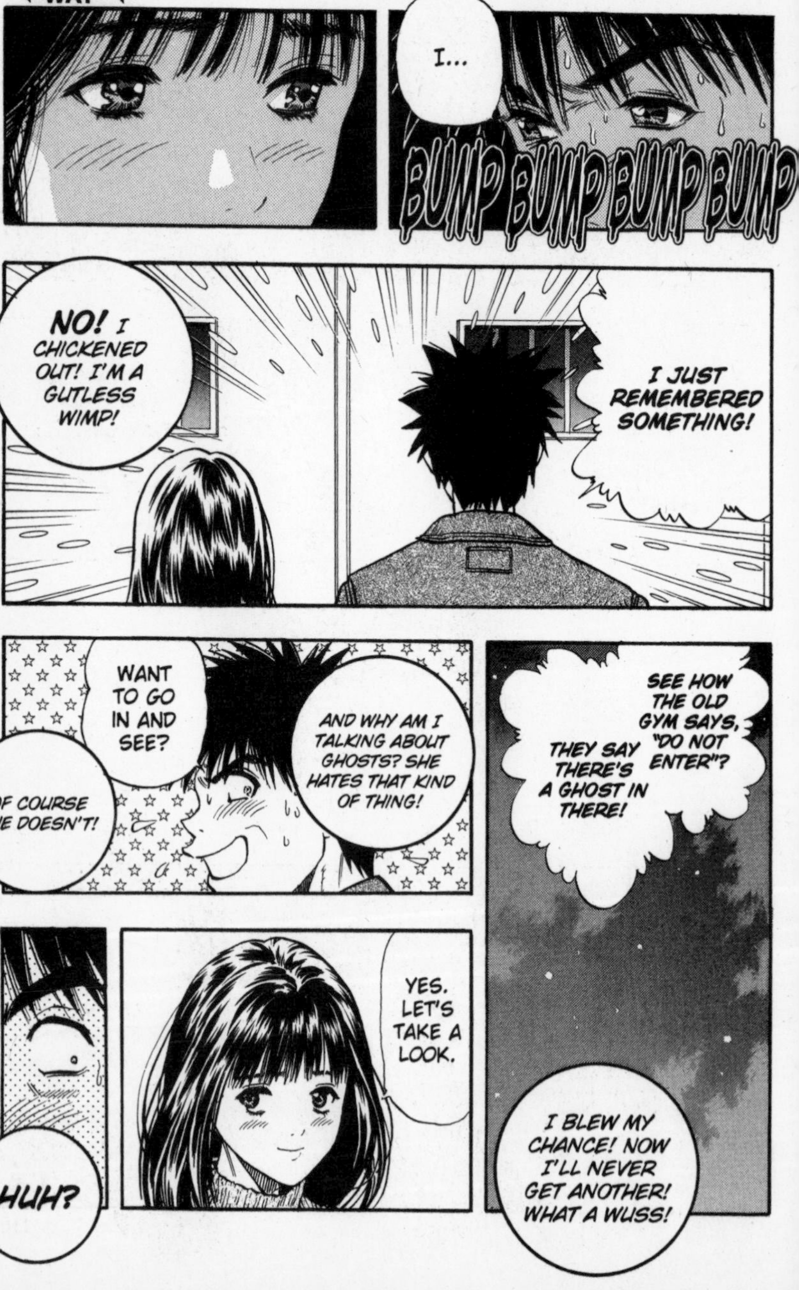
I...
BUMP BUMP BUMP BUMP
I JUST REMEMBERED SOMETHING!
NO! I CHICKENED OUT! I'M A GUTLESS WIMP!
SEE HOW THE OLD GYM SAYS, "DO NOT ENTER"?
THEY SAY THERE'S A GHOST IN THERE!
I BLEW MY CHANCE! NOW I'LL NEVER GET ANOTHER! WHAT A WUSS!
WANT TO GO IN AND SEE?
AND WHY AM I TALKING ABOUT GHOSTS? SHE HATES THAT KIND OF THING!
OF COURSE SHE DOESN'T!
YES. LET'S TAKE A LOOK.
HUH?

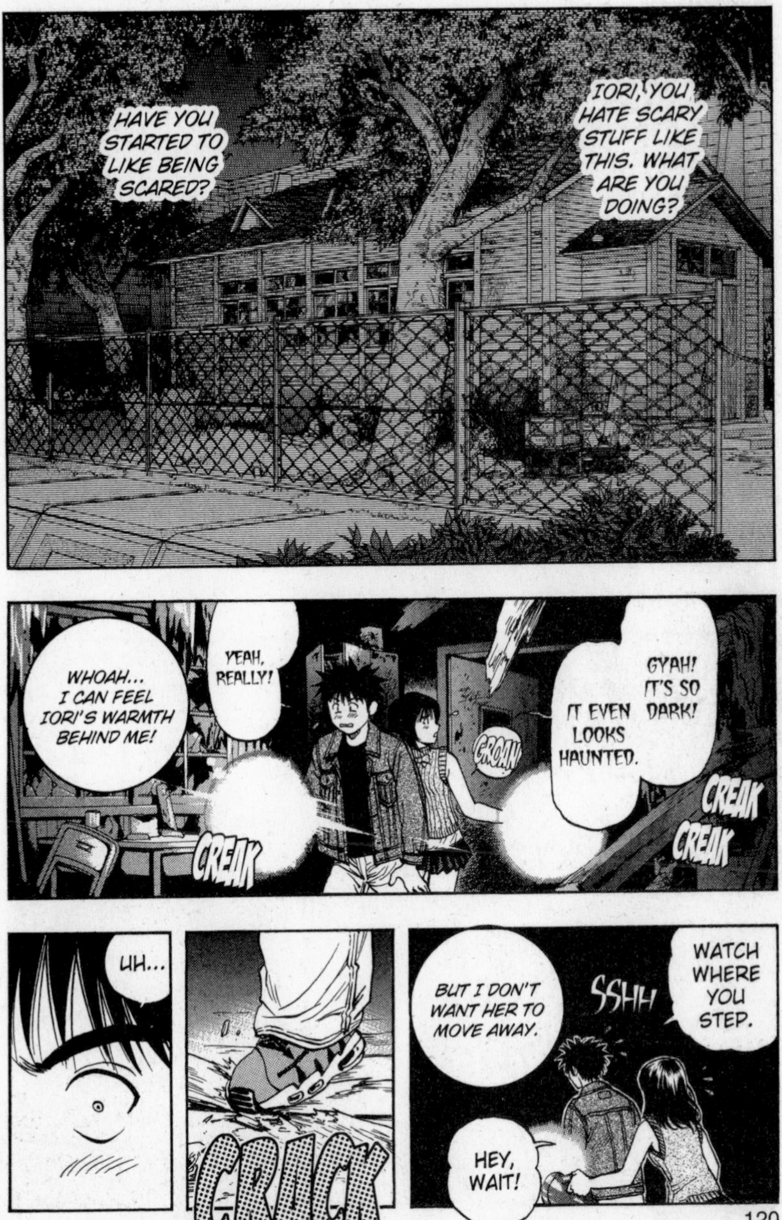
IORI, YOU HATE SCARY STUFF LIKE THIS. WHAT ARE YOU DOING?
HAVE YOU STARTED TO LIKE BEING SCARED?
GYAH! IT'S SO DARK!
IT EVEN LOOKS HAUNTED.
CREAK
CREAK
GROAN
YEAH, REALLY!
WHOAH... I CAN FEEL IORI'S WARMTH BEHIND ME!
CREAK
WATCH WHERE YOU STEP.
SSHH
BUT I DON'T WANT HER TO MOVE AWAY.
HEY, WAIT!
CRACK
UH...

READ THIS WAY

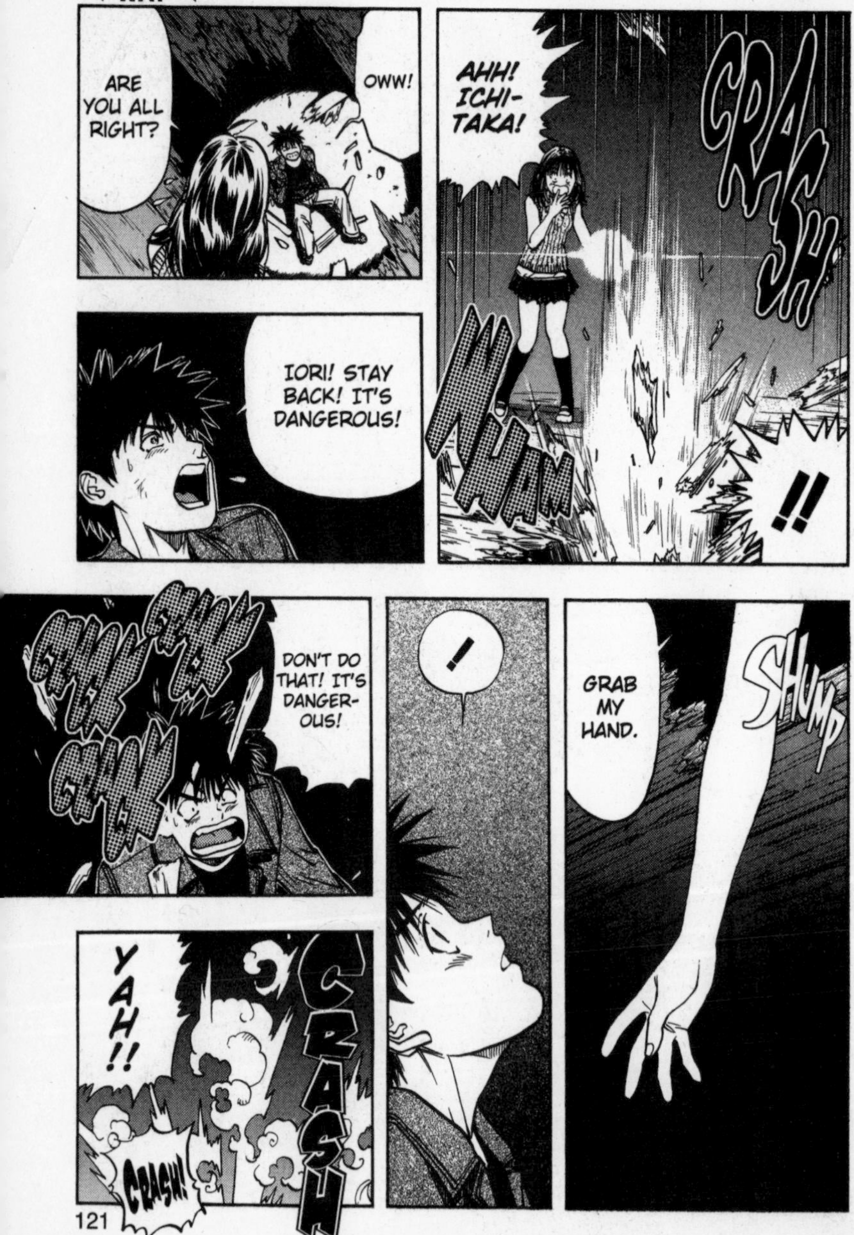
CRASH
AHH! ICHI-TAKA!
WHAM
!!
OWW!
ARE YOU ALL RIGHT?
IORI! STAY BACK! IT'S DANGEROUS!
SHUMP
GRAB MY HAND.
!
DON'T DO THAT! IT'S DANGER-OUS!
CRASH
YAH!!
CRASH!

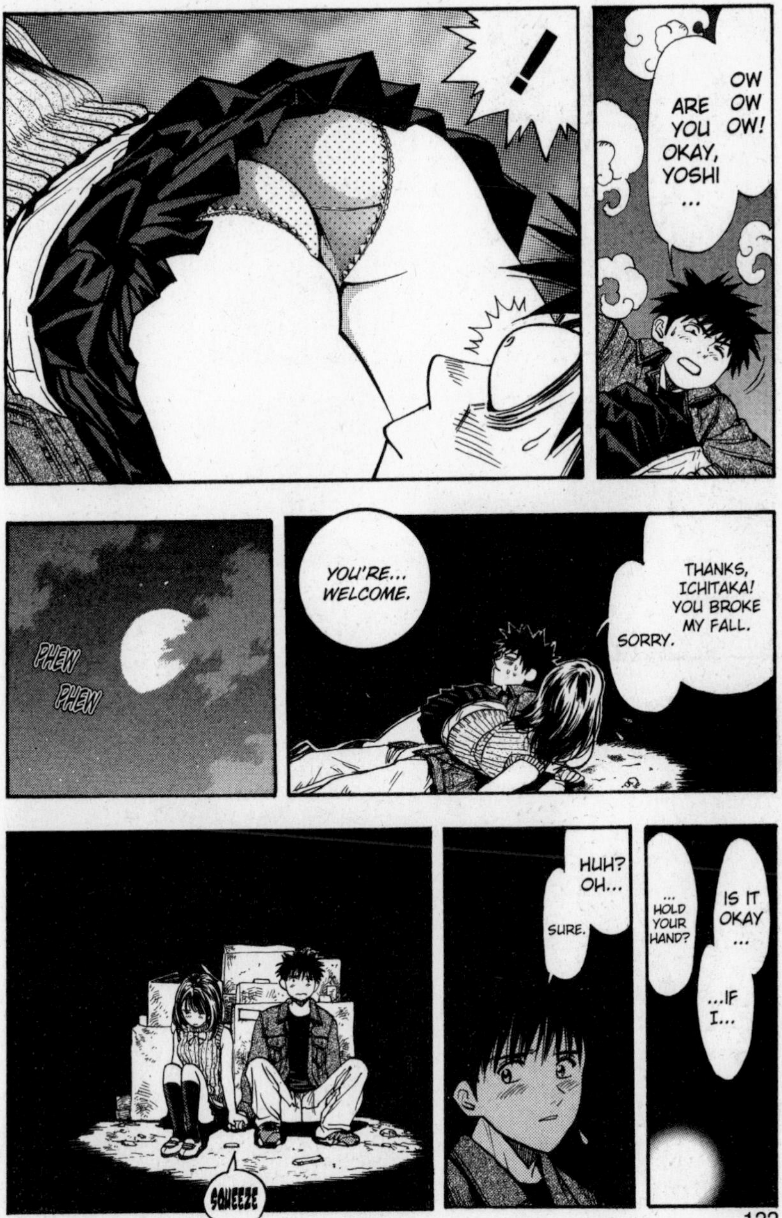

OW OW OW!
ARE YOU OKAY, YOSHI...
!
THANKS, ICHITAKA! YOU BROKE MY FALL.
SORRY.
YOU'RE... WELCOME.
PHEW PHEW
IS IT OKAY...
...IF I...
...HOLD YOUR HAND?
HUH? OH...
SURE.
SQUEEZE

READ THIS WAY

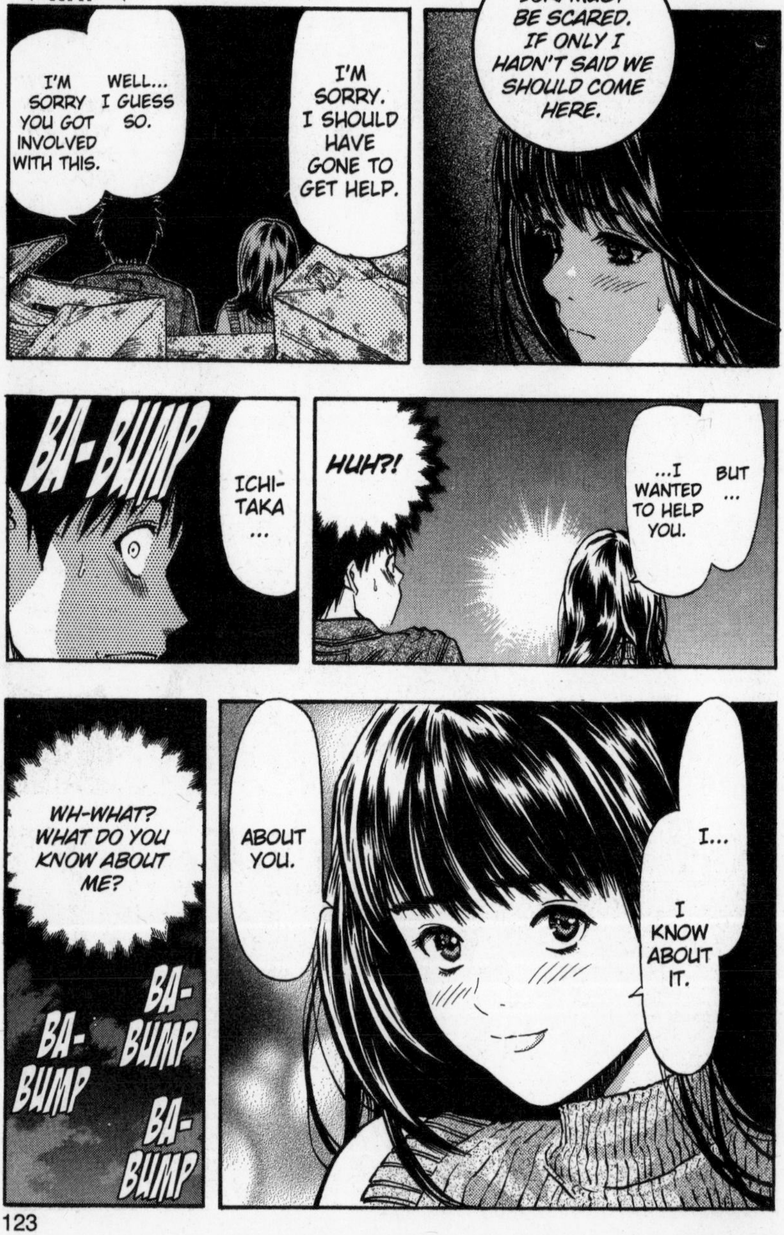
IORI MUST BE SCARED. IF ONLY I HADN'T SAID WE SHOULD COME HERE.
I'M SORRY. I SHOULD HAVE GONE TO GET HELP.
WELL... I GUESS SO.
I'M SORRY YOU GOT INVOLVED WITH THIS.
BUT ...
...I WANTED TO HELP YOU.
HUH?!
ICHI-TAKA ...
BA-BUMP
I...
I KNOW ABOUT IT.
ABOUT YOU.
WH-WHAT? WHAT DO YOU KNOW ABOUT ME?
BA-BUMP
BA-BUMP
BA-BUMP

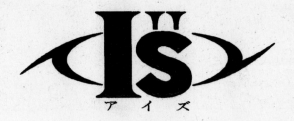

Chapter 61:
The Conversation

READ THIS WAY

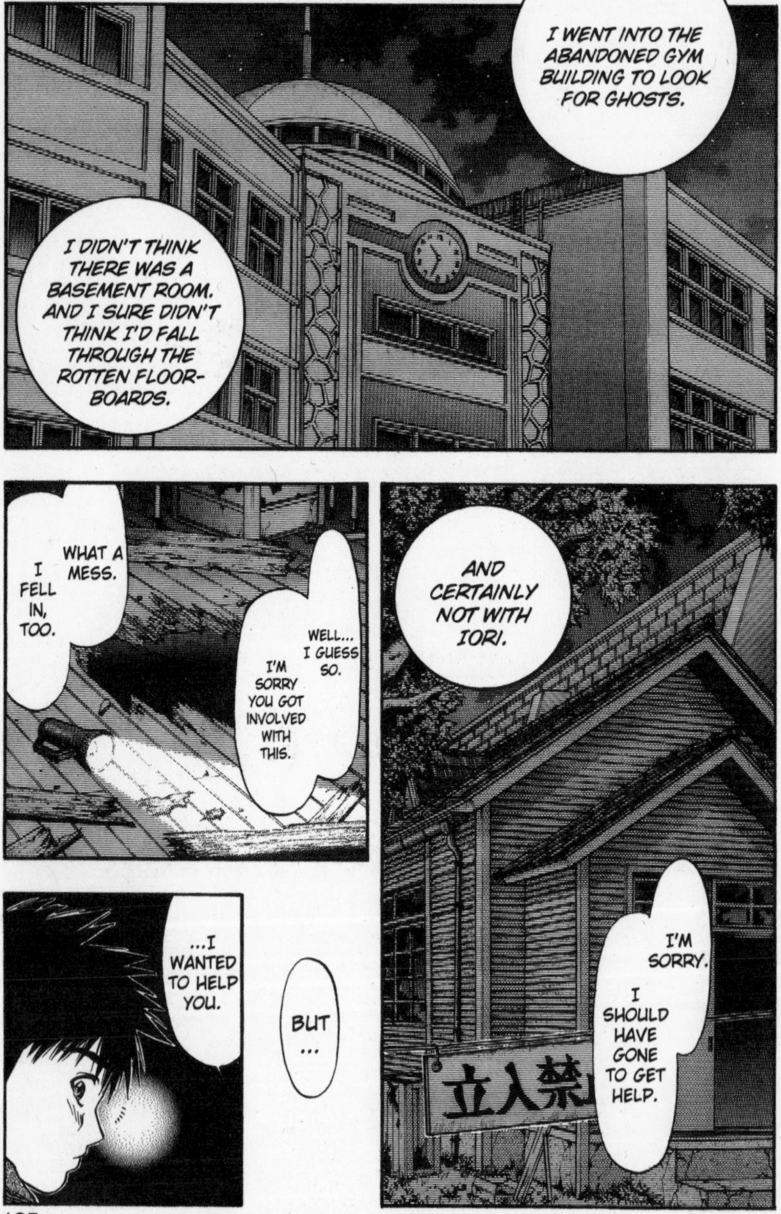
I WENT INTO THE ABANDONED GYM BUILDING TO LOOK FOR GHOSTS.
I DIDN'T THINK THERE WAS A BASEMENT ROOM. AND I SURE DIDN'T THINK I'D FALL THROUGH THE ROTTEN FLOOR-BOARDS.
AND CERTAINLY NOT WITH IORI.
I'M SORRY.
I SHOULD HAVE GONE TO GET HELP.
立入禁
WELL... I GUESS SO.
I'M SORRY YOU GOT INVOLVED WITH THIS.
WHAT A MESS.
I FELL IN, TOO.
...I WANTED TO HELP YOU.
BUT ...

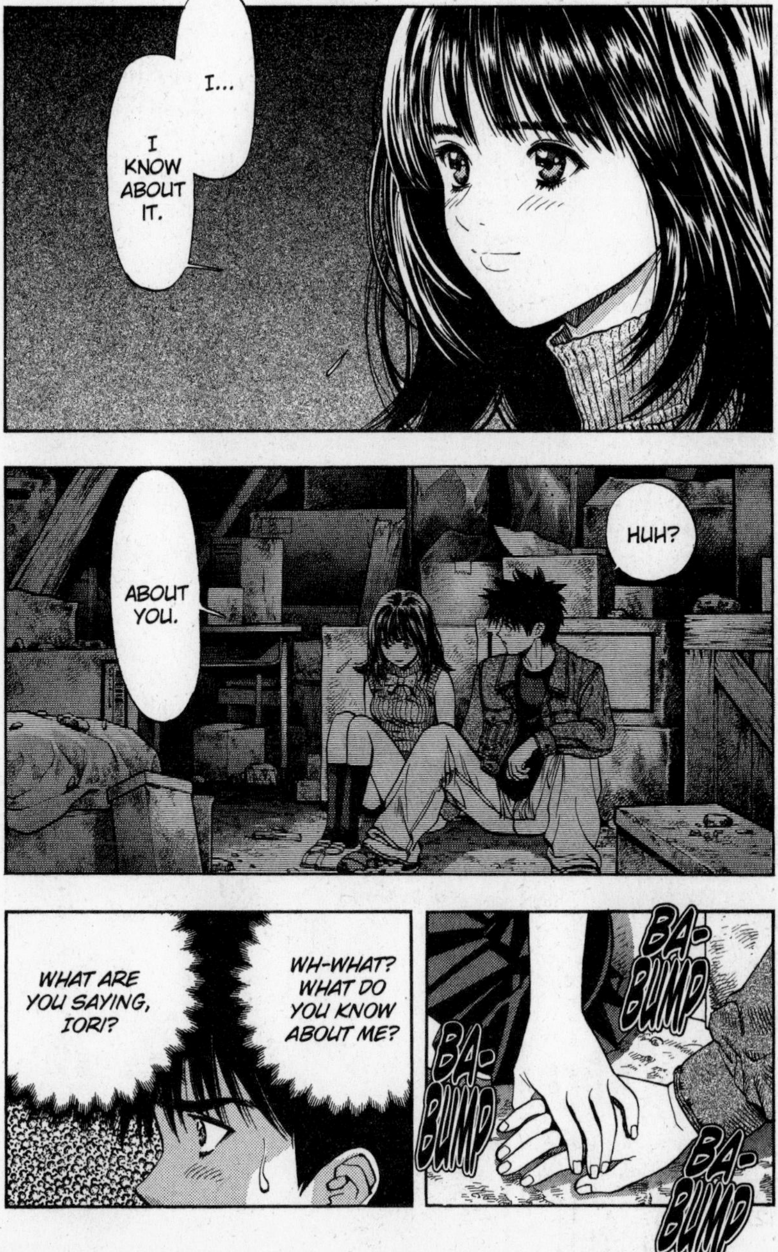
I...
I KNOW ABOUT IT.
ABOUT YOU.
HUH?
BA-BUMP
BA-BUMP
BA-BUMP
WH-WHAT? WHAT DO YOU KNOW ABOUT ME?
WHAT ARE YOU SAYING, IORI?

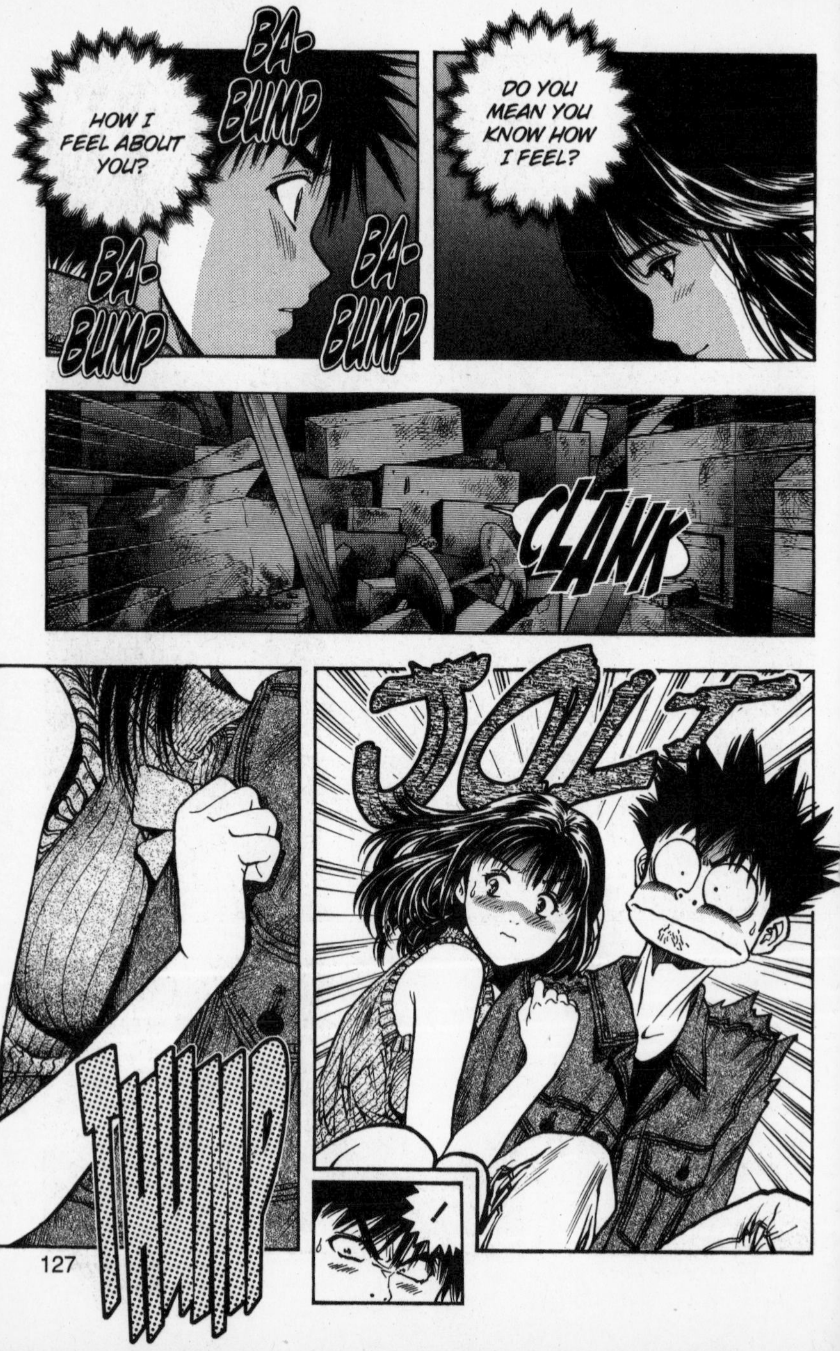
DO YOU MEAN YOU KNOW HOW I FEEL?
BA-BUMP
BA-BUMP
HOW I FEEL ABOUT YOU?
BA-BUMP
CLANK
JOLT
THUMP

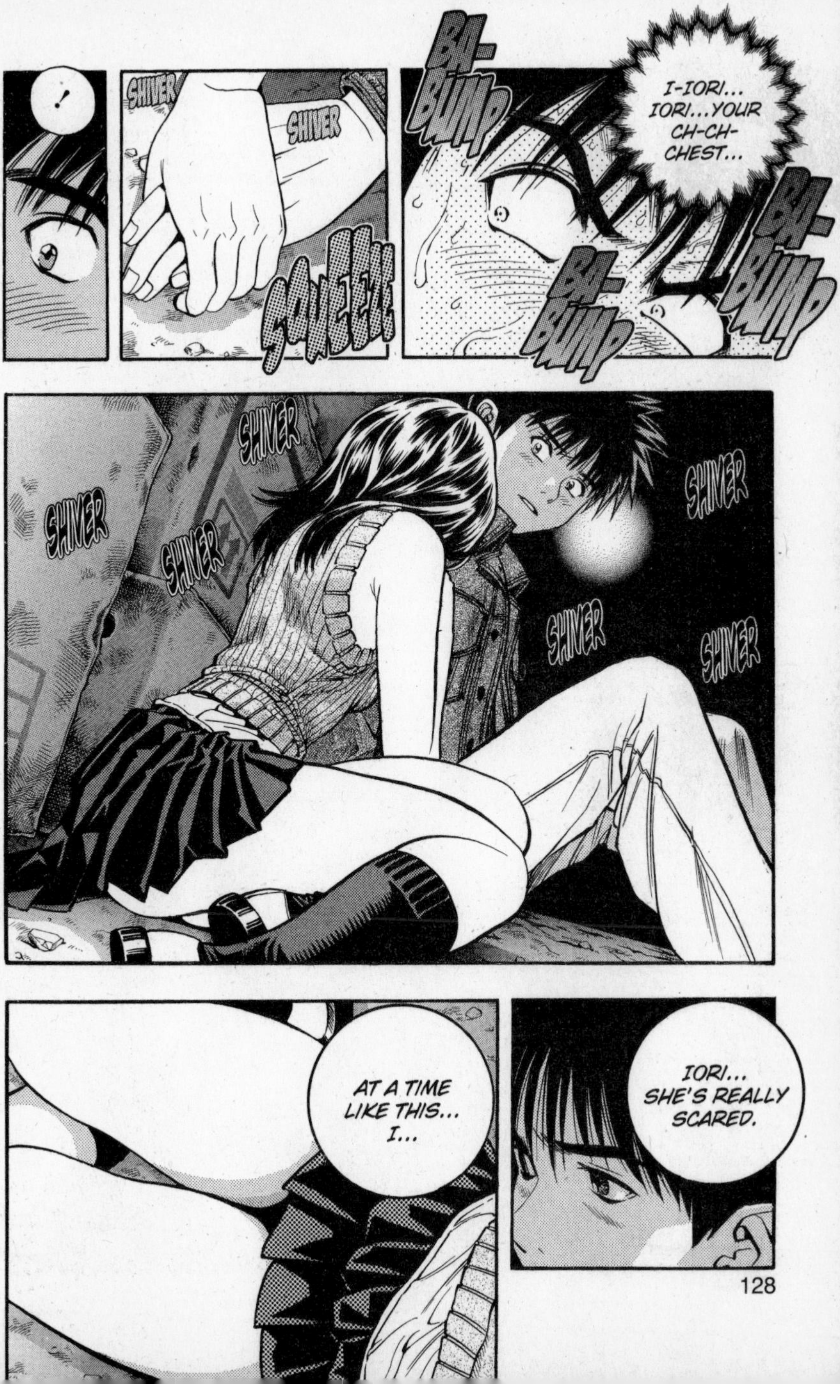
BA-BUMP
I-IORI... IORI...YOUR CH-CH-CHEST...
BA-BUMP
BA-BUMP
SHIVER
SHIVER
SQUEEZE
!
SHIVER
SHIVER
SHIVER
SHIVER
SHIVER
SHIVER
IORI... SHE'S REALLY SCARED.
AT A TIME LIKE THIS... I...

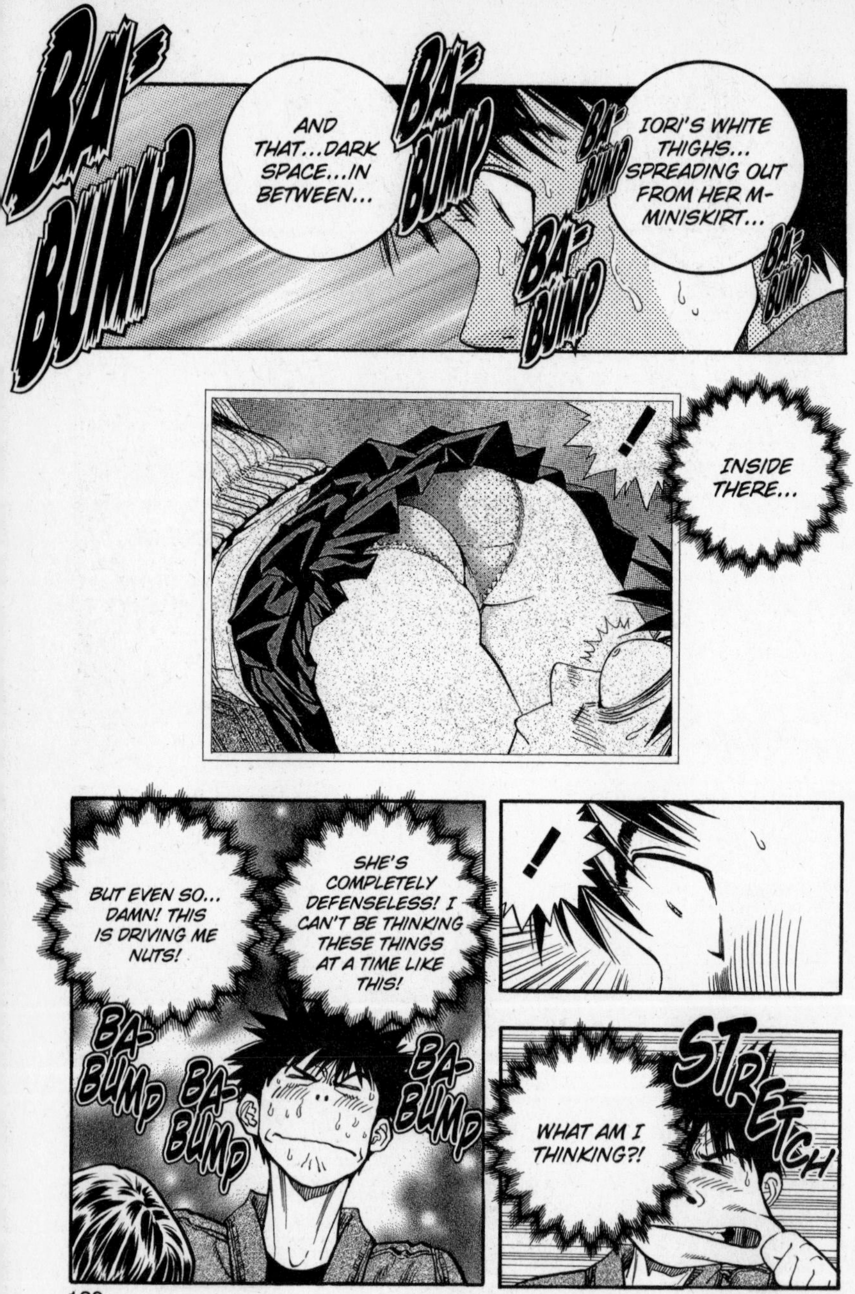
BA-BUMP
IORI'S WHITE THIGHS... SPREADING OUT FROM HER M-MINISKIRT...
BA-BUMP
BA-BUMP
BA-BUMP
AND THAT...DARK SPACE...IN BETWEEN...
BA-BUMP
!
INSIDE THERE...
!
STRETCH
WHAT AM I THINKING?!
SHE'S COMPLETELY DEFENSELESS! I CAN'T BE THINKING THESE THINGS AT A TIME LIKE THIS!
BUT EVEN SO... DAMN! THIS IS DRIVING ME NUTS!
BA-BUMP
BA-BUMP
BA-BUMP

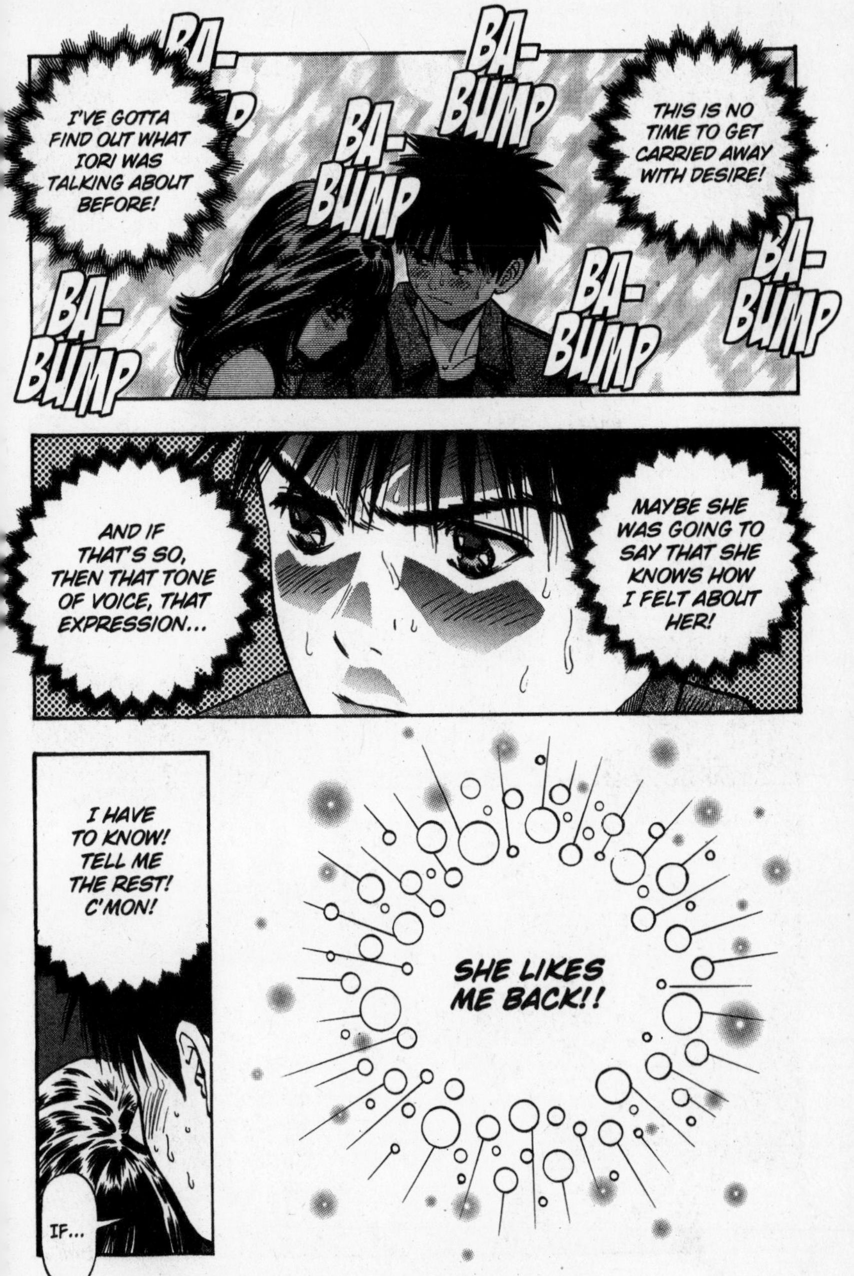
BA-BUMP
THIS IS NO TIME TO GET CARRIED AWAY WITH DESIRE!
BA-BUMP
I'VE GOTTA FIND OUT WHAT IORI WAS TALKING ABOUT BEFORE!
BA-BUMP
BA-BUMP
BA-BUMP
MAYBE SHE WAS GOING TO SAY THAT SHE KNOWS HOW I FELT ABOUT HER!
AND IF THAT'S SO, THEN THAT TONE OF VOICE, THAT EXPRESSION...
SHE LIKES ME BACK!!
I HAVE TO KNOW! TELL ME THE REST! C'MON!
IF...

READ THIS WAY

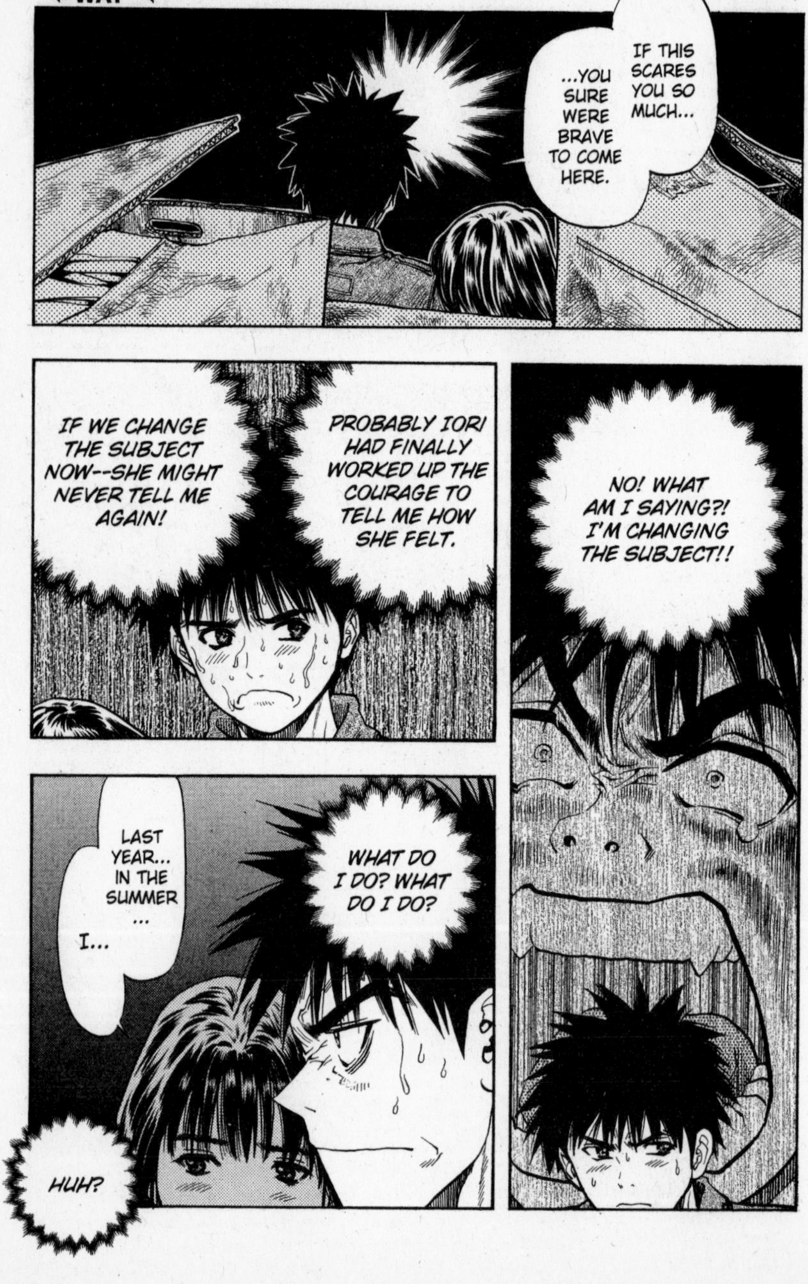
IF THIS SCARES YOU SO MUCH...
...YOU SURE WERE BRAVE TO COME HERE.
NO! WHAT AM I SAYING?! I'M CHANGING THE SUBJECT!!
PROBABLY IORI HAD FINALLY WORKED UP THE COURAGE TO TELL ME HOW SHE FELT.
IF WE CHANGE THE SUBJECT NOW--SHE MIGHT NEVER TELL ME AGAIN!
WHAT DO I DO? WHAT DO I DO?
LAST YEAR... IN THE SUMMER ... I...
HUH?

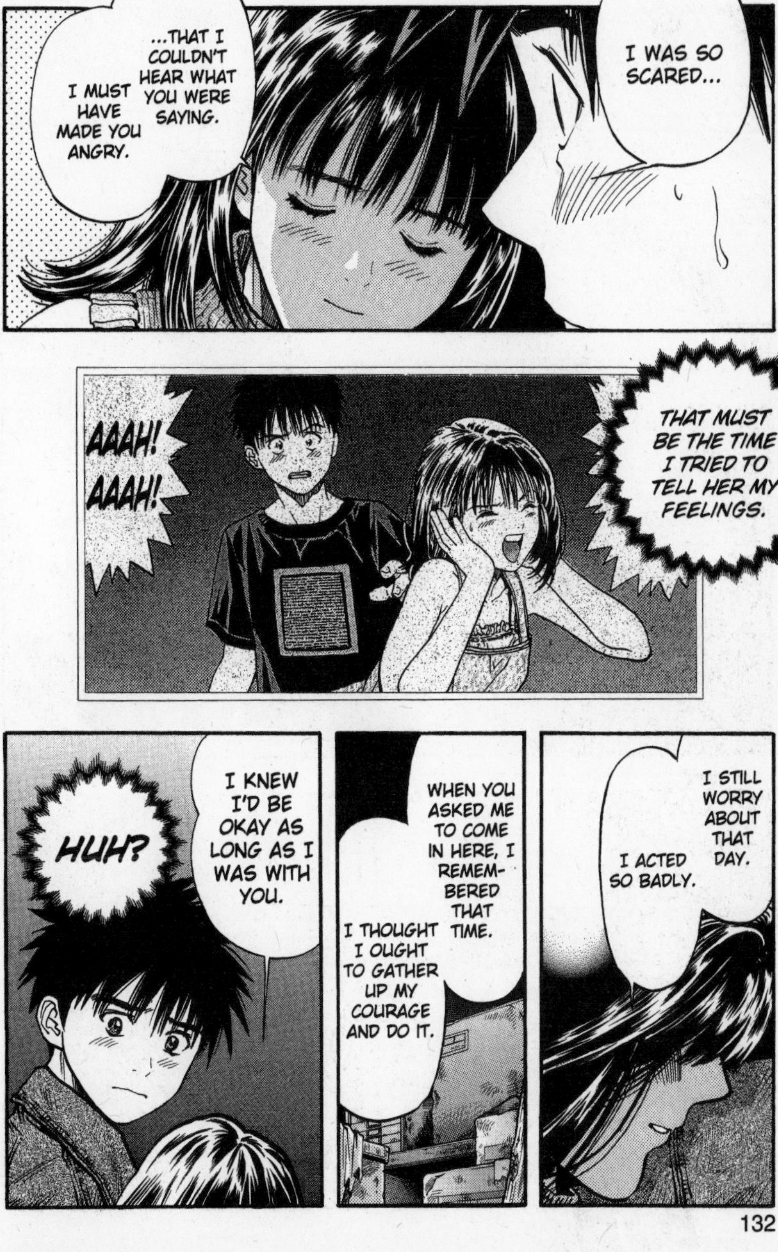
I WAS SO SCARED...
...THAT I COULDN'T HEAR WHAT YOU WERE SAYING.
I MUST HAVE MADE YOU ANGRY.
THAT MUST BE THE TIME I TRIED TO TELL HER MY FEELINGS.
AAAH! AAAH!
I STILL WORRY ABOUT THAT DAY.
I ACTED SO BADLY.
WHEN YOU ASKED ME TO COME IN HERE, I REMEMBERED THAT TIME.
I THOUGHT I OUGHT TO GATHER UP MY COURAGE AND DO IT.
I KNEW I'D BE OKAY AS LONG AS I WAS WITH YOU.
HUH?

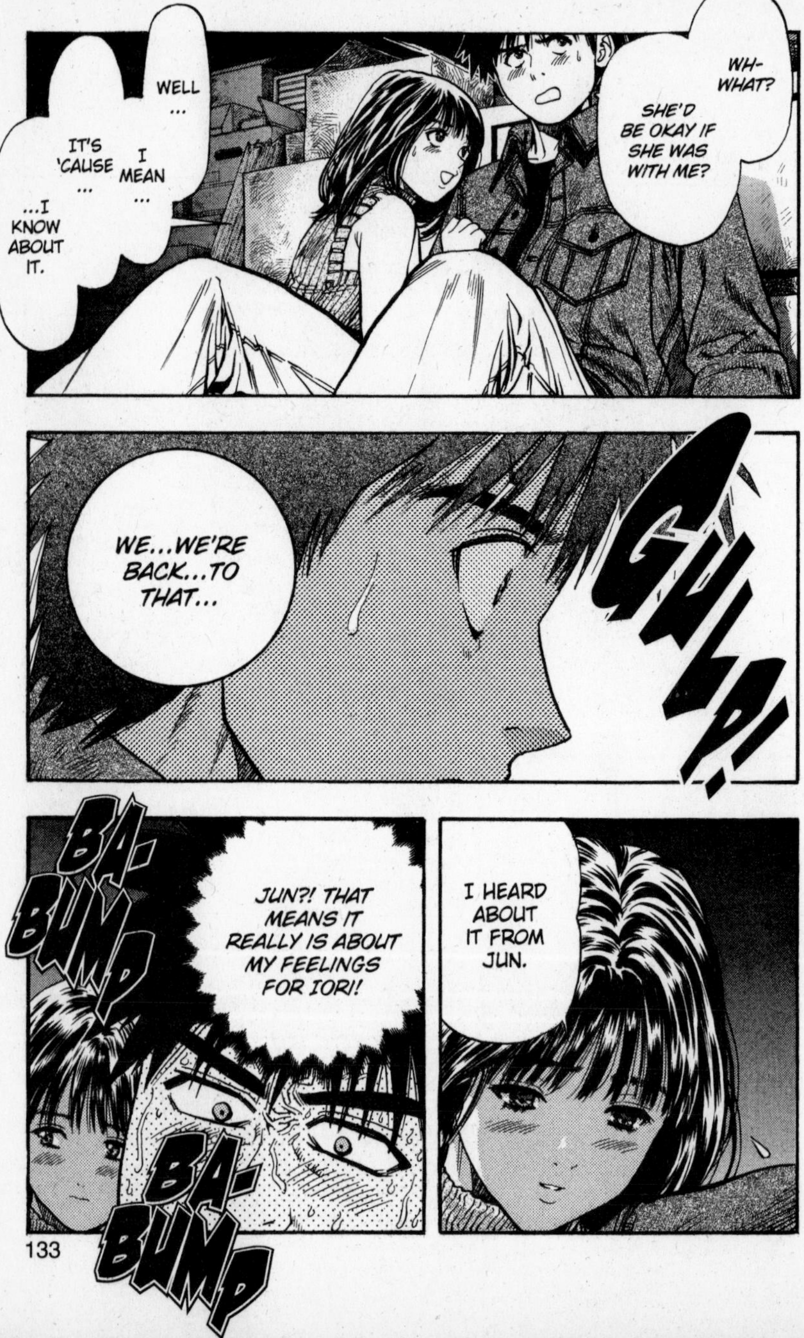
WH-WHAT?
SHE'D BE OKAY IF SHE WAS WITH ME?
WELL ...
I MEAN ...
IT'S 'CAUSE ...
...I KNOW ABOUT IT.
GULP!
WE...WE'RE BACK...TO THAT...
I HEARD ABOUT IT FROM JUN.
JUN?! THAT MEANS IT REALLY IS ABOUT MY FEELINGS FOR IORI!
BA-BUMP
BA-BUMP

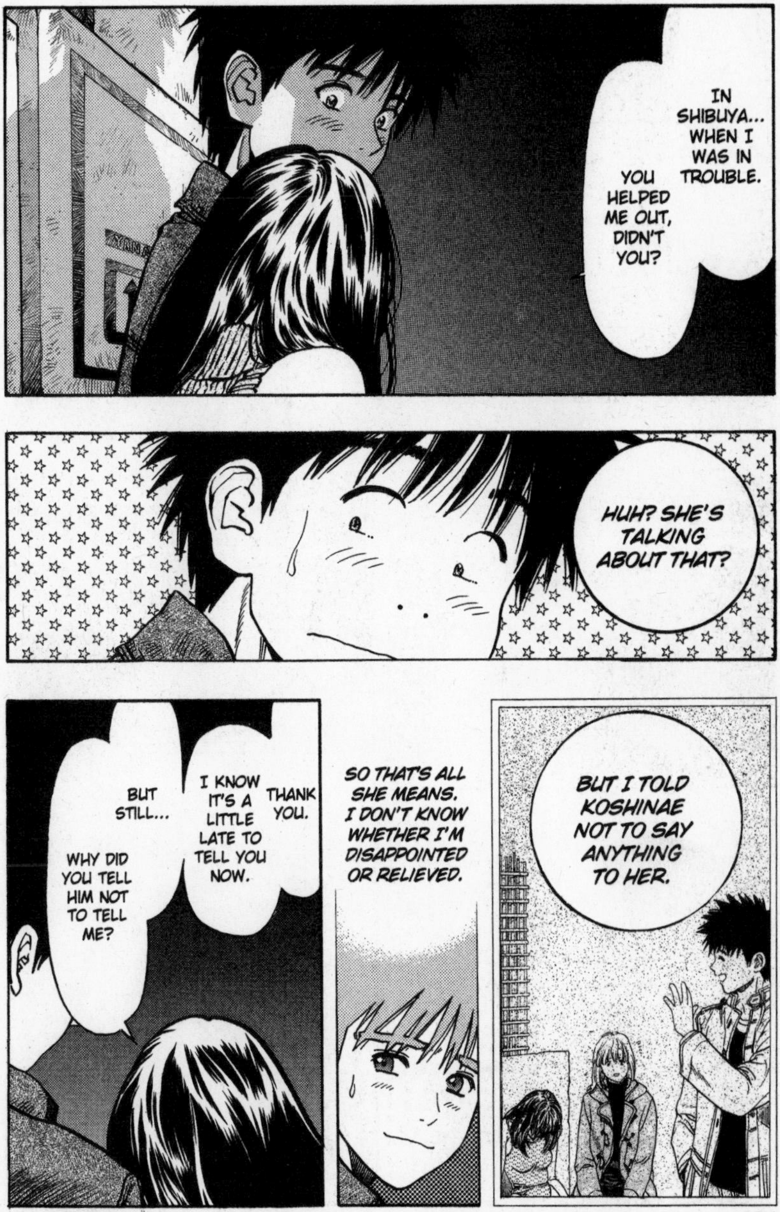
IN SHIBUYA... WHEN I WAS IN TROUBLE.
YOU HELPED ME OUT, DIDN'T YOU?
HUH? SHE'S TALKING ABOUT THAT?
BUT I TOLD KOSHINAE NOT TO SAY ANYTHING TO HER.
SO THAT'S ALL SHE MEANS. I DON'T KNOW WHETHER I'M DISAPPOINTED OR RELIEVED.
THANK YOU.
I KNOW IT'S A LITTLE LATE TO TELL YOU NOW.
BUT STILL...
WHY DID YOU TELL HIM NOT TO TELL ME?

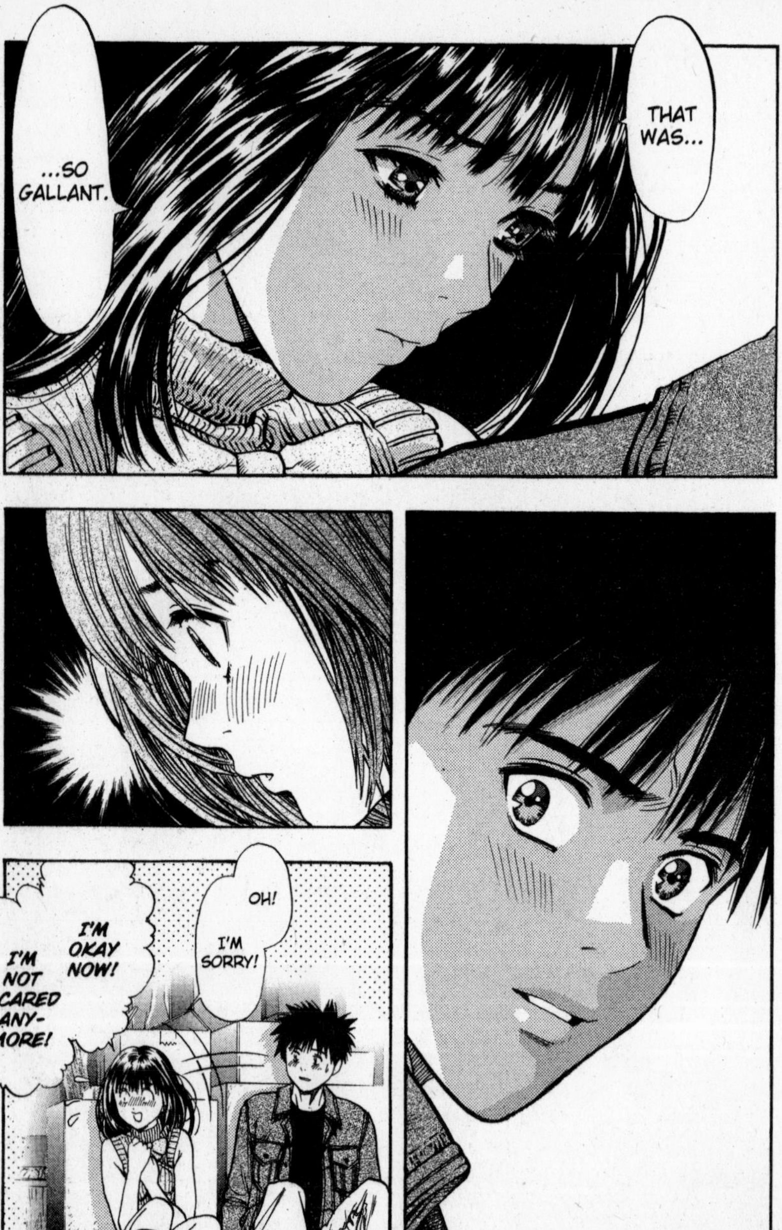
THAT WAS...
...SO GALLANT.
OH! I'M SORRY!
I'M OKAY NOW! I'M NOT SCARED ANY-MORE!

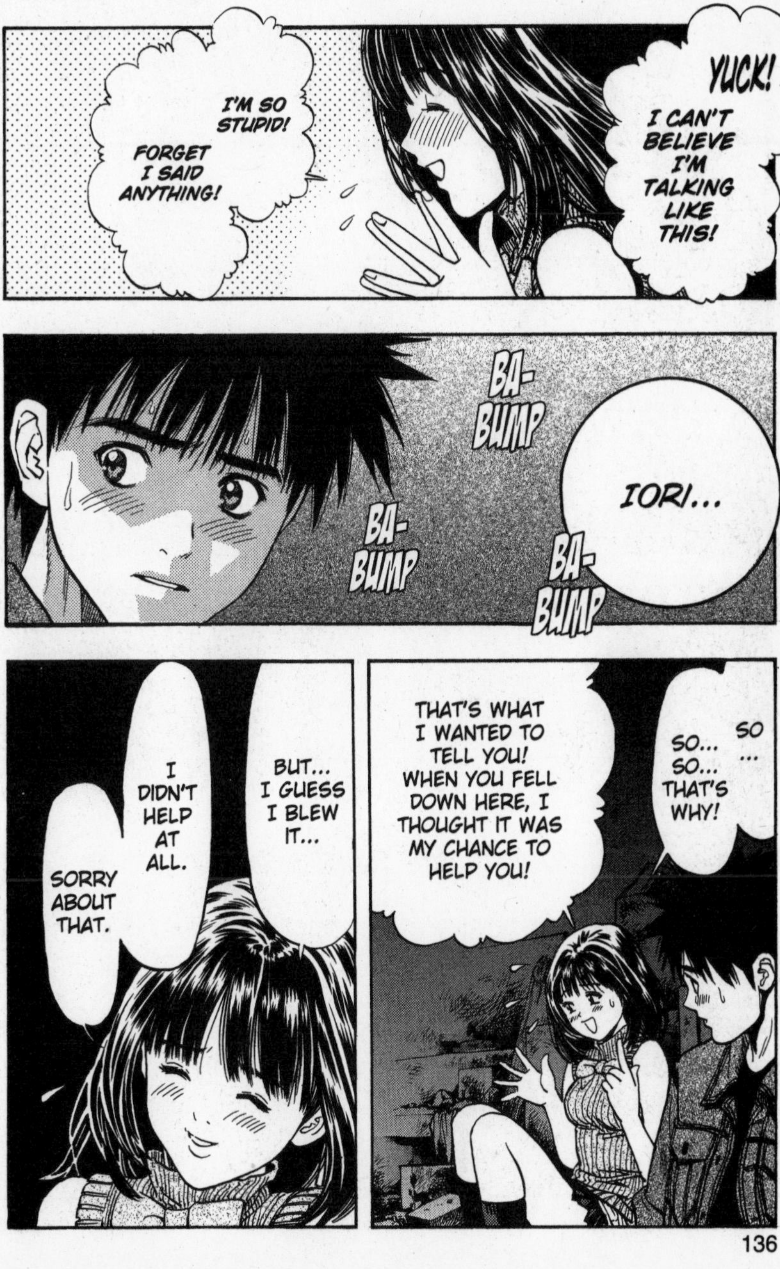
YUCK! I CAN'T BELIEVE I'M TALKING LIKE THIS!
I'M SO STUPID!
FORGET I SAID ANYTHING!
BA-BUMP
IORI...
BA-BUMP
BA-BUMP
SO ...
SO... SO... THAT'S WHY!
THAT'S WHAT I WANTED TO TELL YOU! WHEN YOU FELL DOWN HERE, I THOUGHT IT WAS MY CHANCE TO HELP YOU!
BUT... I GUESS I BLEW IT...
I DIDN'T HELP AT ALL.
SORRY ABOUT THAT.

READ THIS WAY

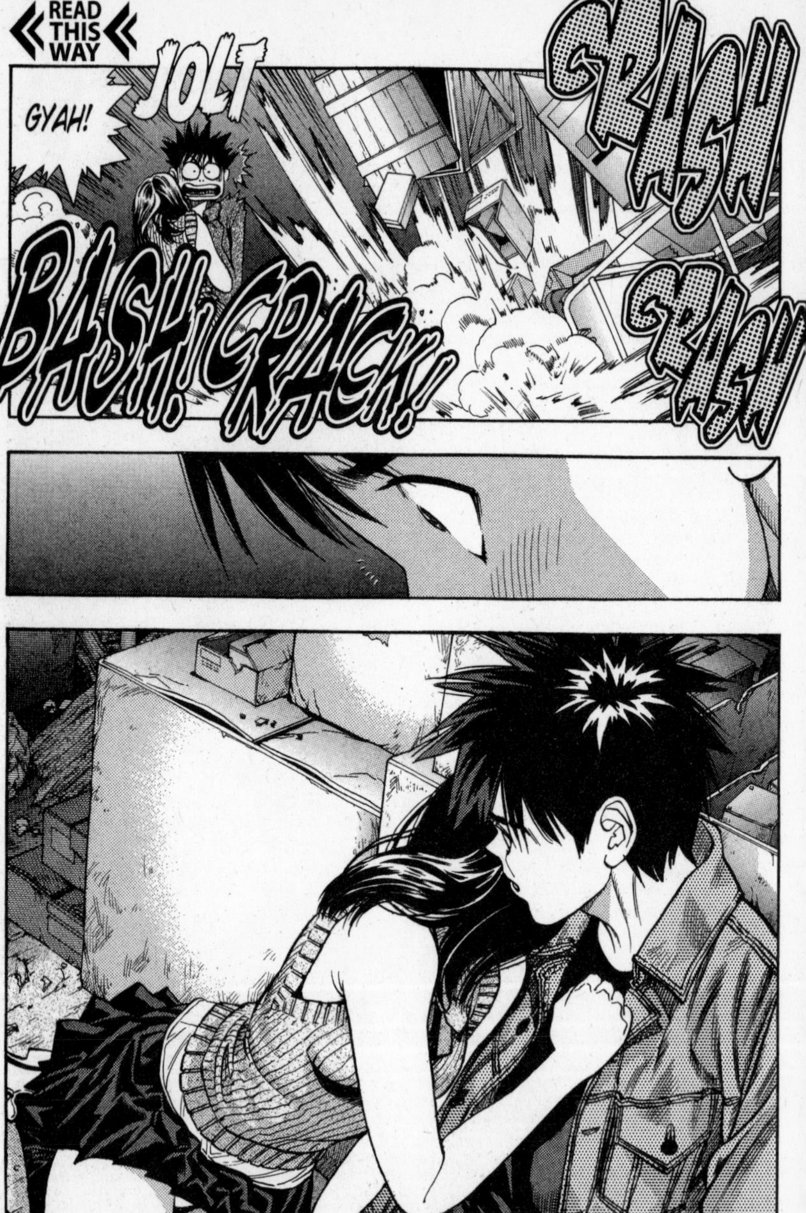
CRASH
CRASH
JOLT
GYAH!
BASH! CRACK!

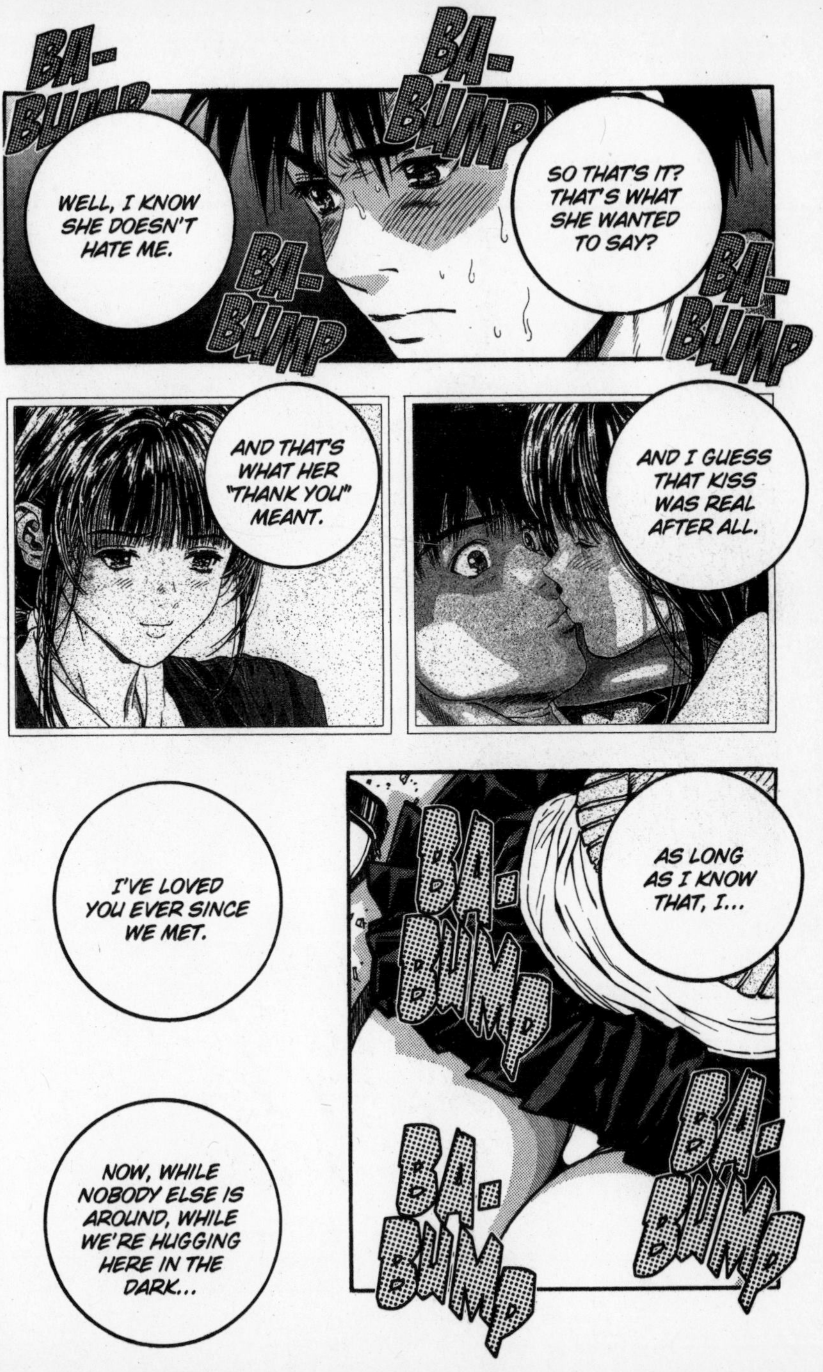
BA-BUMP
SO THAT'S IT? THAT'S WHAT SHE WANTED TO SAY?
BA-BUMP
BA-BUMP
WELL, I KNOW SHE DOESN'T HATE ME.
AND I GUESS THAT KISS WAS REAL AFTER ALL.
AND THAT'S WHAT HER "THANK YOU" MEANT.
AS LONG AS I KNOW THAT, I...
BA-BUMP
BA-BUMP
BA-BUMP
I'VE LOVED YOU EVER SINCE WE MET.
NOW, WHILE NOBODY ELSE IS AROUND, WHILE WE'RE HUGGING HERE IN THE DARK...

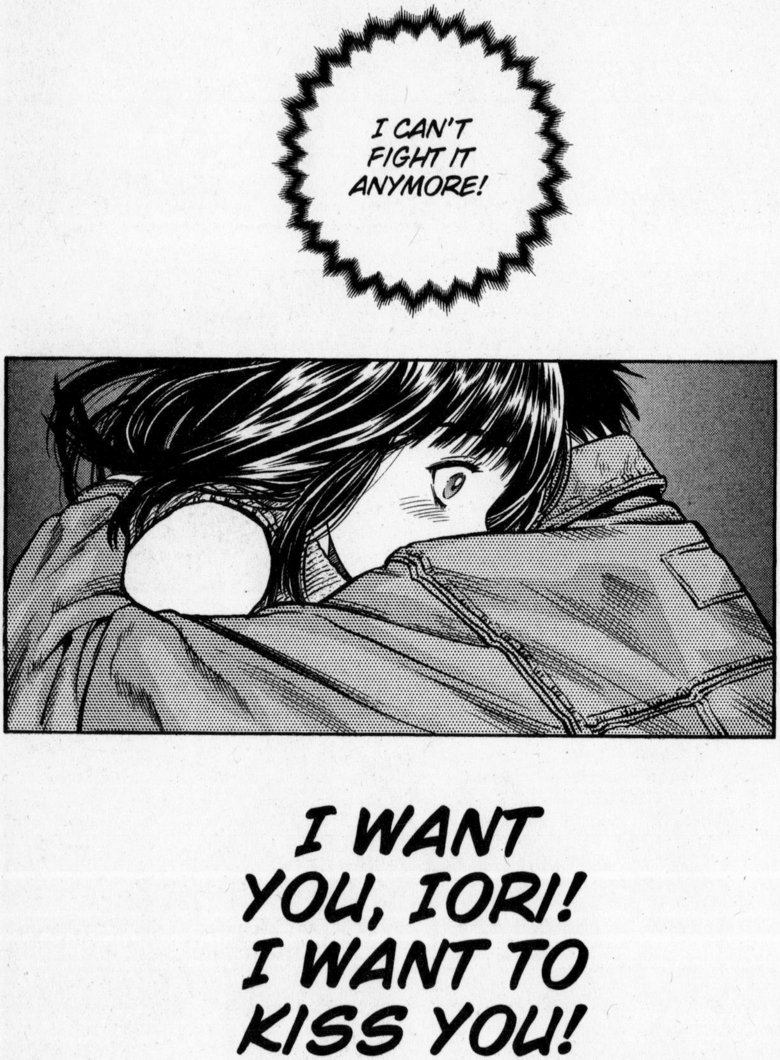
I CAN'T FIGHT IT ANYMORE!
I WANT YOU, IORI! I WANT TO KISS YOU!

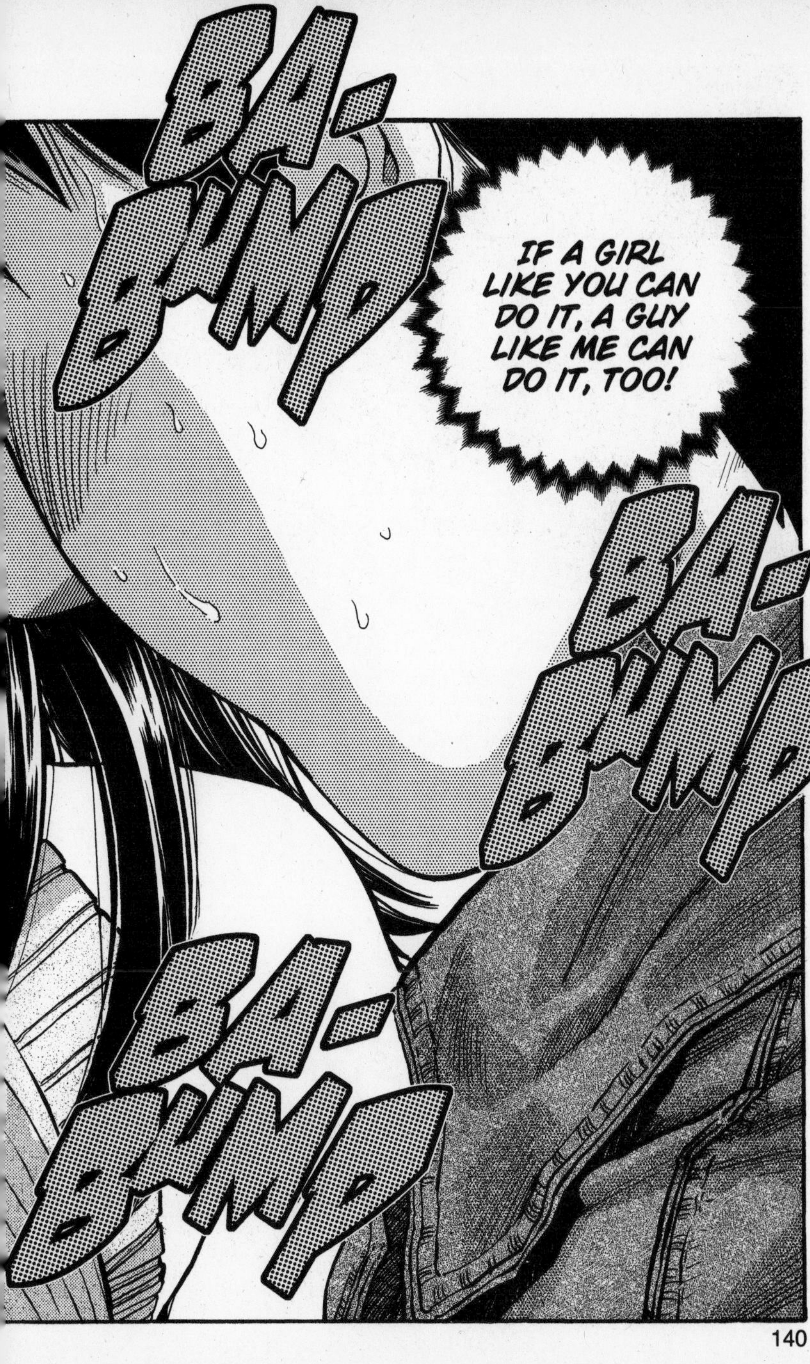
BA-BUMP
IF A GIRL LIKE YOU CAN DO IT, A GUY LIKE ME CAN DO IT, TOO!
BA-BUMP
BA-BUMP

READ THIS WAY

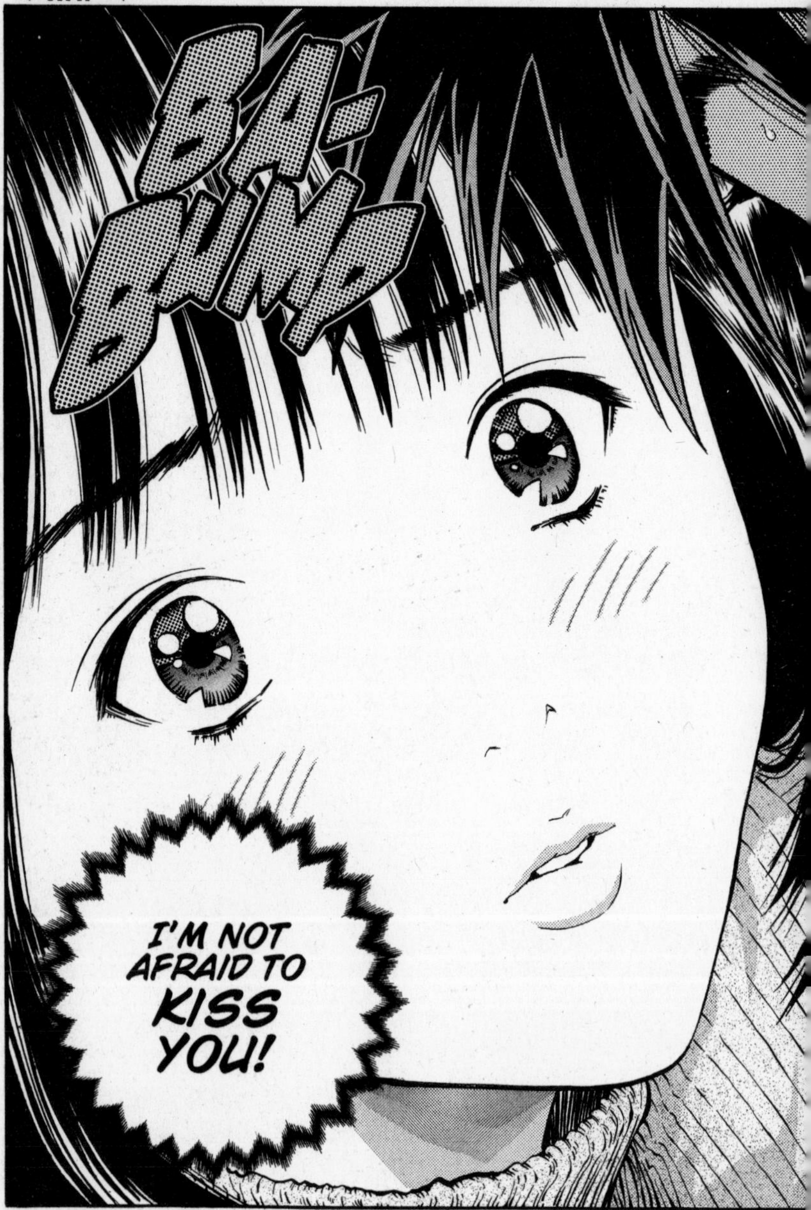
BA-BUMP
I'M NOT AFRAID TO KISS YOU!

I"s

アイズ

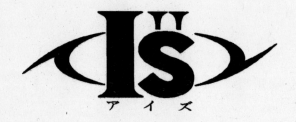

Chapter 62: Blame Me

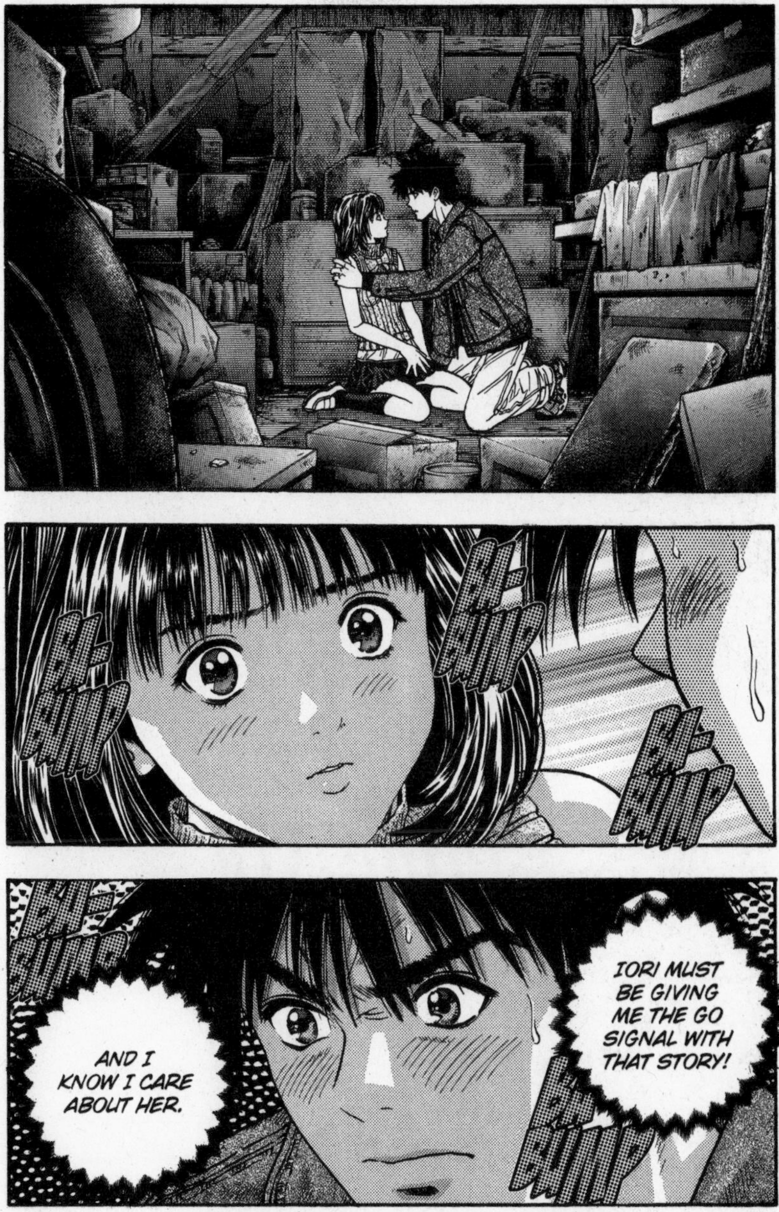
IORI MUST BE GIVING ME THE GO SIGNAL WITH THAT STORY!
AND I KNOW I CARE ABOUT HER.

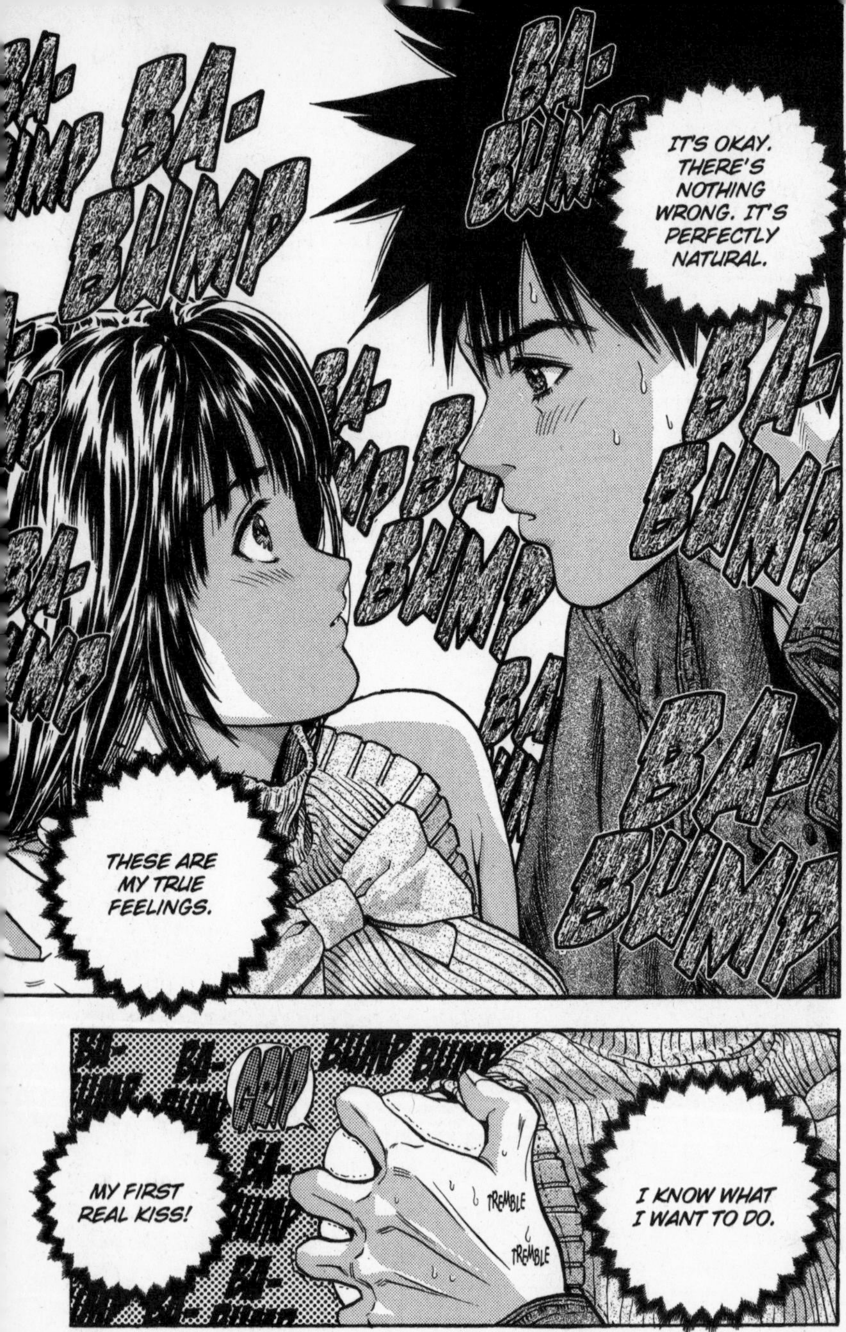
BA-BUMP
IT'S OKAY. THERE'S NOTHING WRONG. IT'S PERFECTLY NATURAL.
BA-BUMP
BA-BUMP
BA-BUMP
BA-BUMP
BA-BUMP
THESE ARE MY TRUE FEELINGS.
I KNOW WHAT I WANT TO DO.
TREMBLE
TREMBLE
BUMP BUMP
GRIP
BA-BUMP
MY FIRST REAL KISS!

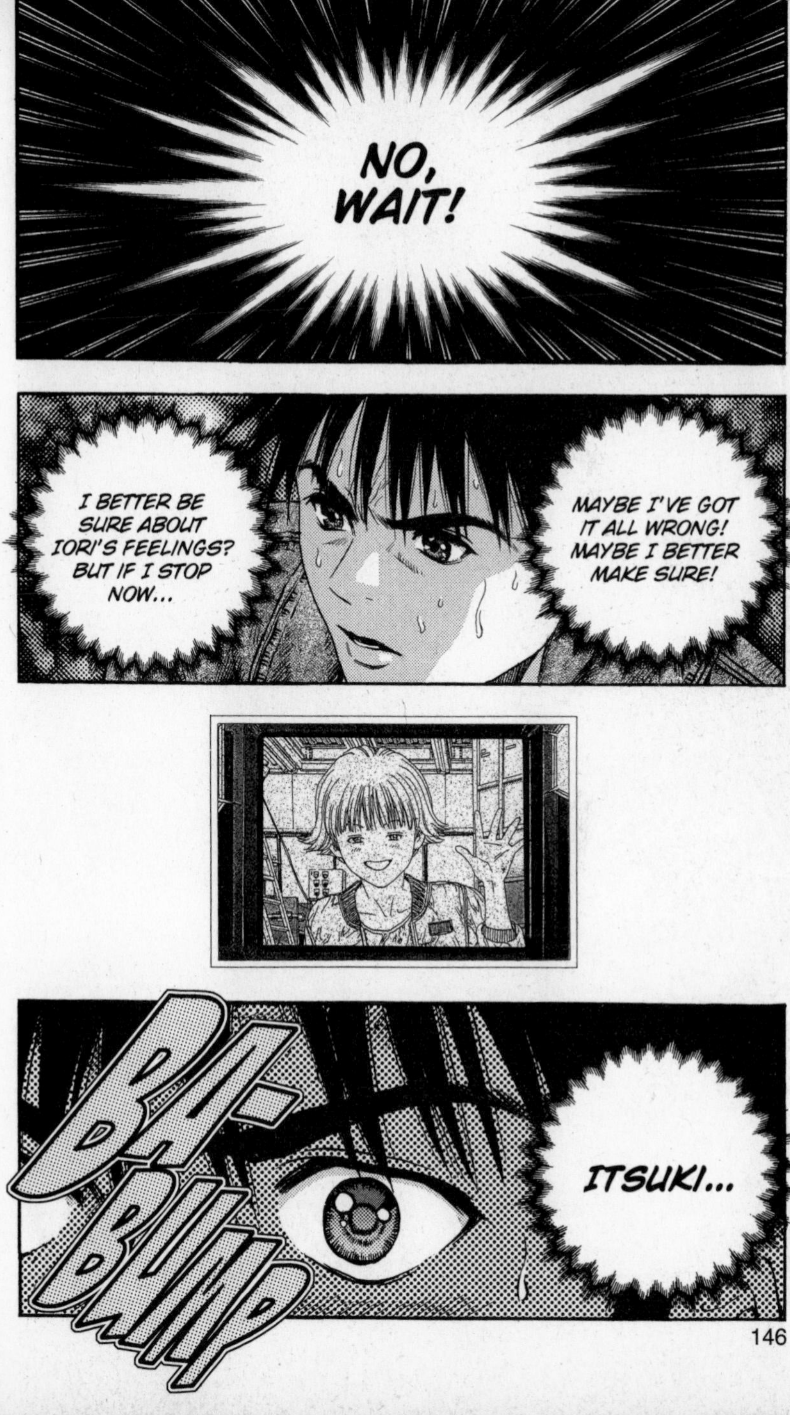
NO, WAIT!
MAYBE I'VE GOT IT ALL WRONG! MAYBE I BETTER MAKE SURE!
I BETTER BE SURE ABOUT IORI'S FEELINGS? BUT IF I STOP NOW...
ITSUKI...
BA-BUMP

READ THIS WAY

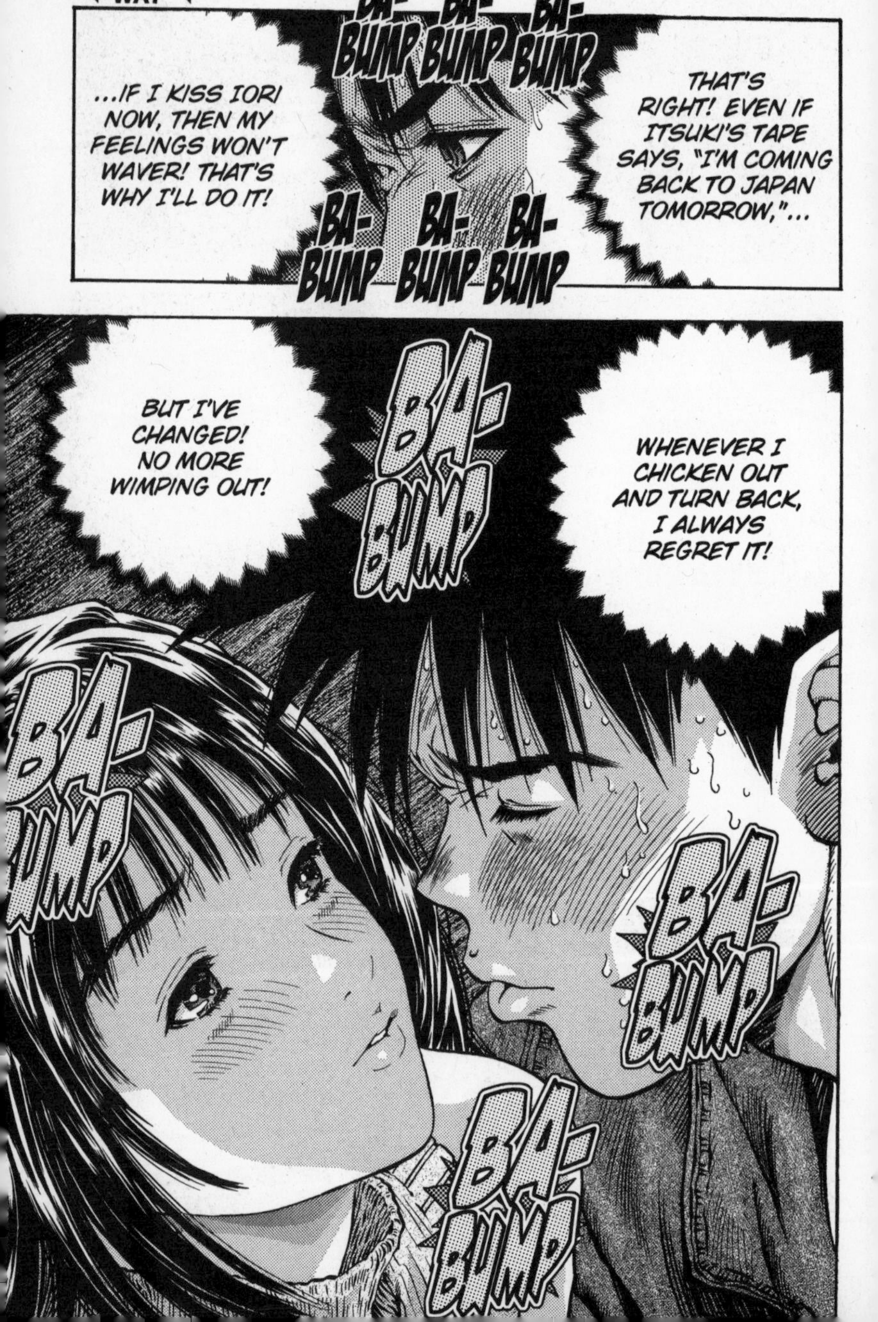
THAT'S RIGHT! EVEN IF ITSUKI'S TAPE SAYS, "I'M COMING BACK TO JAPAN TOMORROW,"...
BA-BUMP BA-BUMP BA-BUMP
...IF I KISS IORI NOW, THEN MY FEELINGS WON'T WAVER! THAT'S WHY I'LL DO IT!
BA-BUMP BA-BUMP BA-BUMP
WHENEVER I CHICKEN OUT AND TURN BACK, I ALWAYS REGRET IT!
BA-BUMP
BUT I'VE CHANGED! NO MORE WIMPING OUT!
BA-BUMP
BA-BUMP
BA-BUMP

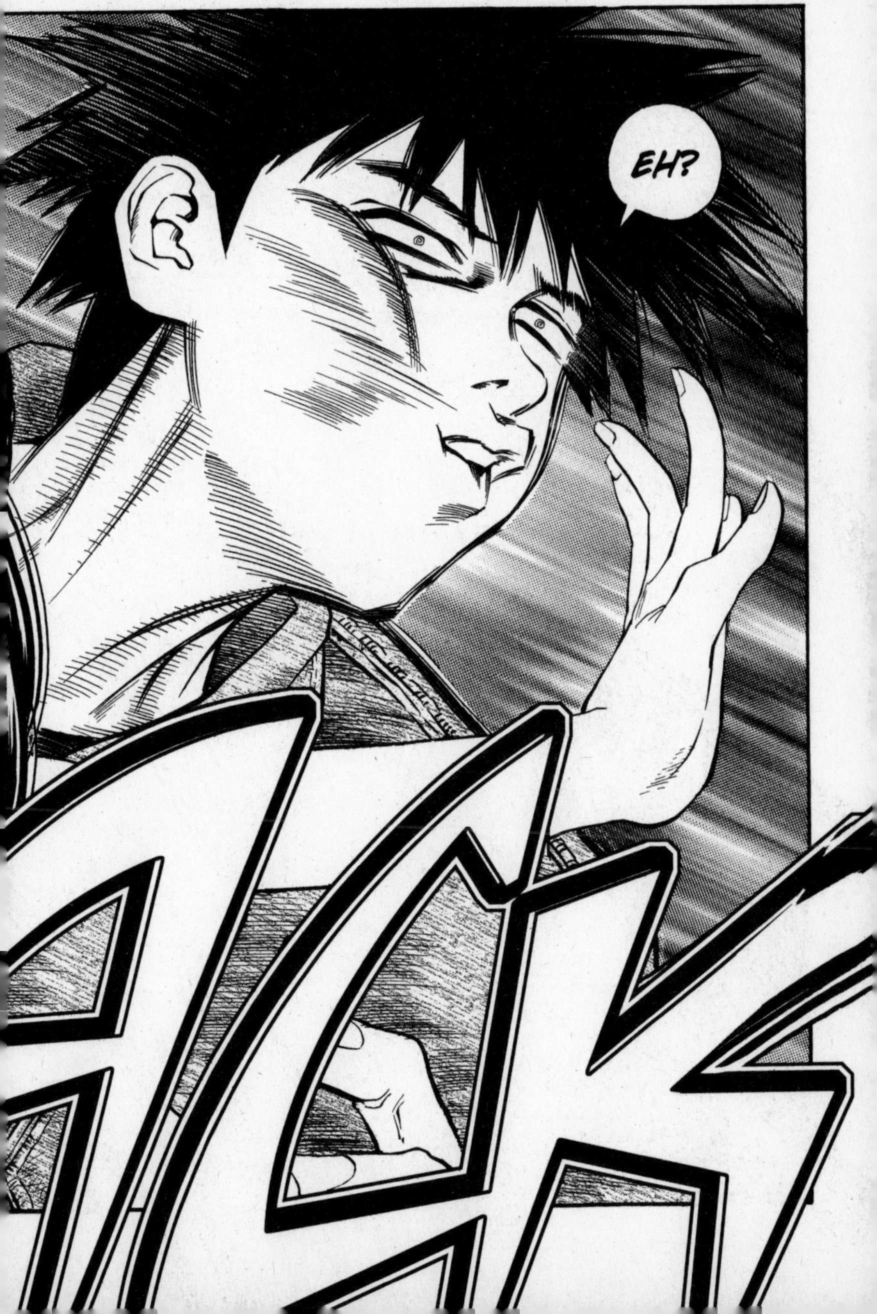
EH?

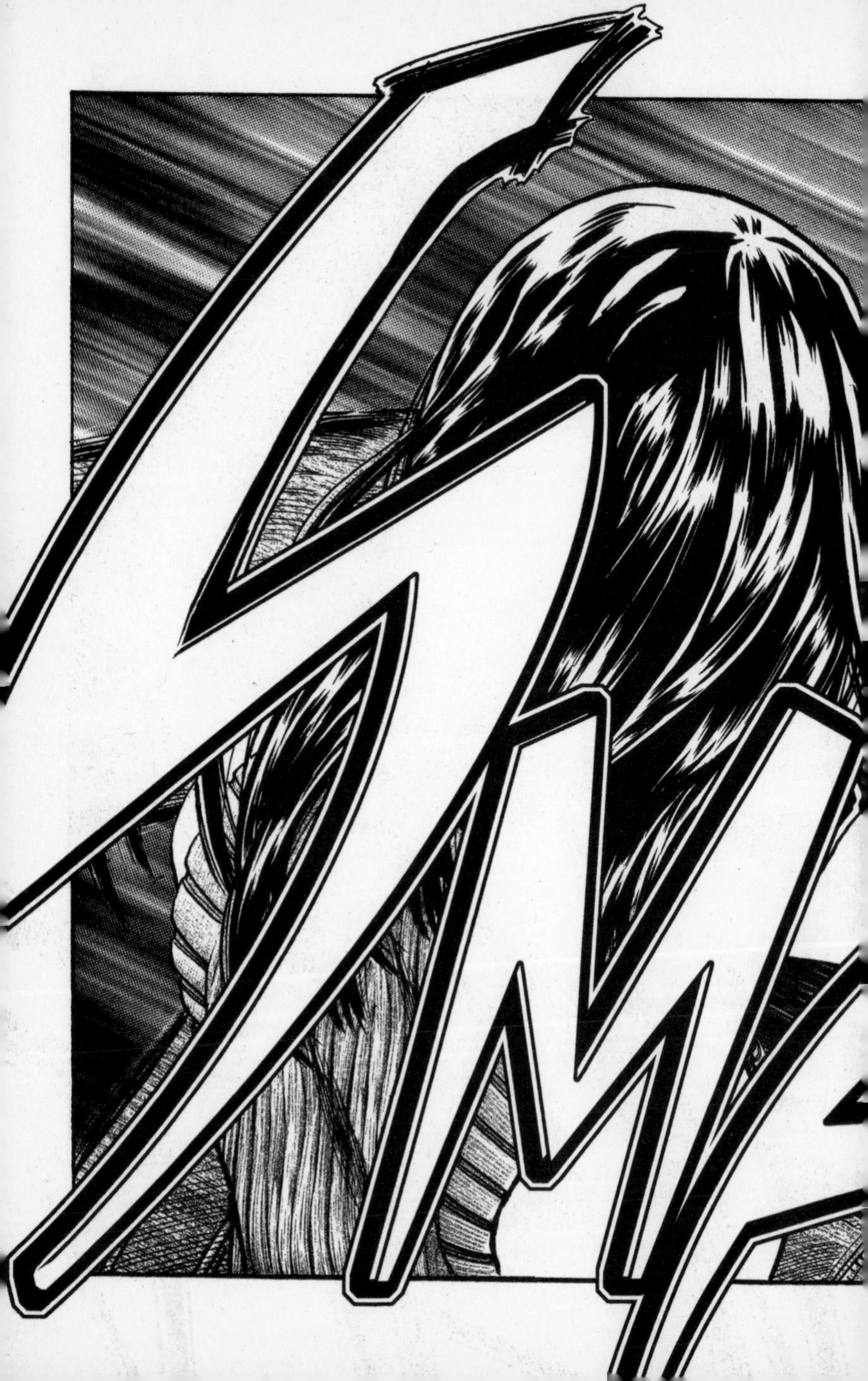
SMA

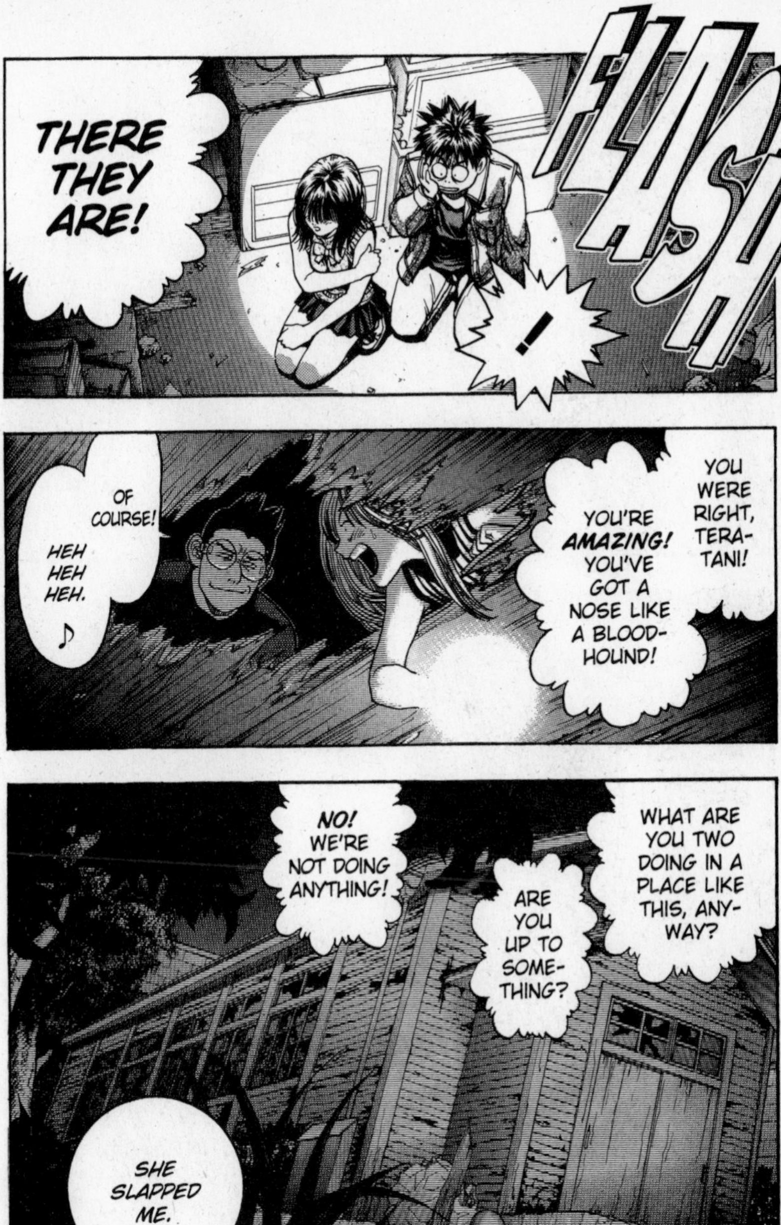
FLASH
THERE THEY ARE!
!
YOU WERE RIGHT, TERA-TANI!
YOU'RE AMAZING! YOU'VE GOT A NOSE LIKE A BLOOD-HOUND!
OF COURSE!
HEH HEH HEH. ♪
WHAT ARE YOU TWO DOING IN A PLACE LIKE THIS, ANY-WAY?
ARE YOU UP TO SOME-THING?
NO! WE'RE NOT DOING ANYTHING!
SHE SLAPPED ME.

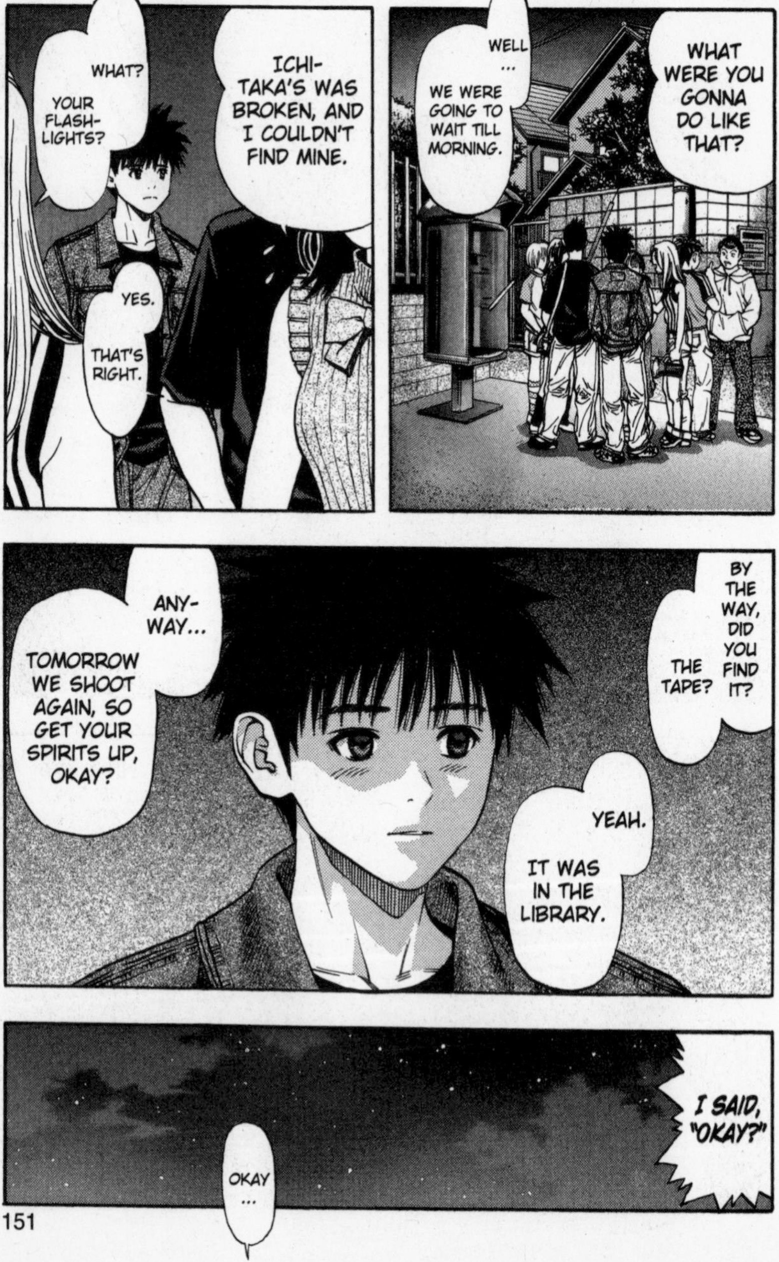

WHAT WERE YOU GONNA DO LIKE THAT?
WELL ... WE WERE GOING TO WAIT TILL MORNING.
ICHI-TAKA'S WAS BROKEN, AND I COULDN'T FIND MINE.
WHAT? YOUR FLASH-LIGHTS?
YES. THAT'S RIGHT.
BY THE WAY, DID YOU FIND IT? THE TAPE?
YEAH. IT WAS IN THE LIBRARY.
ANY-WAY... TOMORROW WE SHOOT AGAIN, SO GET YOUR SPIRITS UP, OKAY?
I SAID, "OKAY?"
OKAY ...

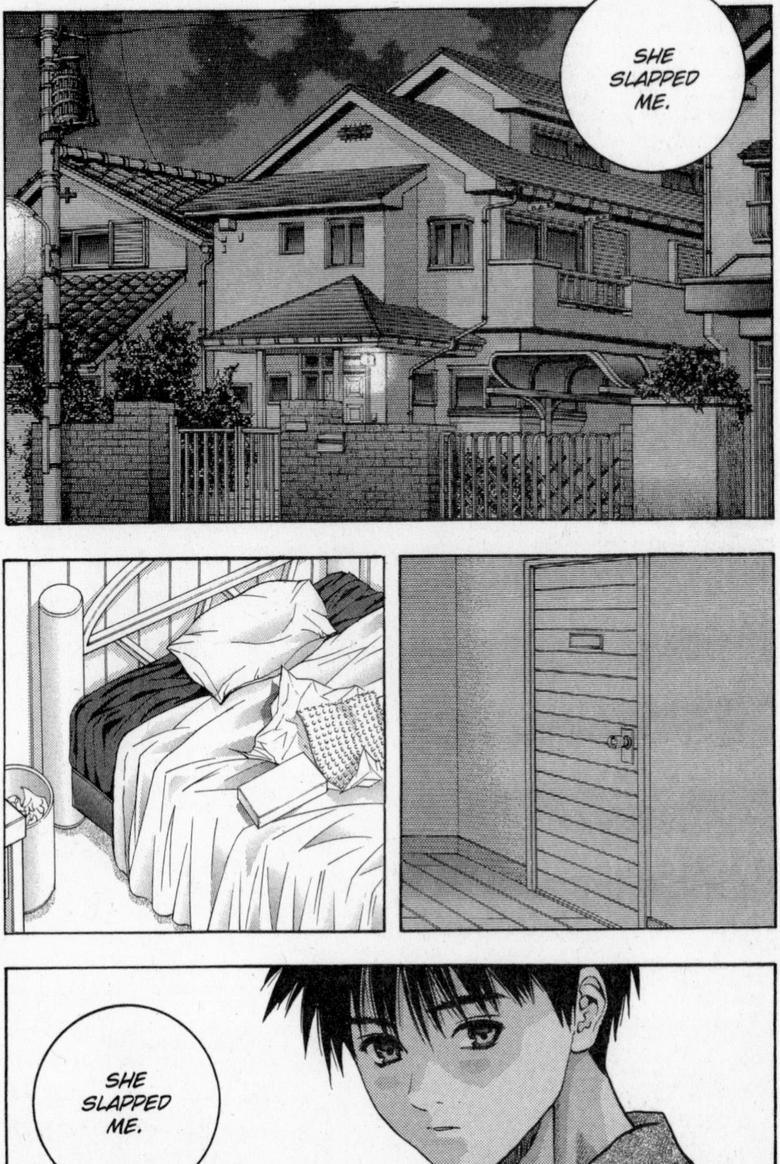
SHE SLAPPED ME.
SHE SLAPPED ME.

READ THIS WAY

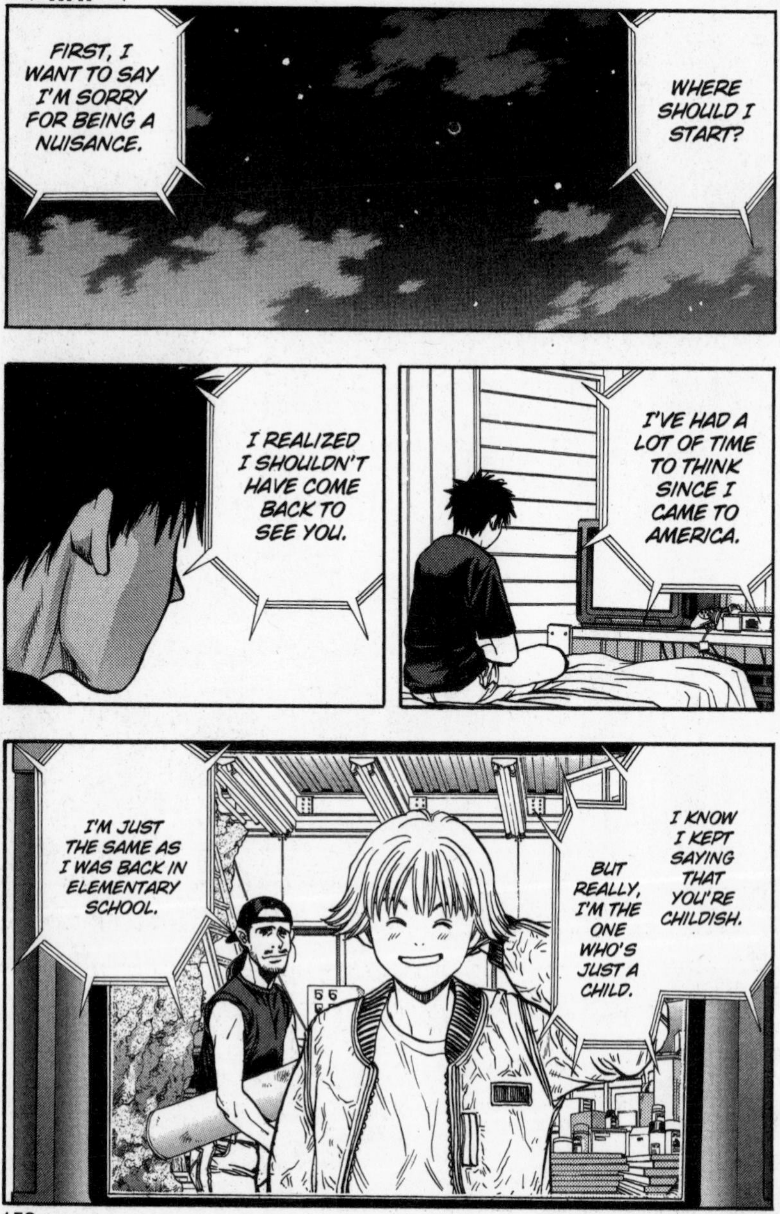
WHERE SHOULD I START?
FIRST, I WANT TO SAY I'M SORRY FOR BEING A NUISANCE.
I'VE HAD A LOT OF TIME TO THINK SINCE I CAME TO AMERICA.
I REALIZED I SHOULDN'T HAVE COME BACK TO SEE YOU.
I KNOW I KEPT SAYING THAT YOU'RE CHILDISH.
BUT REALLY, I'M THE ONE WHO'S JUST A CHILD.
I'M JUST THE SAME AS I WAS BACK IN ELEMENTARY SCHOOL.

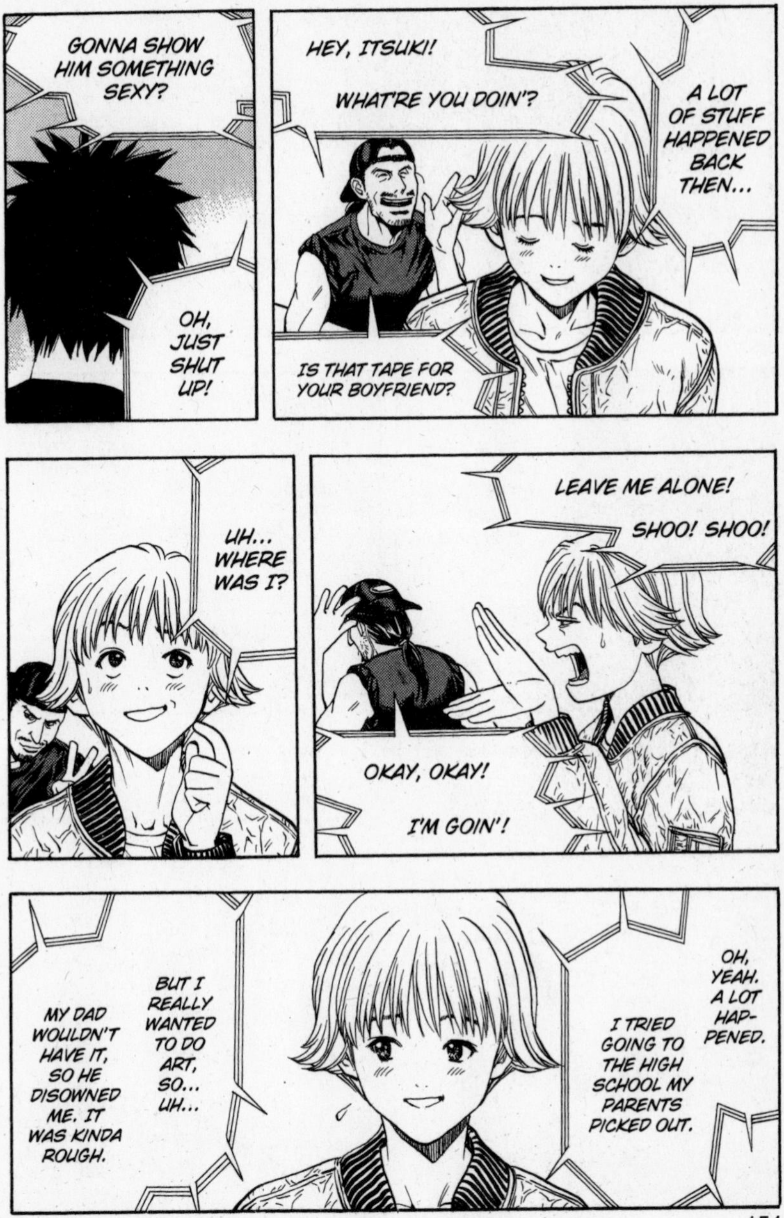
A LOT OF STUFF HAPPENED BACK THEN...
HEY, ITSUKI!
WHAT'RE YOU DOIN'?
IS THAT TAPE FOR YOUR BOYFRIEND?
GONNA SHOW HIM SOMETHING SEXY?
OH, JUST SHUT UP!
LEAVE ME ALONE!
SHOO! SHOO!
OKAY, OKAY!
I'M GOIN'!
UH... WHERE WAS I?
OH, YEAH. A LOT HAP-PENED.
I TRIED GOING TO THE HIGH SCHOOL MY PARENTS PICKED OUT.
BUT I REALLY WANTED TO DO ART, SO... UH...
MY DAD WOULDN'T HAVE IT, SO HE DISOWNED ME. IT WAS KINDA ROUGH.

READ THIS WAY

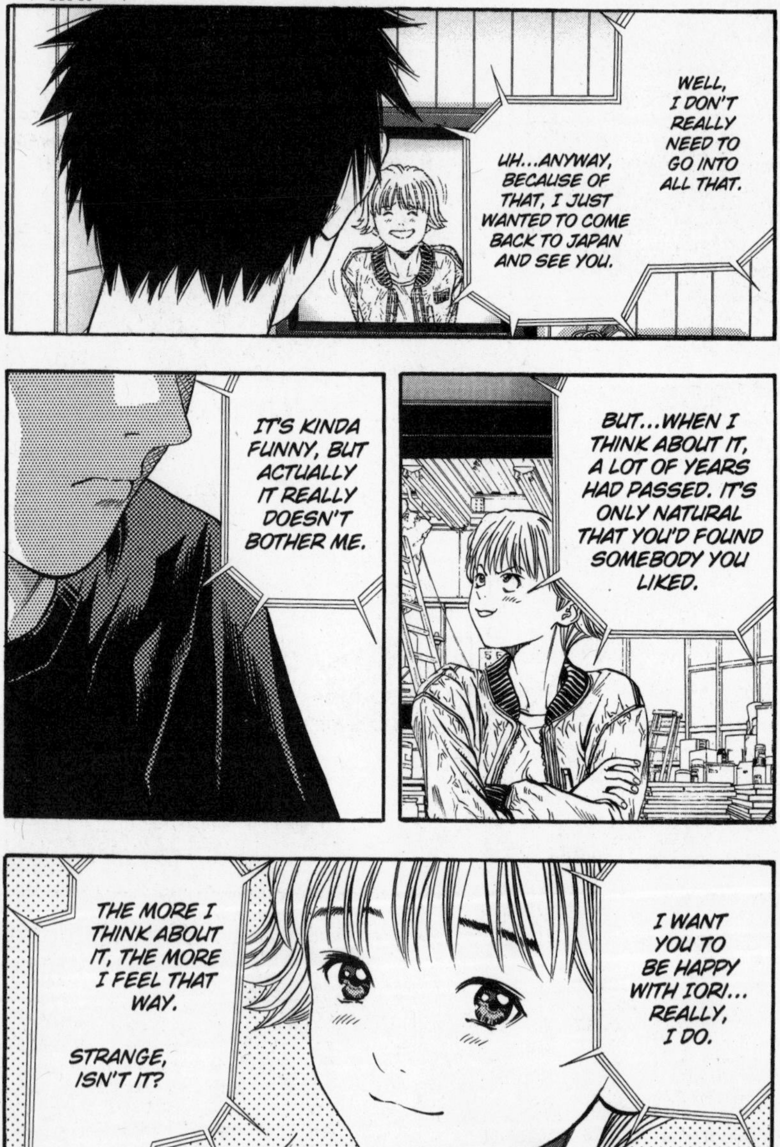

WELL, I DON'T REALLY NEED TO GO INTO ALL THAT.
UH...ANYWAY, BECAUSE OF THAT, I JUST WANTED TO COME BACK TO JAPAN AND SEE YOU.
BUT...WHEN I THINK ABOUT IT, A LOT OF YEARS HAD PASSED. IT'S ONLY NATURAL THAT YOU'D FOUND SOMEBODY YOU LIKED.
IT'S KINDA FUNNY, BUT ACTUALLY IT REALLY DOESN'T BOTHER ME.
I WANT YOU TO BE HAPPY WITH IORI... REALLY, I DO.
THE MORE I THINK ABOUT IT, THE MORE I FEEL THAT WAY.
STRANGE, ISN'T IT?

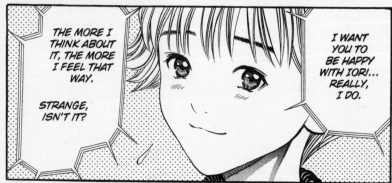

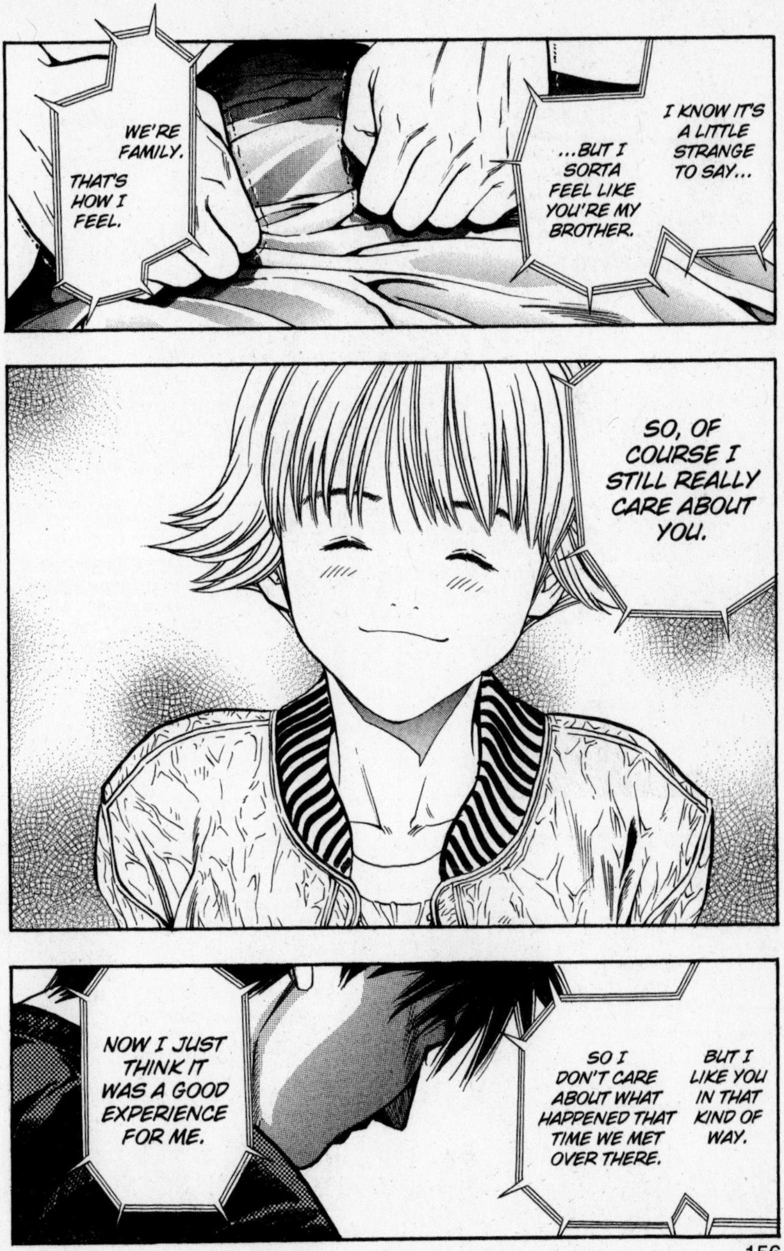
I KNOW IT'S A LITTLE STRANGE TO SAY...
...BUT I SORTA FEEL LIKE YOU'RE MY BROTHER.
WE'RE FAMILY.
THAT'S HOW I FEEL.
SO, OF COURSE I STILL REALLY CARE ABOUT YOU.
BUT I LIKE YOU IN THAT KIND OF WAY.
SO I DON'T CARE ABOUT WHAT HAPPENED THAT TIME WE MET OVER THERE.
NOW I JUST THINK IT WAS A GOOD EXPERIENCE FOR ME.

READ THIS WAY

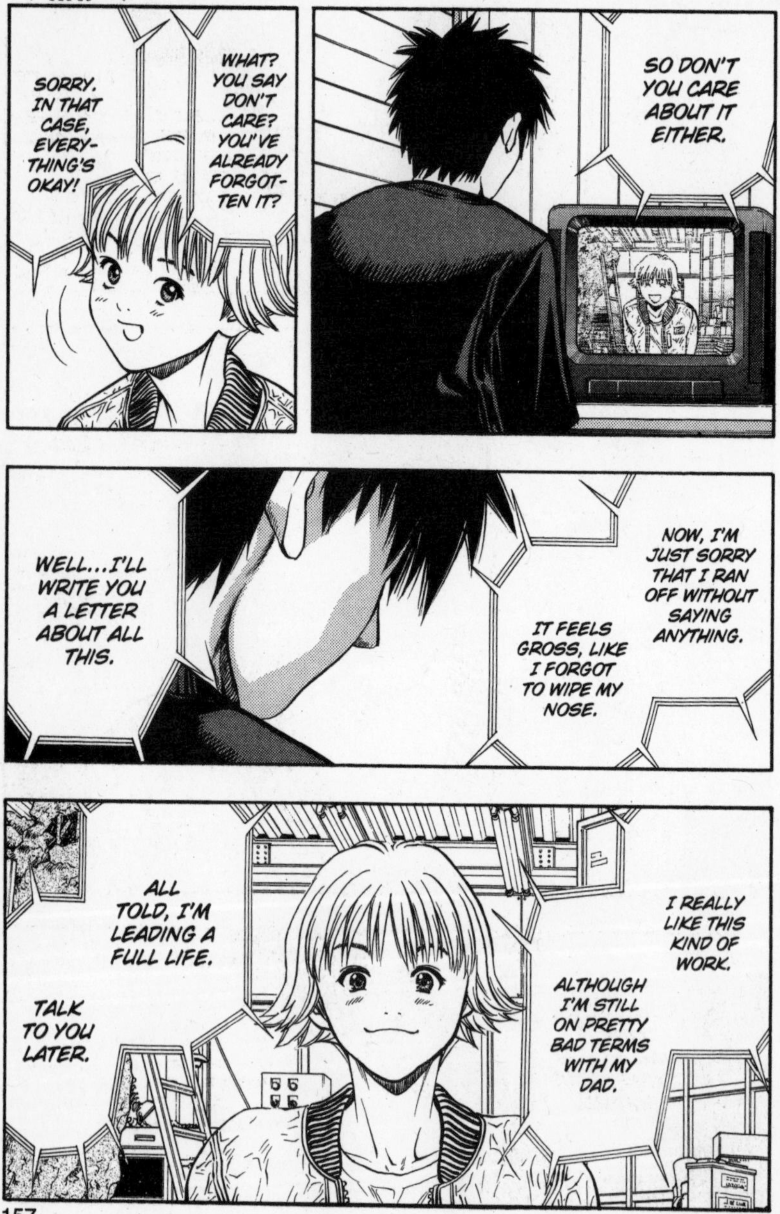
SO DON'T YOU CARE ABOUT IT EITHER.
WHAT? YOU SAY DON'T CARE? YOU'VE ALREADY FORGOT-TEN IT?
SORRY. IN THAT CASE, EVERY-THING'S OKAY!
NOW, I'M JUST SORRY THAT I RAN OFF WITHOUT SAYING ANYTHING.
IT FEELS GROSS, LIKE I FORGOT TO WIPE MY NOSE.
WELL...I'LL WRITE YOU A LETTER ABOUT ALL THIS.
I REALLY LIKE THIS KIND OF WORK.
ALTHOUGH I'M STILL ON PRETTY BAD TERMS WITH MY DAD.
ALL TOLD, I'M LEADING A FULL LIFE.
TALK TO YOU LATER.

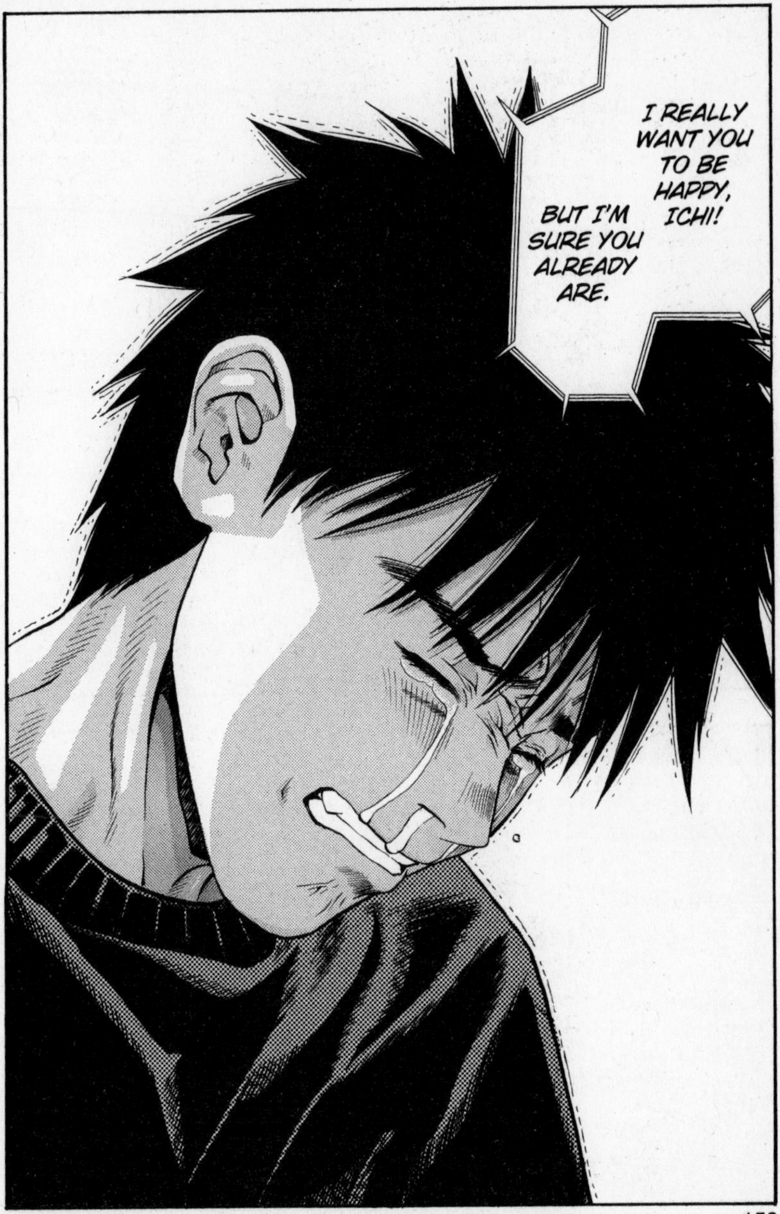
I REALLY WANT YOU TO BE HAPPY, ICHI!
BUT I'M SURE YOU ALREADY ARE.

READ THIS WAY

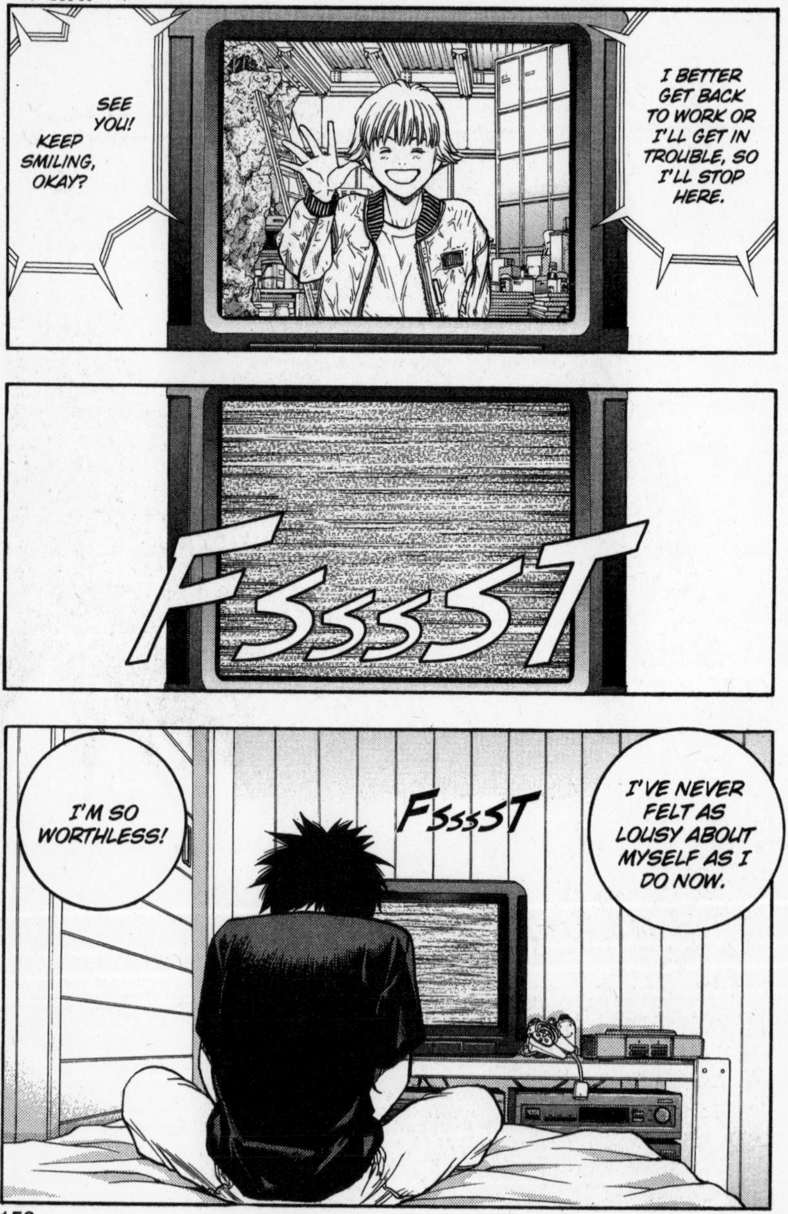
I BETTER GET BACK TO WORK OR I'LL GET IN TROUBLE, SO I'LL STOP HERE.
SEE YOU!
KEEP SMILING, OKAY?
FSSSST
I'VE NEVER FELT AS LOUSY ABOUT MYSELF AS I DO NOW.
FSSSST
I'M SO WORTHLESS!

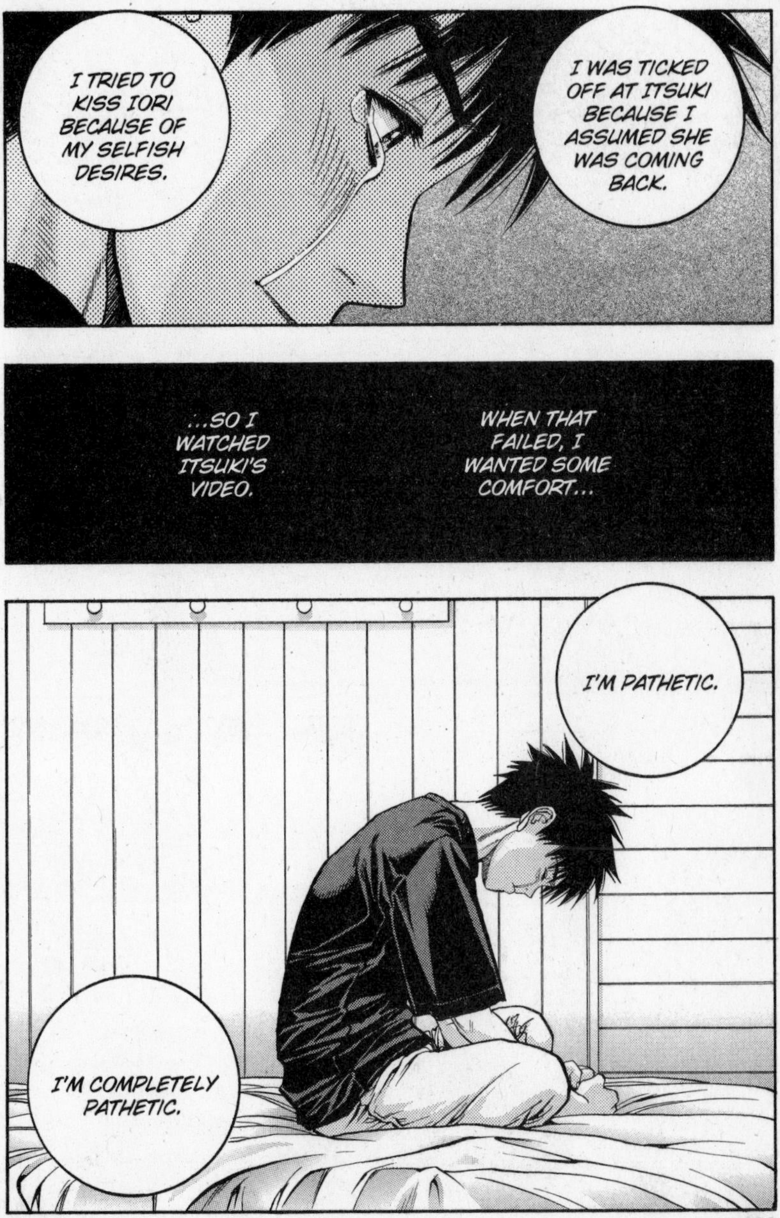
I WAS TICKED OFF AT ITSUKI BECAUSE I ASSUMED SHE WAS COMING BACK.
I TRIED TO KISS IORI BECAUSE OF MY SELFISH DESIRES.
WHEN THAT FAILED, I WANTED SOME COMFORT...
...SO I WATCHED ITSUKI'S VIDEO.
I'M PATHETIC.
I'M COMPLETELY PATHETIC.

Ïš

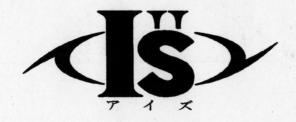

Chapter 63:
Return to the Inn

READ THIS WAY

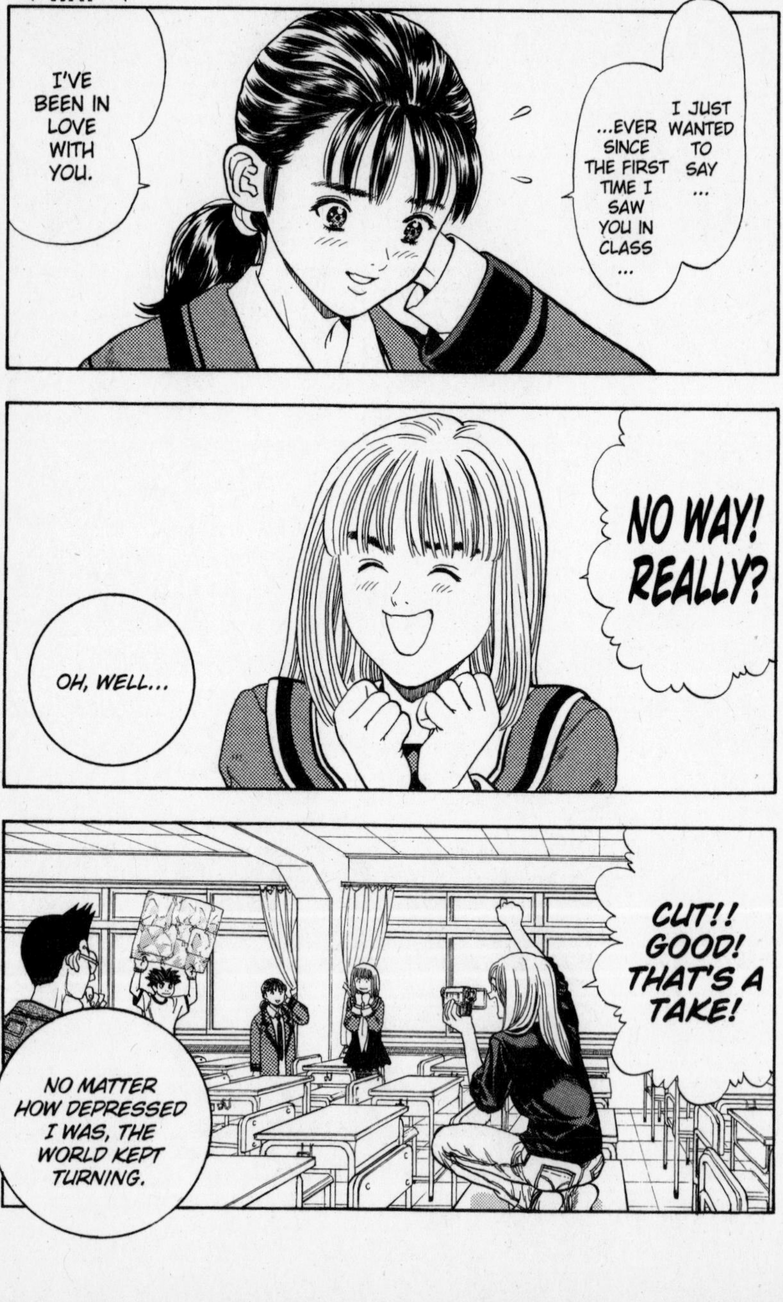
I JUST WANTED TO SAY ...
...EVER SINCE THE FIRST TIME I SAW YOU IN CLASS ...
I'VE BEEN IN LOVE WITH YOU.
NO WAY! REALLY?
OH, WELL...
CUT!! GOOD! THAT'S A TAKE!
NO MATTER HOW DEPRESSED I WAS, THE WORLD KEPT TURNING.

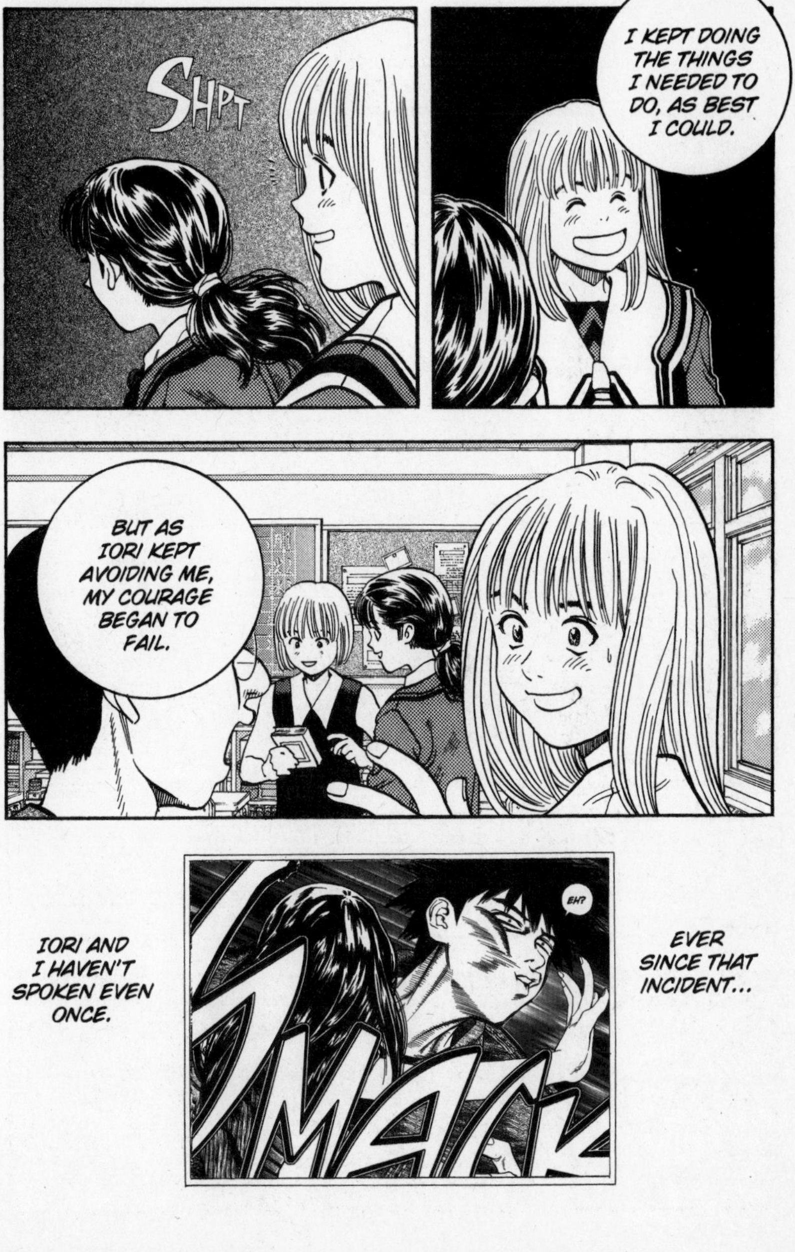
I KEPT DOING THE THINGS I NEEDED TO DO, AS BEST I COULD.
SHPT
BUT AS IORI KEPT AVOIDING ME, MY COURAGE BEGAN TO FAIL.
EVER SINCE THAT INCIDENT...
EH?
SMACK
IORI AND I HAVEN'T SPOKEN EVEN ONCE.

WELL, ANYWAY, THE MOVIE WAS COMPLETED.

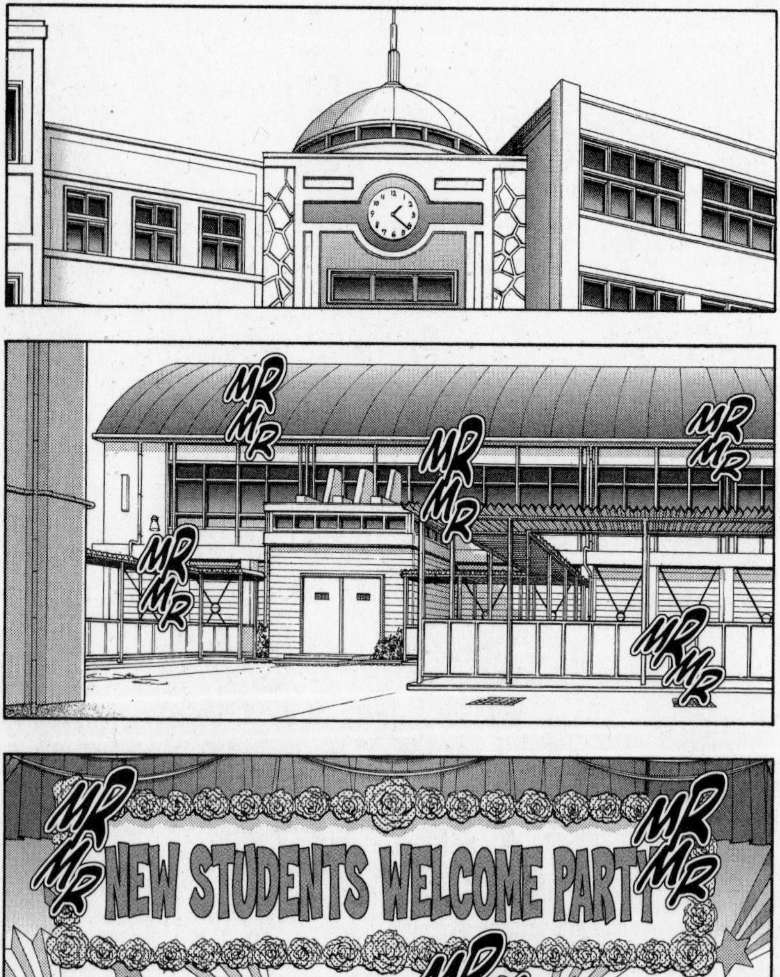
MR MR
MR MR
MR MR
MR MR
MR MR
NEW STUDENTS WELCOME PARTY
MR MR
MR MR
MR MR

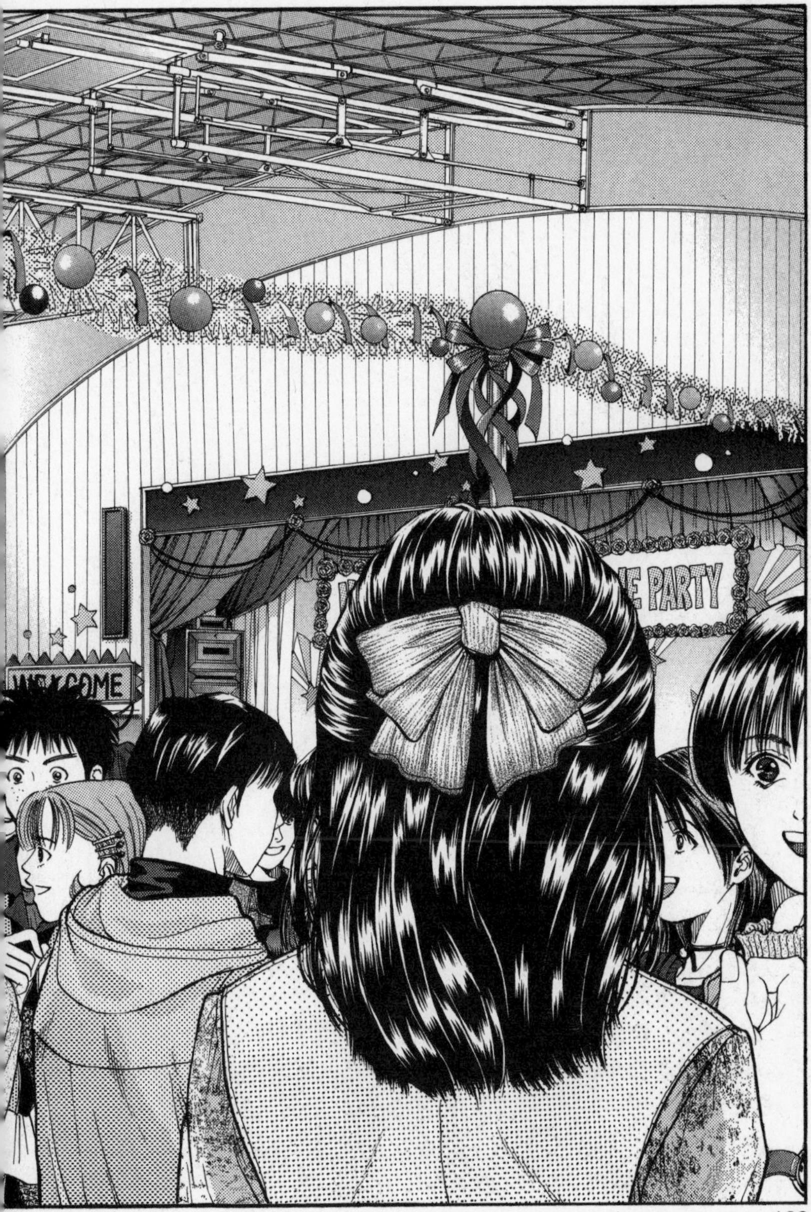
PARTY

READ THIS WAY

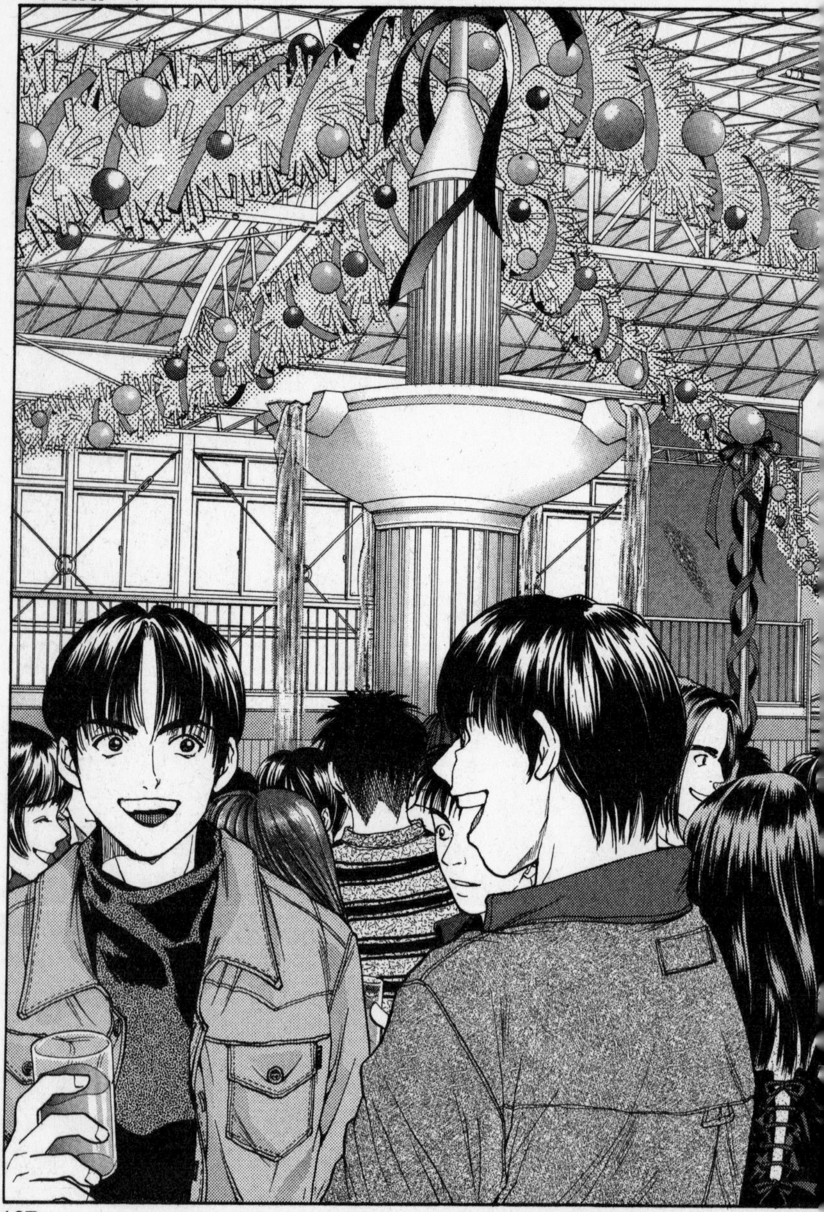

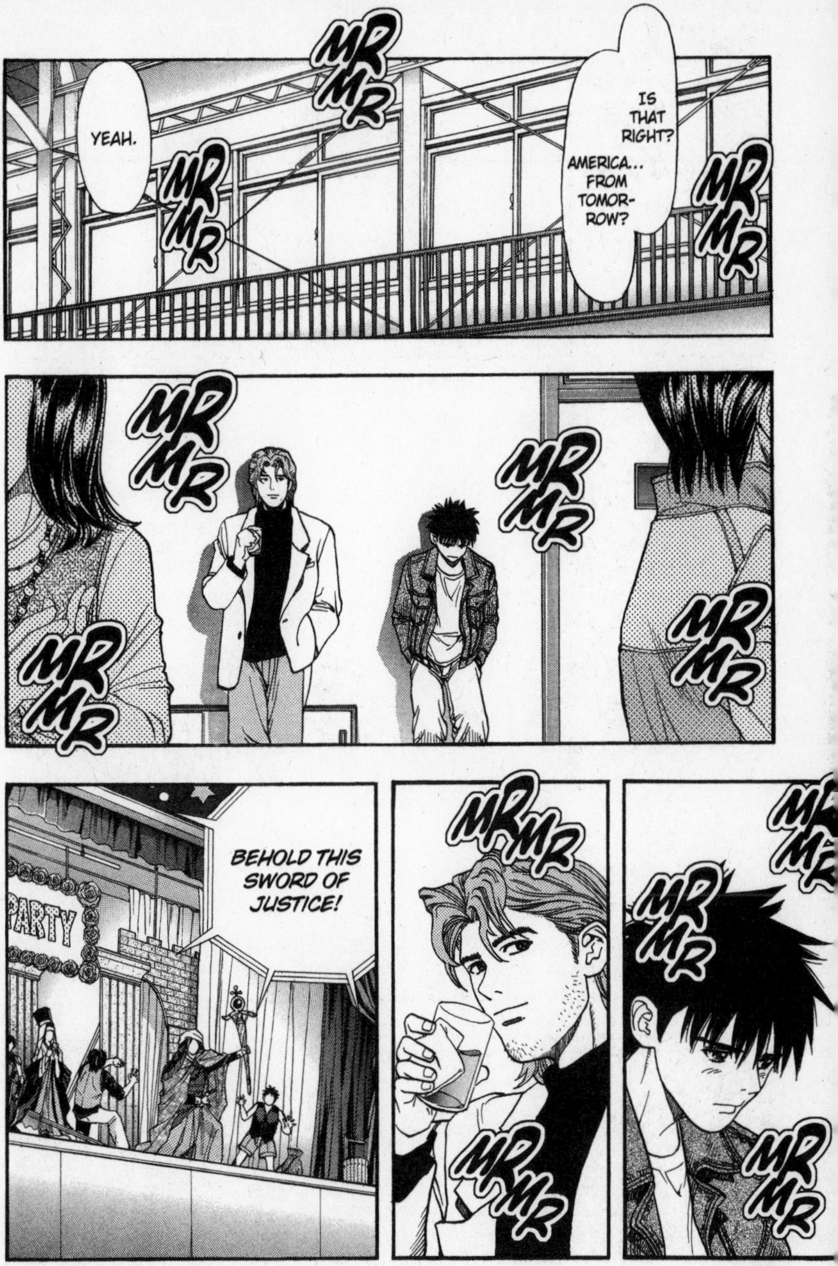
MR MR
IS THAT RIGHT? AMERICA... FROM TOMORROW?
MR MR
MR MR
YEAH.
MR MR
MR MR
MR MR
MR MR
MR MR
MR MR
MR MR
MR MR
MR MR
BEHOLD THIS SWORD OF JUSTICE!

READ THIS WAY

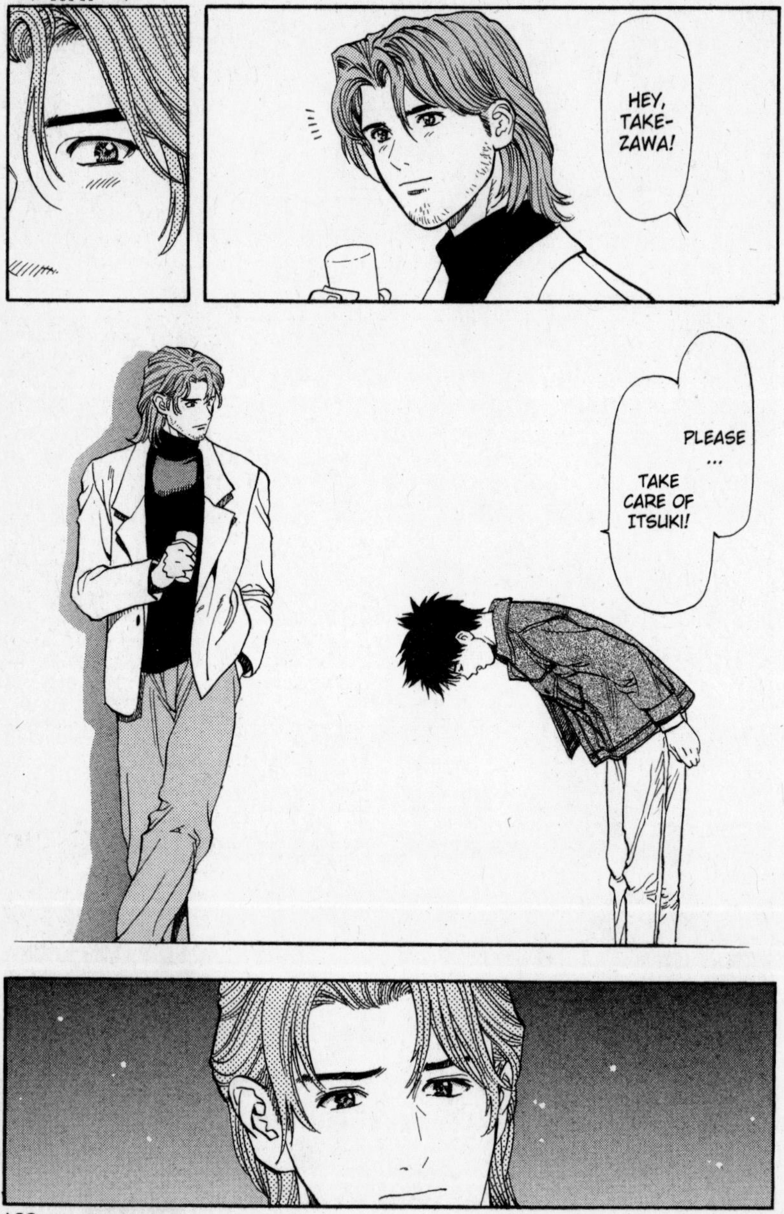
HEY, TAKE-ZAWA!
PLEASE ... TAKE CARE OF ITSUKI!

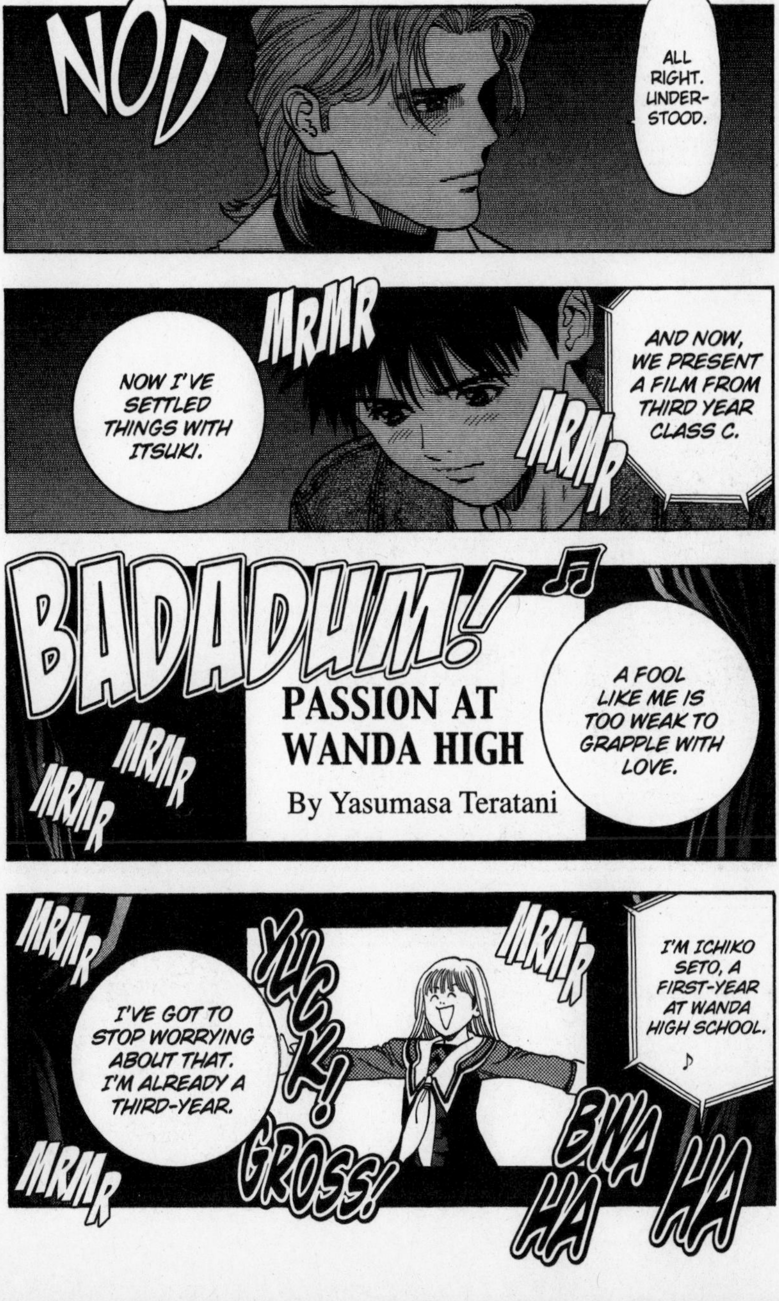
ALL RIGHT. UNDERSTOOD.
NOD
AND NOW, WE PRESENT A FILM FROM THIRD YEAR CLASS C.
MRMR
MRMR
NOW I'VE SETTLED THINGS WITH ITSUKI.
A FOOL LIKE ME IS TOO WEAK TO GRAPPLE WITH LOVE.
PASSION AT WANDA HIGH
By Yasumasa Teratani
BADADUM! ♫
MRMR
MRMR
I'M ICHIKO SETO, A FIRST-YEAR AT WANDA HIGH SCHOOL. ♪
MRMR
BWA HA HA HA
YUCK! GROSS!
I'VE GOT TO STOP WORRYING ABOUT THAT. I'M ALREADY A THIRD-YEAR.
MRMR
MRMR

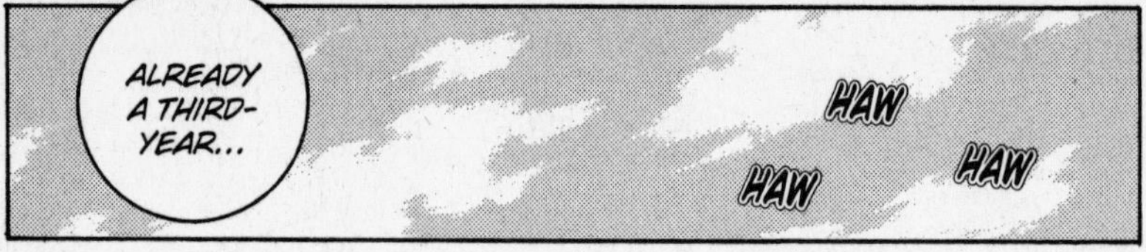
ALREADY A THIRD-YEAR...
HAW
HAW
HAW

Summer...

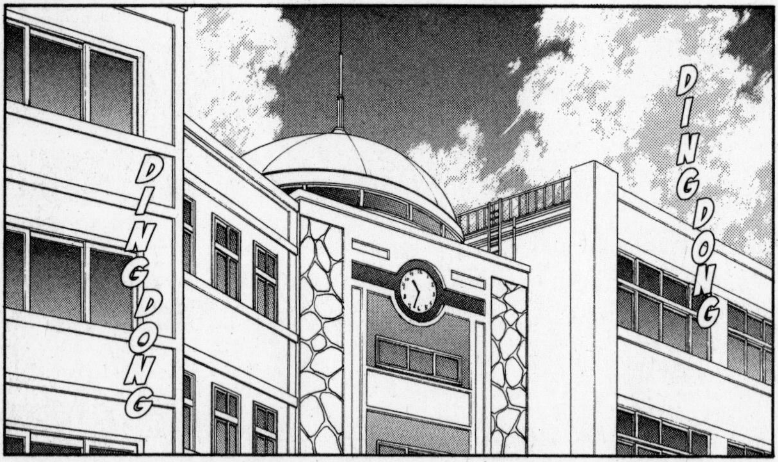
DING DONG
DING DONG

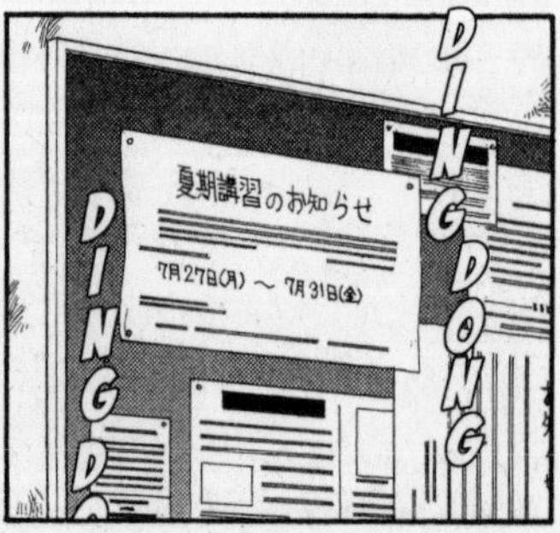
DING DONG
夏期講習のお知らせ
7月27日(月) ～ 7月31日(金)
DING

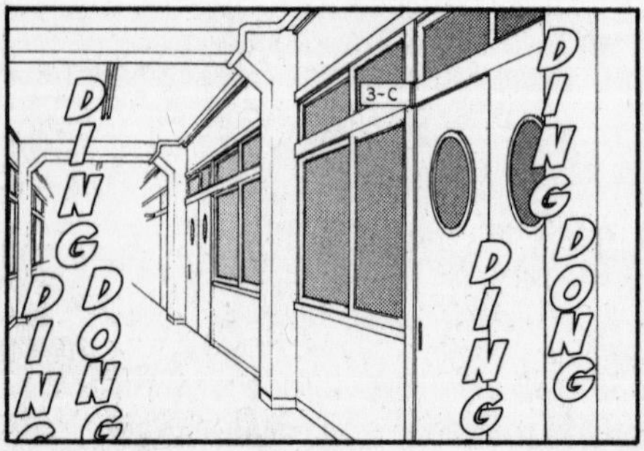
3-C
DING DONG
DING
DING
DING DONG

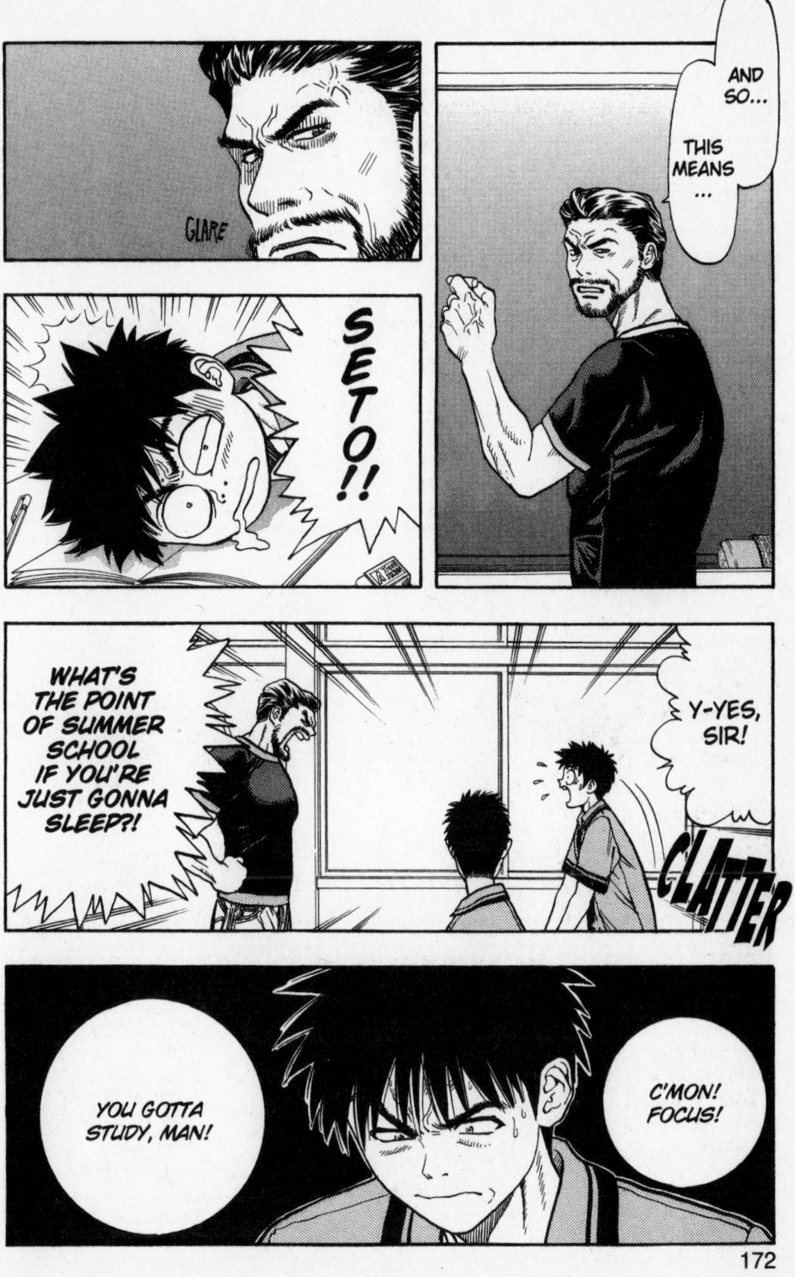
AND SO...
THIS MEANS ...
GLARE
SETO!!
Y-YES, SIR!
CLATTER
WHAT'S THE POINT OF SUMMER SCHOOL IF YOU'RE JUST GONNA SLEEP?!
C'MON! FOCUS!
YOU GOTTA STUDY, MAN!

READ THIS WAY

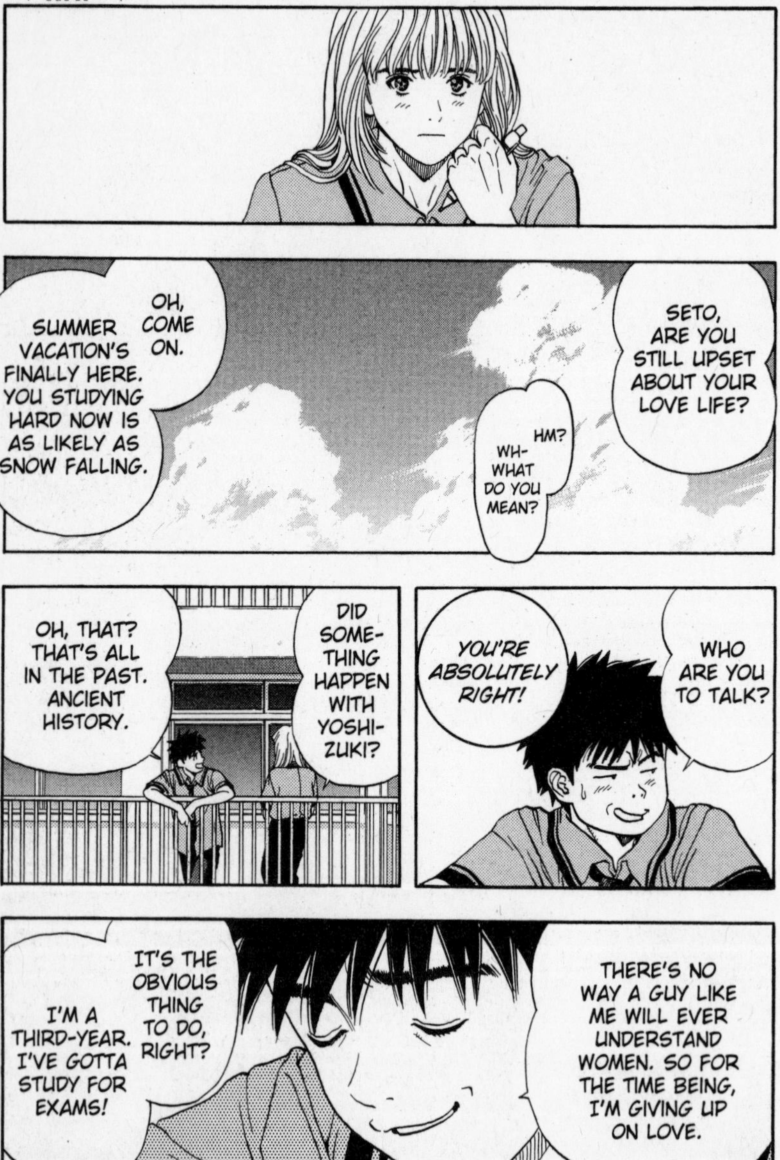
SETO, ARE YOU STILL UPSET ABOUT YOUR LOVE LIFE?
HM? WH-WHAT DO YOU MEAN?
OH, COME ON.
SUMMER VACATION'S FINALLY HERE. YOU STUDYING HARD NOW IS AS LIKELY AS SNOW FALLING.
WHO ARE YOU TO TALK?
YOU'RE ABSOLUTELY RIGHT!
DID SOME-THING HAPPEN WITH YOSHI-ZUKI?
OH, THAT? THAT'S ALL IN THE PAST. ANCIENT HISTORY.
THERE'S NO WAY A GUY LIKE ME WILL EVER UNDERSTAND WOMEN. SO FOR THE TIME BEING, I'M GIVING UP ON LOVE.
IT'S THE OBVIOUS THING TO DO, RIGHT?
I'M A THIRD-YEAR. I'VE GOTTA STUDY FOR EXAMS!

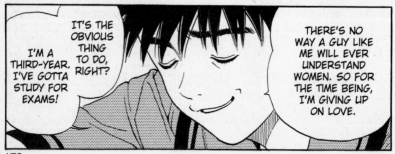

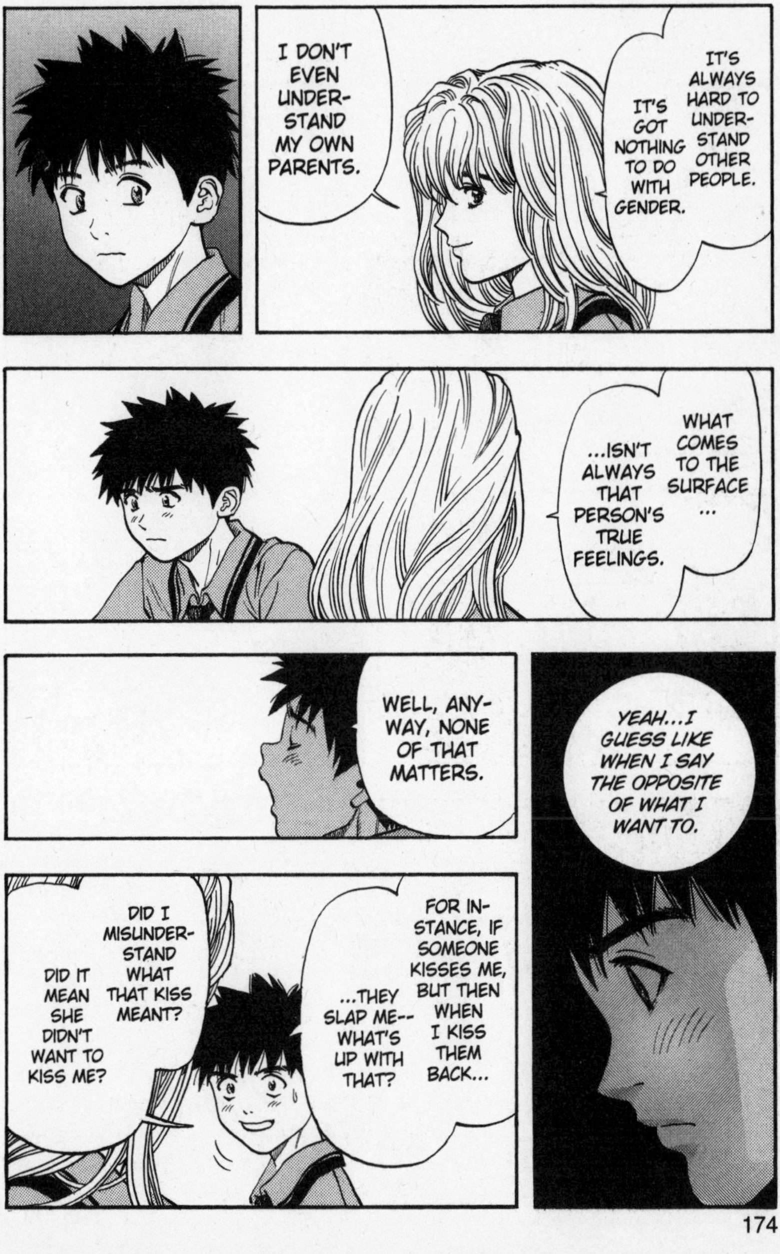
IT'S ALWAYS HARD TO UNDERSTAND OTHER PEOPLE.
IT'S GOT NOTHING TO DO WITH GENDER.
I DON'T EVEN UNDERSTAND MY OWN PARENTS.
WHAT COMES TO THE SURFACE...
...ISN'T ALWAYS THAT PERSON'S TRUE FEELINGS.
YEAH...I GUESS LIKE WHEN I SAY THE OPPOSITE OF WHAT I WANT TO.
WELL, ANYWAY, NONE OF THAT MATTERS.
FOR INSTANCE, IF SOMEONE KISSES ME, BUT THEN WHEN I KISS THEM BACK...
...THEY SLAP ME--WHAT'S UP WITH THAT?
DID I MISUNDERSTAND WHAT THAT KISS MEANT?
DID IT MEAN SHE DIDN'T WANT TO KISS ME?

READ THIS WAY

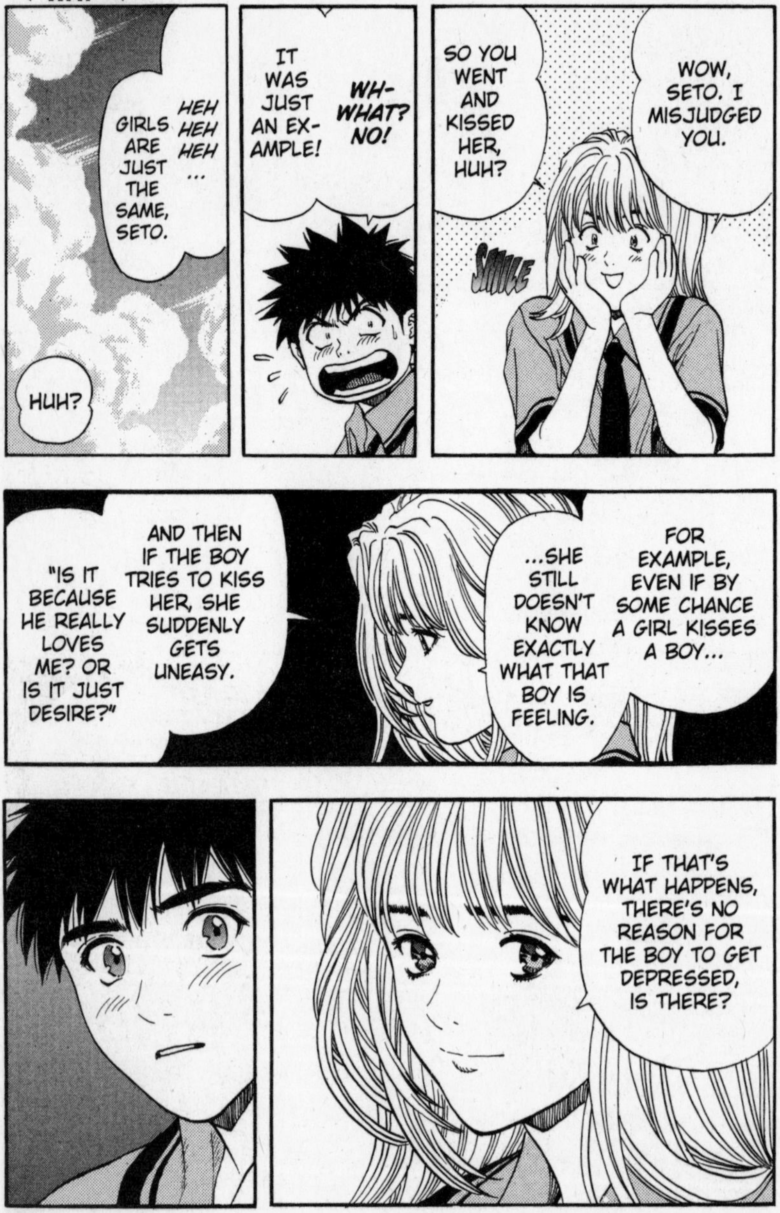
WOW, SETO. I MISJUDGED YOU.
SO YOU WENT AND KISSED HER, HUH?
SMILE
WH-WHAT? NO!
IT WAS JUST AN EX-AMPLE!
HEH HEH HEH ...
GIRLS ARE JUST THE SAME, SETO.
HUH?
FOR EXAMPLE, EVEN IF BY SOME CHANCE A GIRL KISSES A BOY...
...SHE STILL DOESN'T KNOW EXACTLY WHAT THAT BOY IS FEELING.
AND THEN IF THE BOY TRIES TO KISS HER, SHE SUDDENLY GETS UNEASY.
"IS IT BECAUSE HE REALLY LOVES ME? OR IS IT JUST DESIRE?"
IF THAT'S WHAT HAPPENS, THERE'S NO REASON FOR THE BOY TO GET DEPRESSED, IS THERE?

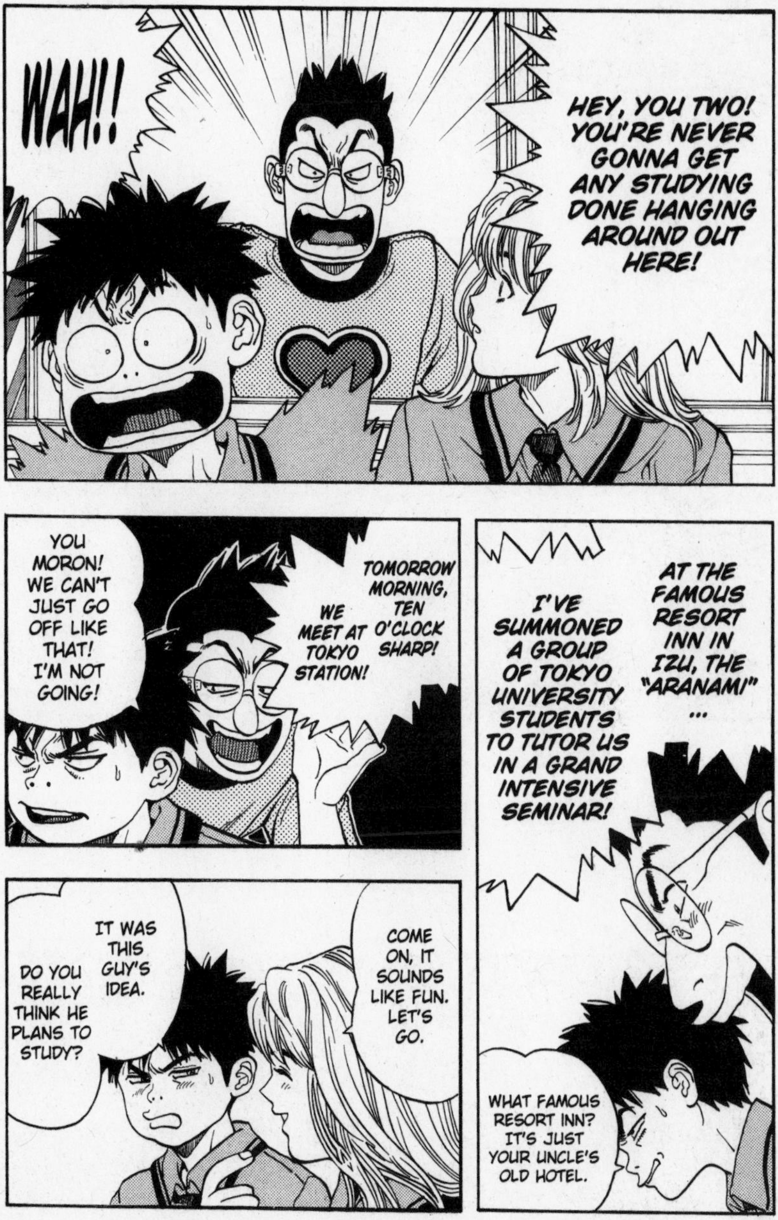
HEY, YOU TWO! YOU'RE NEVER GONNA GET ANY STUDYING DONE HANGING AROUND OUT HERE!
WAH!!
AT THE FAMOUS RESORT INN IN IZU, THE "ARANAMI"...
I'VE SUMMONED A GROUP OF TOKYO UNIVERSITY STUDENTS TO TUTOR US IN A GRAND INTENSIVE SEMINAR!
WHAT FAMOUS RESORT INN? IT'S JUST YOUR UNCLE'S OLD HOTEL.
TOMORROW MORNING, TEN O'CLOCK SHARP!
WE MEET AT TOKYO STATION!
YOU MORON! WE CAN'T JUST GO OFF LIKE THAT! I'M NOT GOING!
COME ON, IT SOUNDS LIKE FUN. LET'S GO.
IT WAS THIS GUY'S IDEA.
DO YOU REALLY THINK HE PLANS TO STUDY?

READ THIS WAY

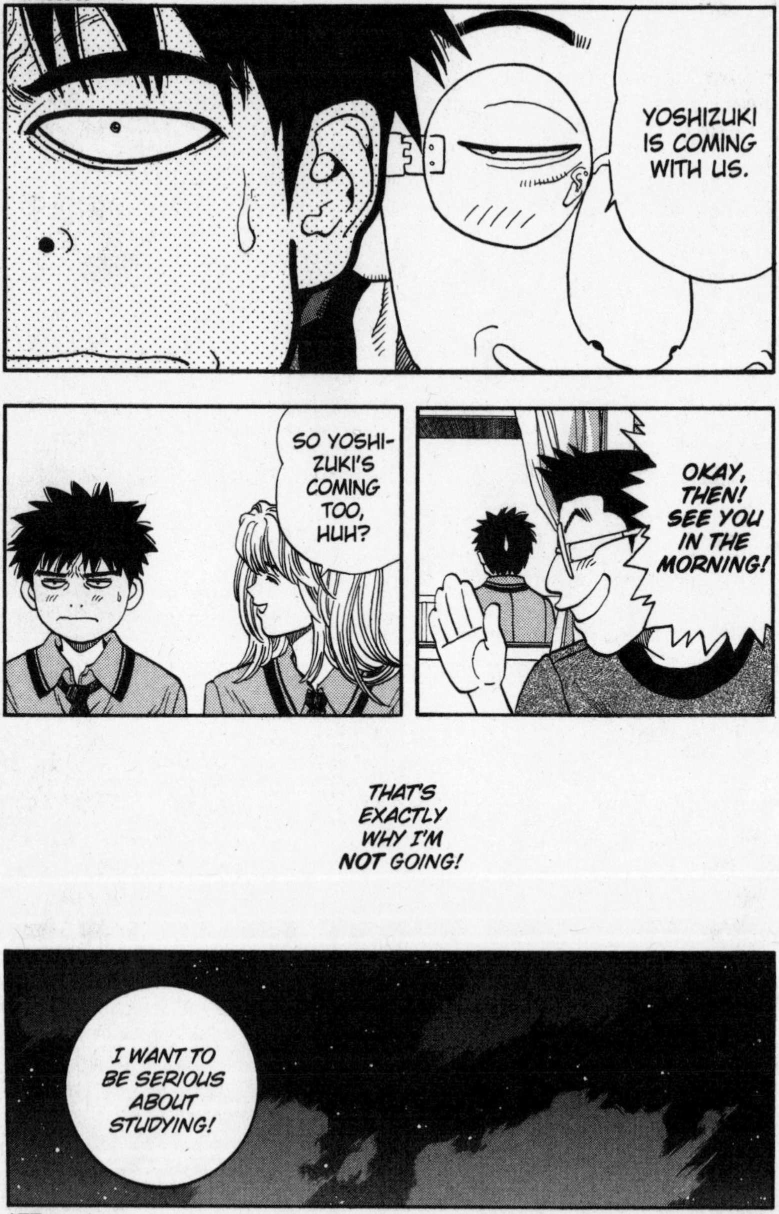

YOSHIZUKI IS COMING WITH US.
OKAY, THEN! SEE YOU IN THE MORNING!
SO YOSHI-ZUKI'S COMING TOO, HUH?
THAT'S EXACTLY WHY I'M NOT GOING!
I WANT TO BE SERIOUS ABOUT STUDYING!

The next day...

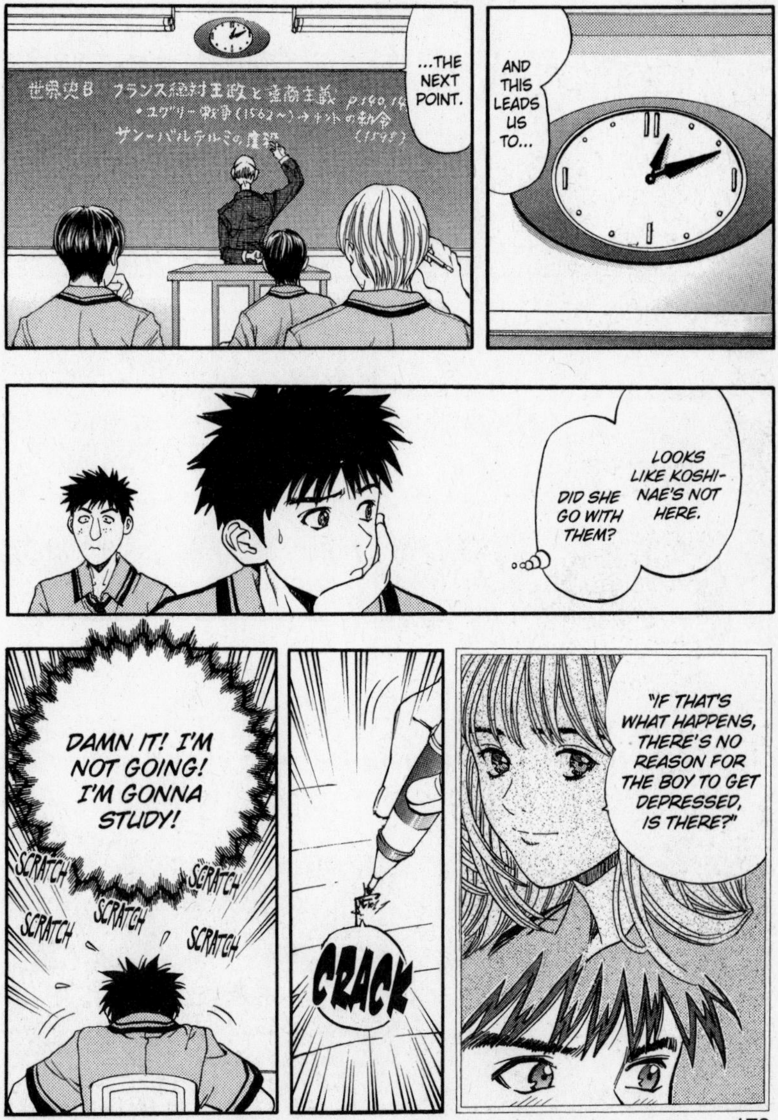

AND THIS LEADS US TO...
...THE NEXT POINT.
LOOKS LIKE KOSHI-NAE'S NOT HERE.
DID SHE GO WITH THEM?
"IF THAT'S WHAT HAPPENS, THERE'S NO REASON FOR THE BOY TO GET DEPRESSED, IS THERE?"
CRACK
DAMN IT! I'M NOT GOING! I'M GONNA STUDY!
SCRATCH
SCRATCH
SCRATCH
SCRATCH
SCRATCH

The next day...

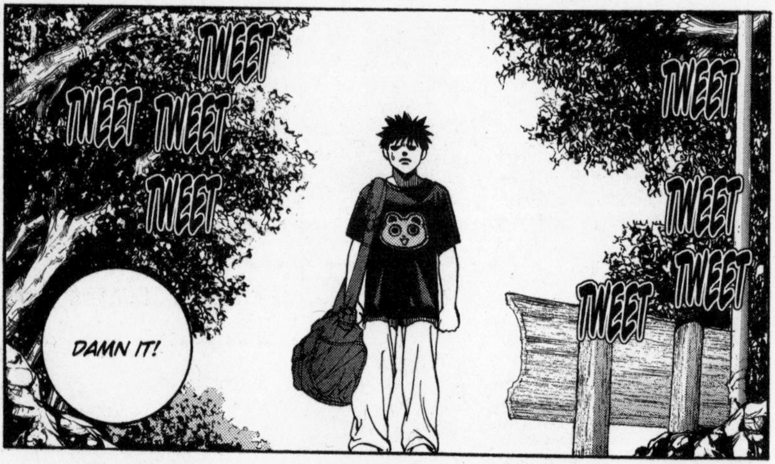
TWEET
TWEET
TWEET
TWEET
TWEET
TWEET
TWEET
TWEET
DAMN IT!

*SIGN: HEAVY SEAS BED & BREAKFAST

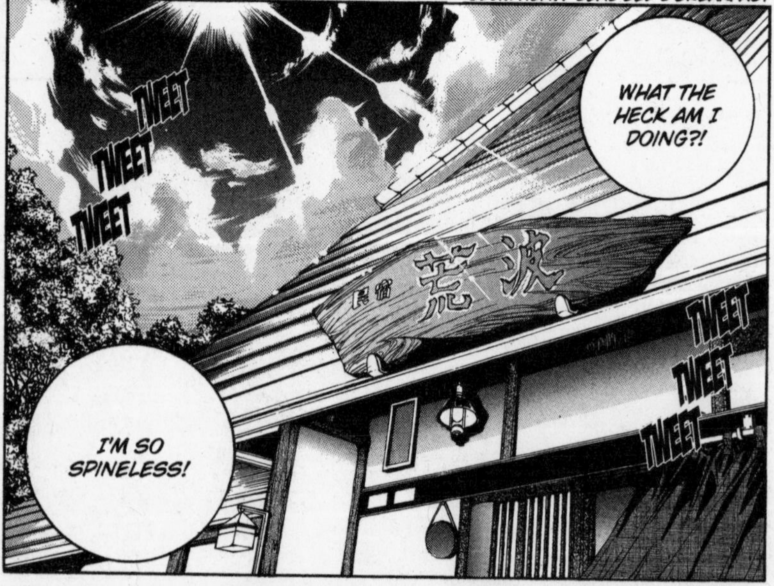
WHAT THE HECK AM I DOING?!
TWEET
TWEET
TWEET
TWEET
TWEET
TWEET
I'M SO SPINELESS!

To be continued in Vol. 8!

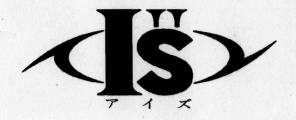

アイズ

I"s Illustration
Collection

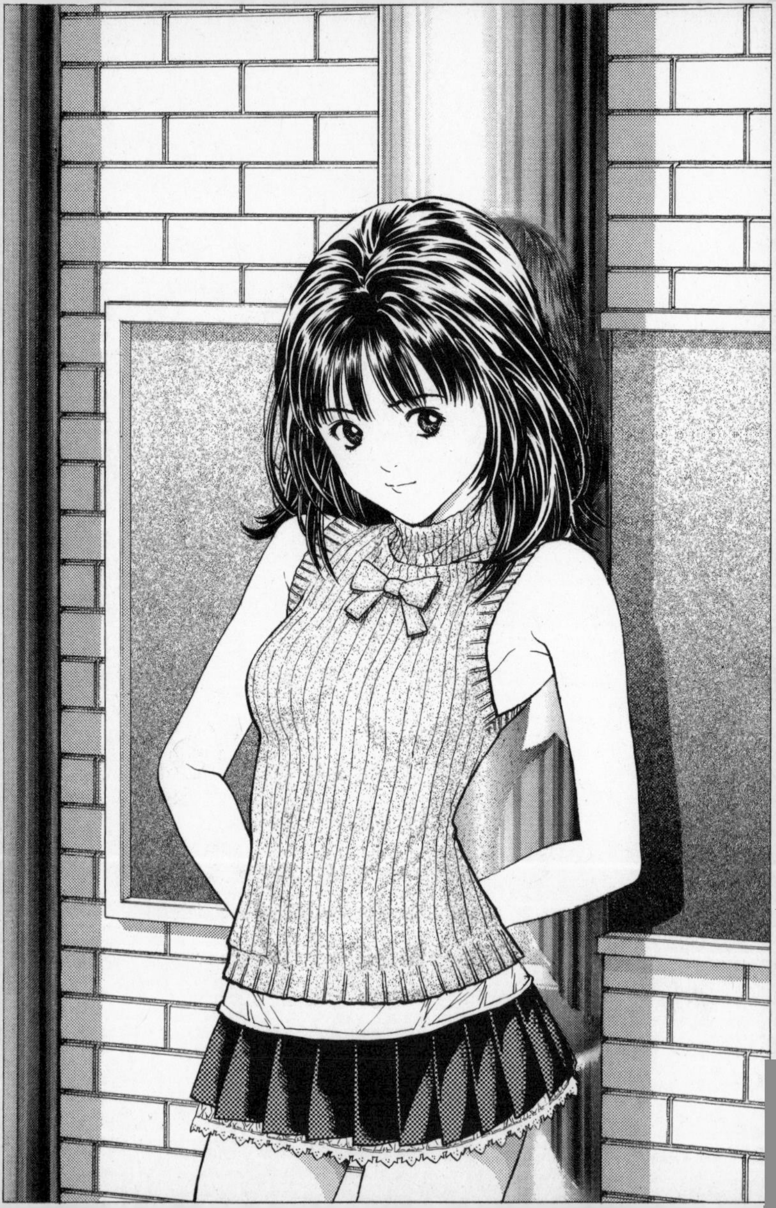

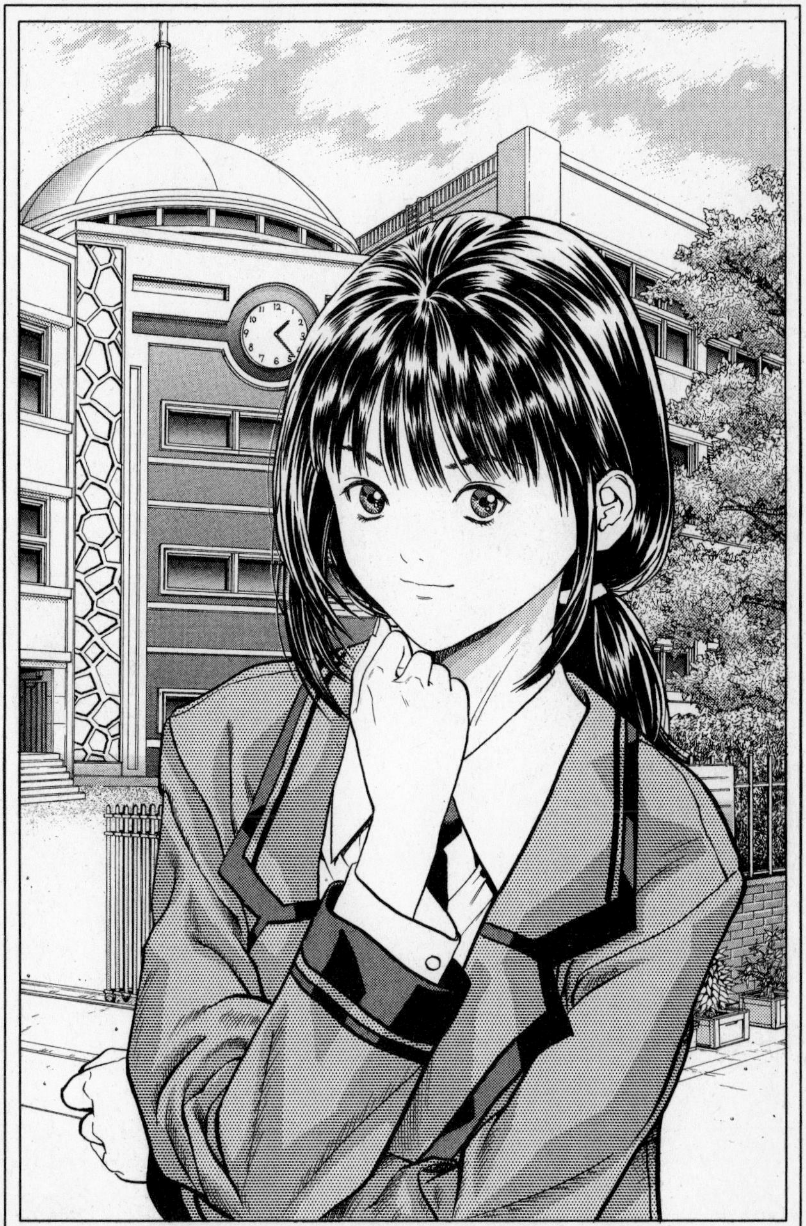

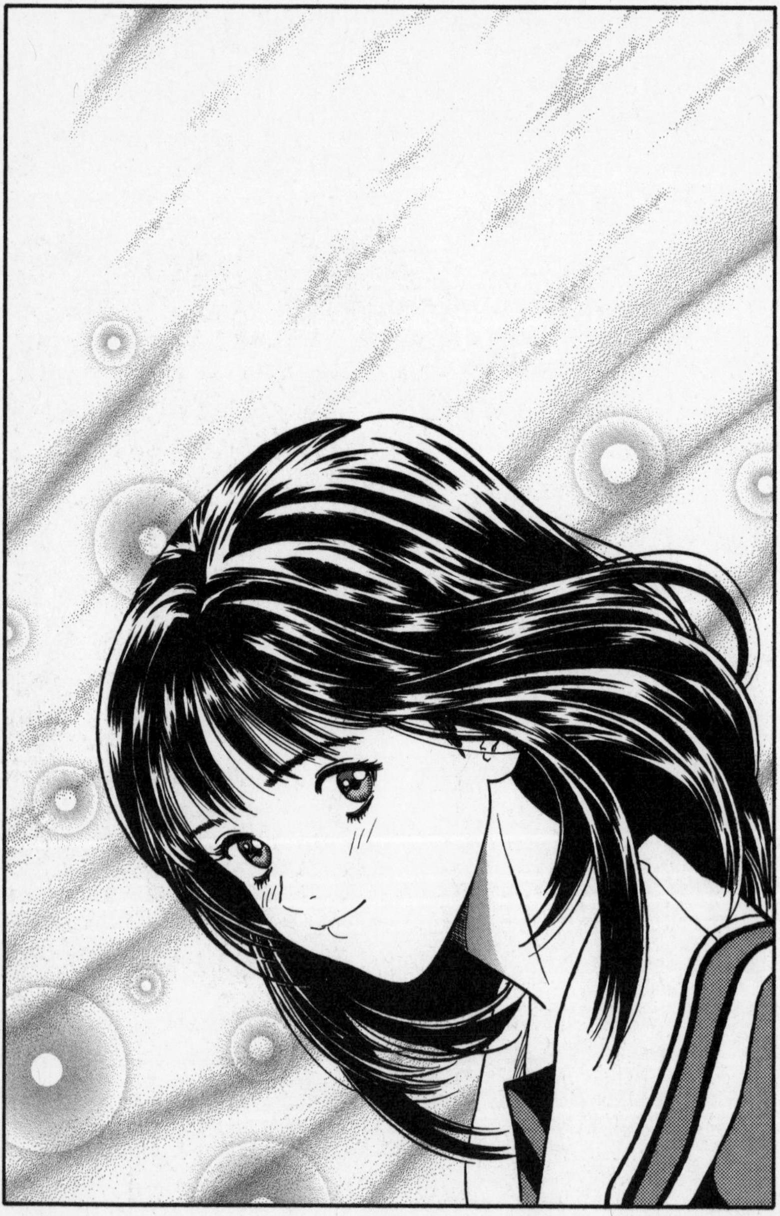

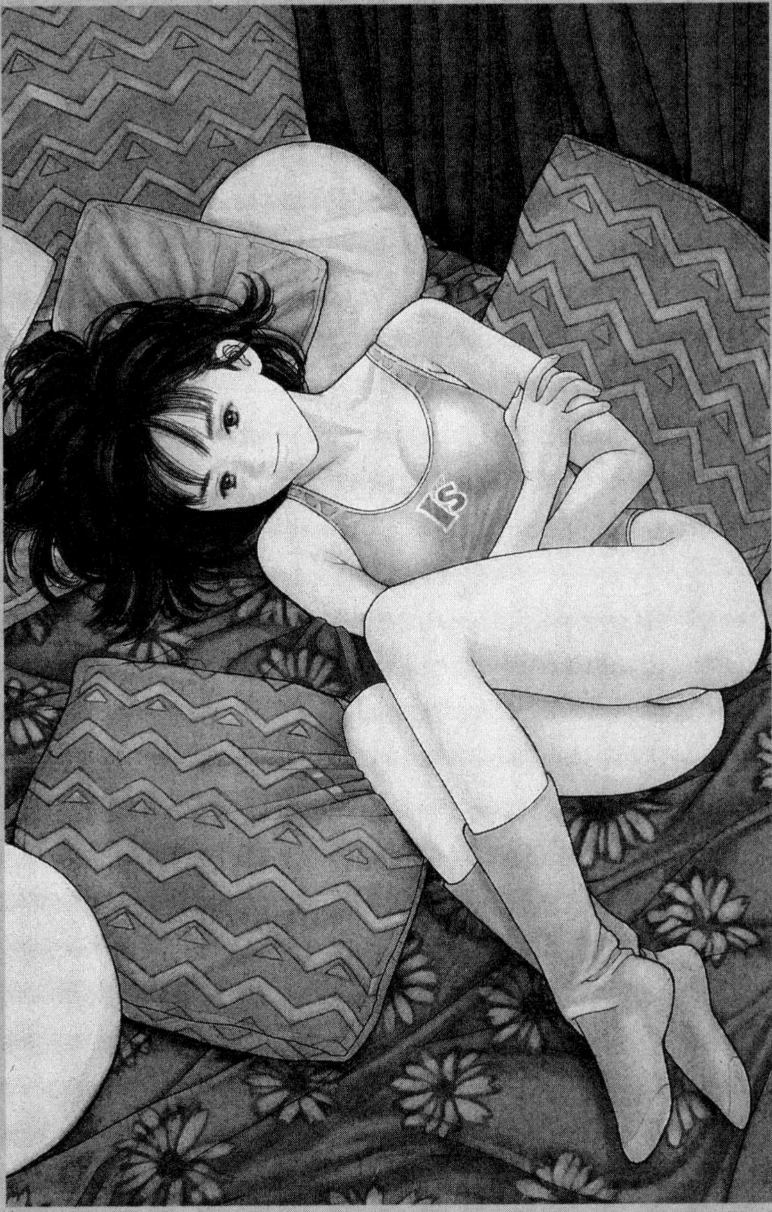

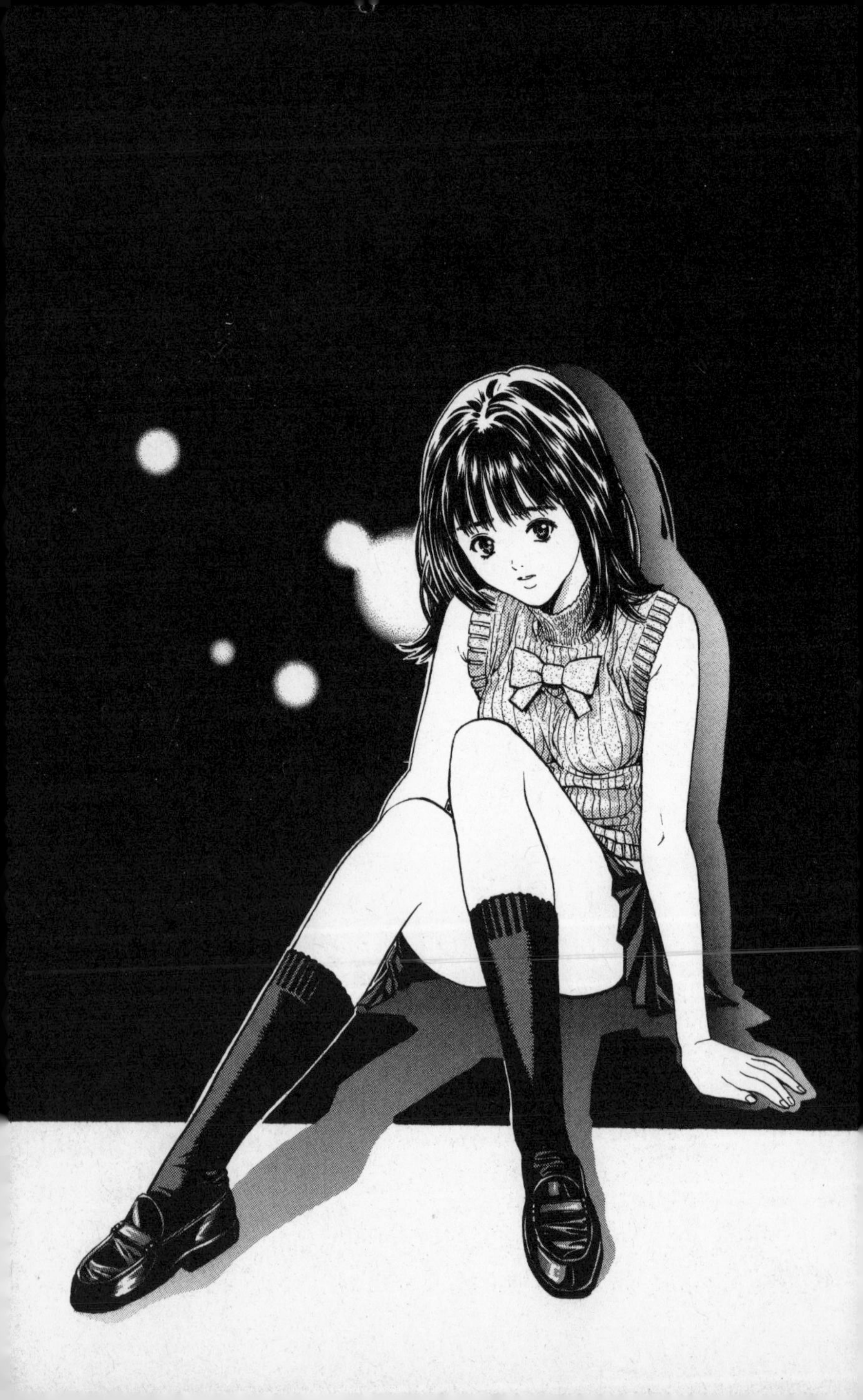

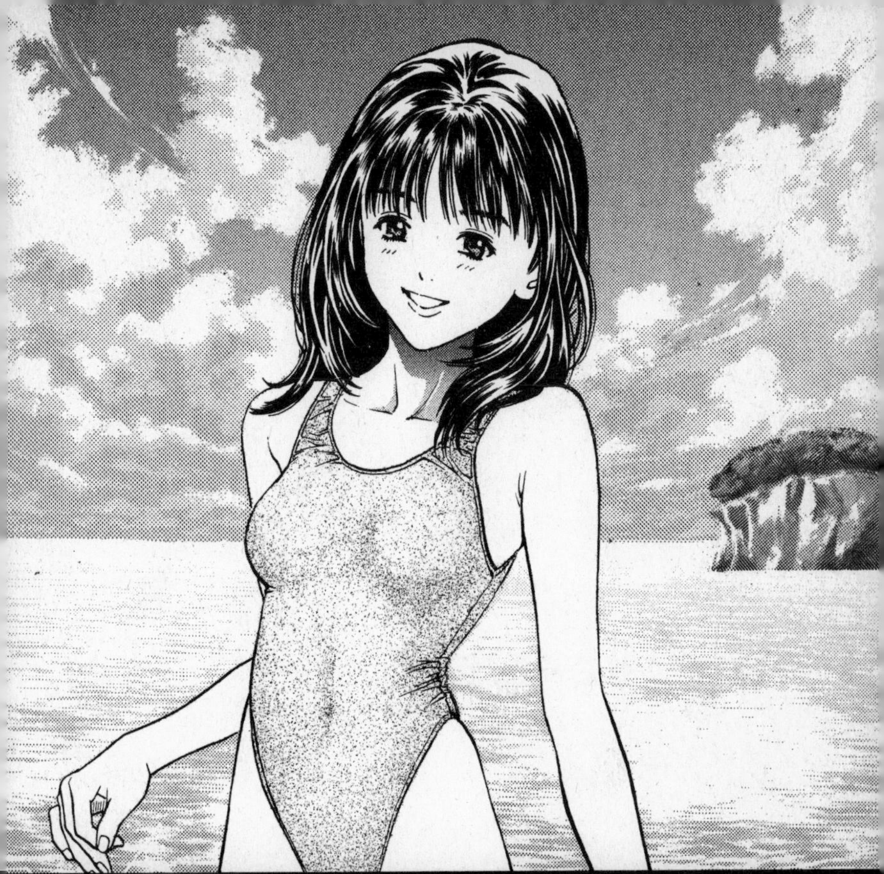

NEXT VOLUME PREVIEW

Ichitaka isn't sure why he came to the seaside resort to join the rest of the gang. His relationship with Iori seems at an all-time low. And before he even has a chance to see her, he runs across a brand-new obstacle—the vivacious Izumi. Izumi has just broken up with her boyfriend and is looking for a new guy in her life. Before he knows it, Ichitaka has become her target. Izumi manages to get in the way every time Ichitaka thinks he has a chance to patch things up with Iori. And just when it seems he may have another opportunity, a prank by Teratani puts him in hot water with Iori—literally!

Available in July 2006

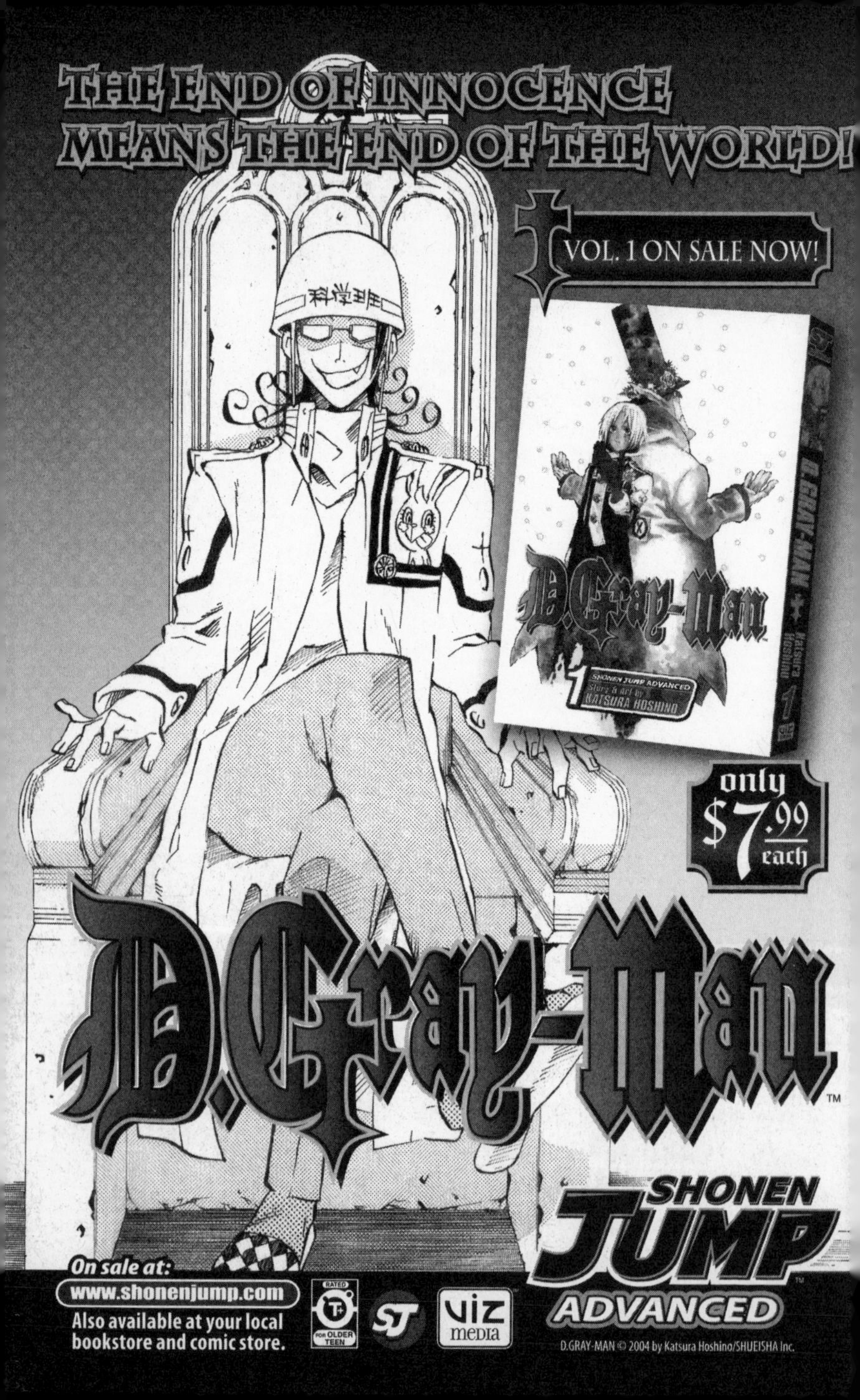

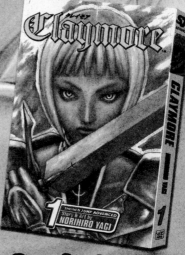
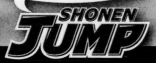

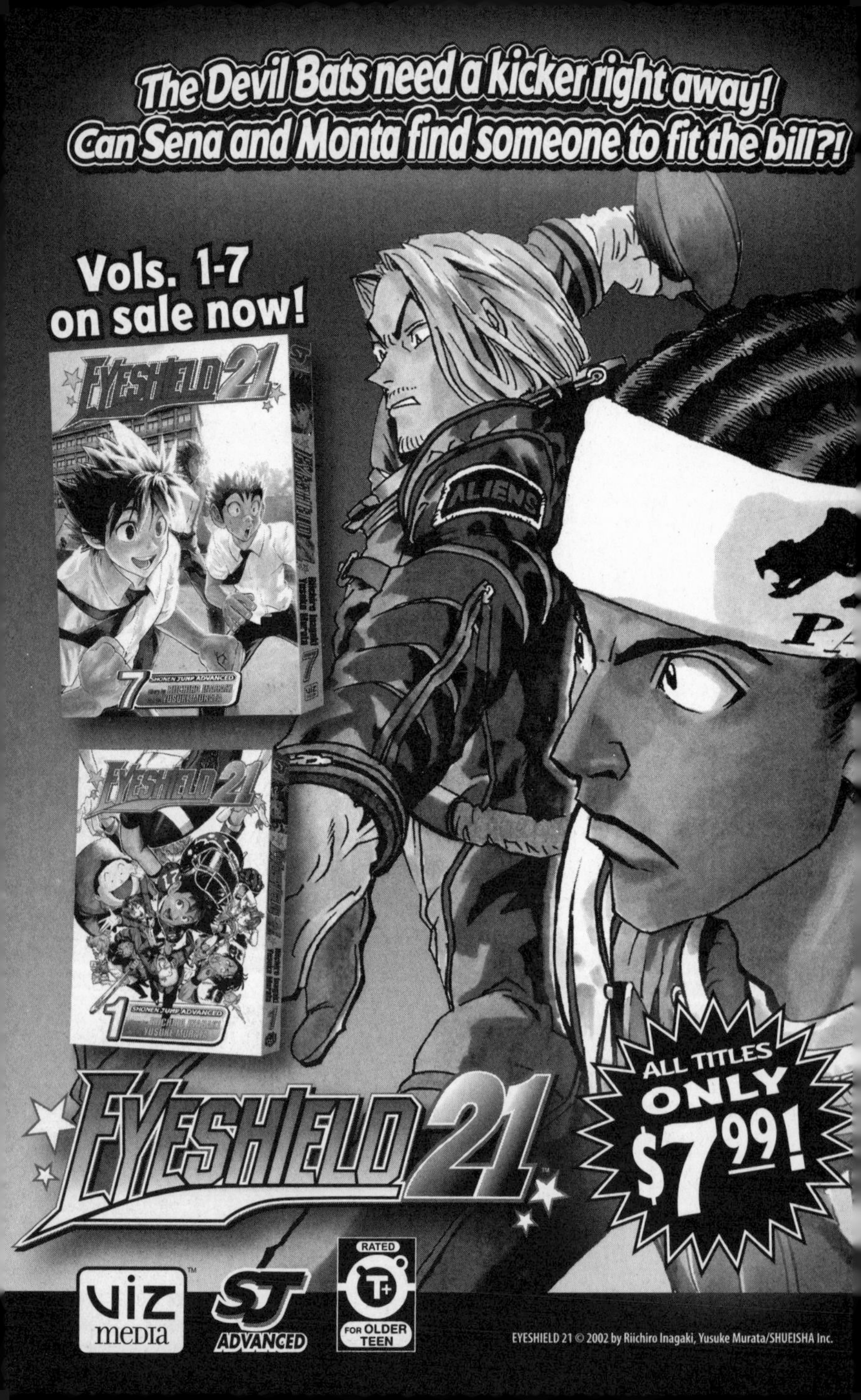
The Devil Bats need a kicker right away!
Can Sena and Monta find someone to fit the bill?!
Vols. 1-7 on sale now!
EYESHIELD 21
ALIENS
EYESHIELD 21
ALL TITLES ONLY $7.99!
viz media
SJ ADVANCED
RATED T+ FOR OLDER TEEN
EYESHIELD 21 © 2002 by Riichiro Inagaki, Yusuke Murata/SHUEISHA Inc.

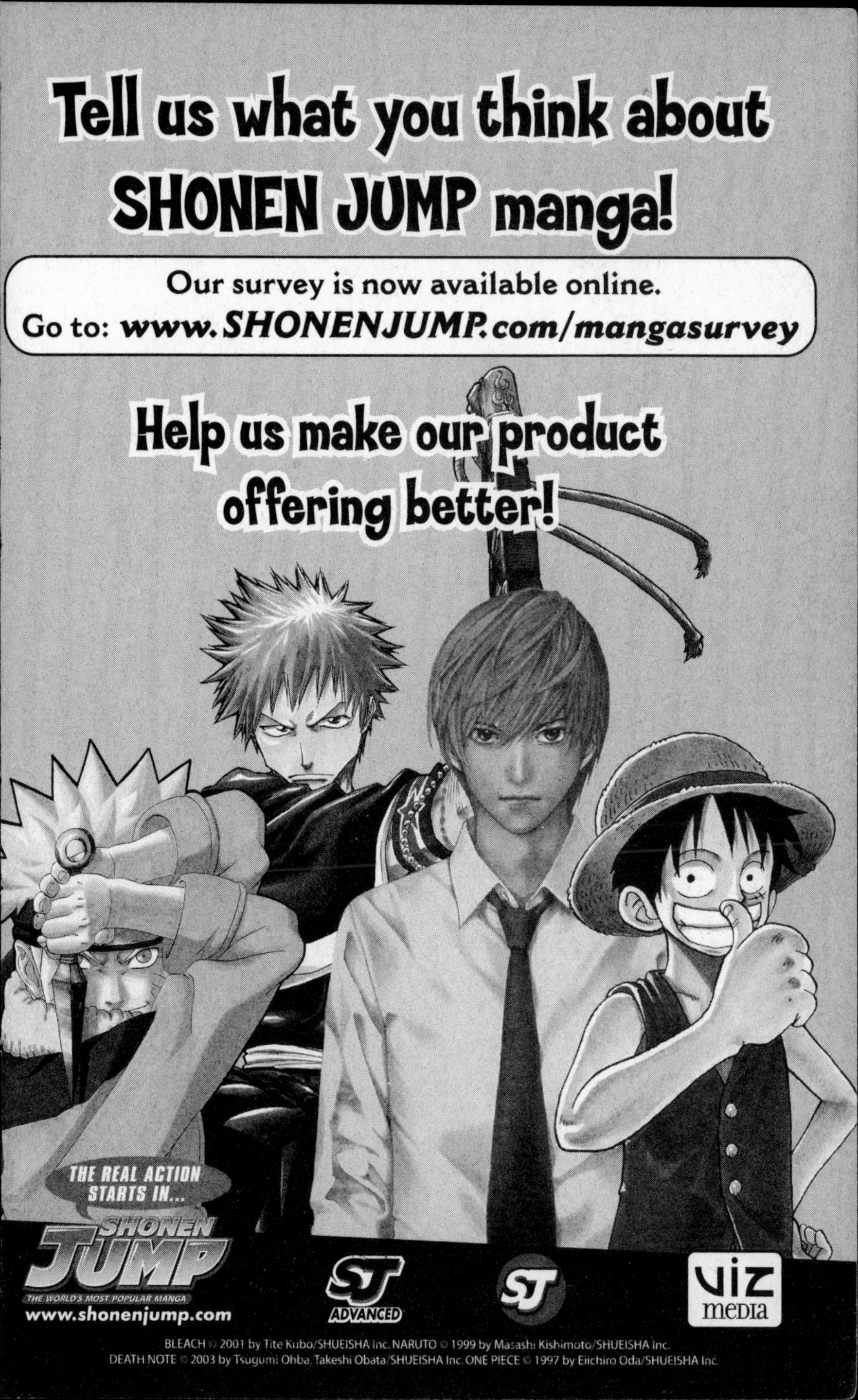
Tell us what you think about SHONEN JUMP manga!
Our survey is now available online.
Go to: www.SHONENJUMP.com/mangasurvey
Help us make our product offering better!
THE REAL ACTION STARTS IN...
SHONEN JUMP
THE WORLD'S MOST POPULAR MANGA
www.shonenjump.com
SJ ADVANCED
SJ
viz media
BLEACH © 2001 by Tite Kubo/SHUEISHA Inc. NARUTO © 1999 by Masashi Kishimoto/SHUEISHA Inc.
DEATH NOTE © 2003 by Tsugumi Ohba, Takeshi Obata/SHUEISHA Inc. ONE PIECE © 1997 by Eiichiro Oda/SHUEISHA Inc.

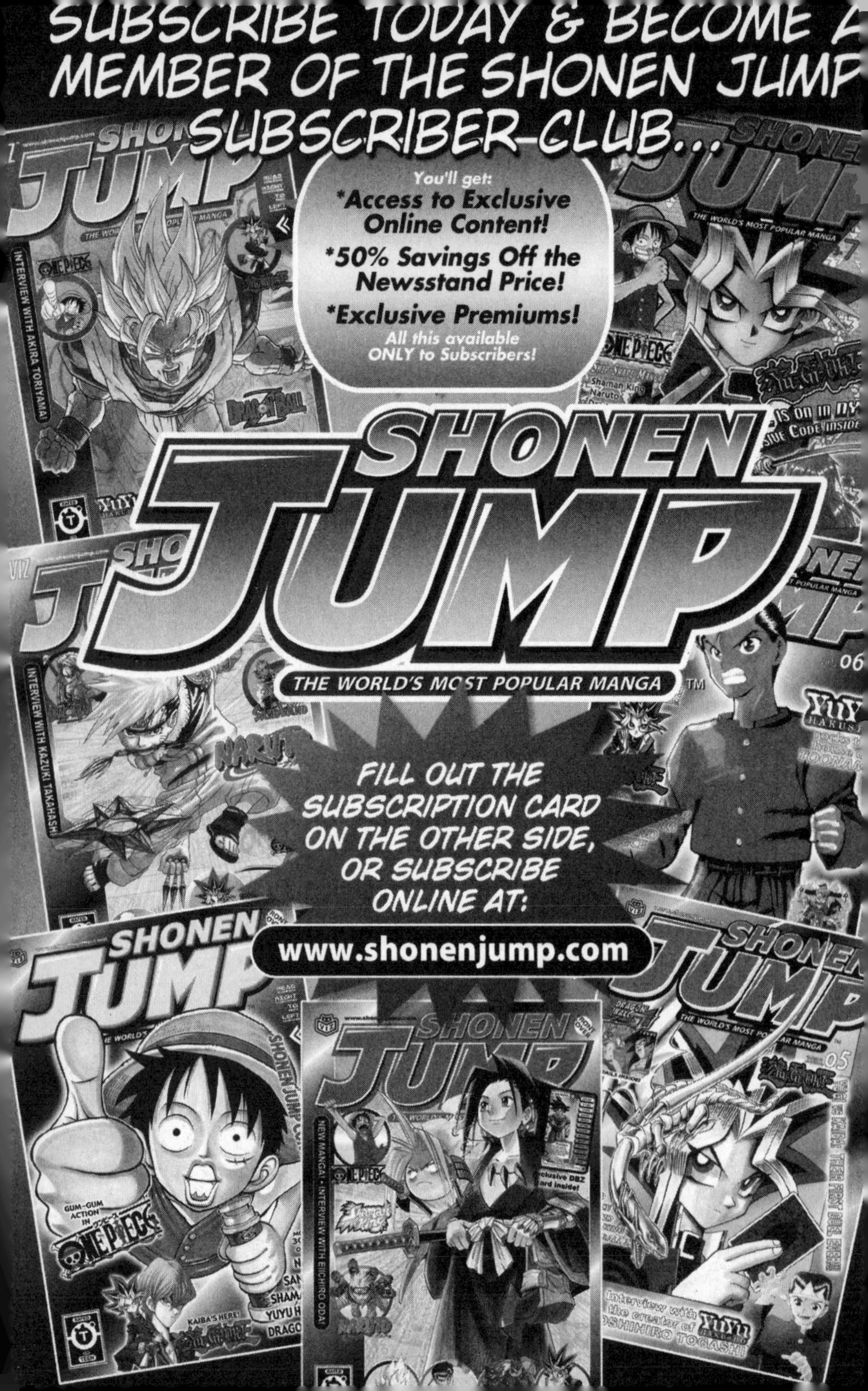
SUBSCRIBE TODAY & BECOME A MEMBER OF THE SHONEN JUMP SUBSCRIBER CLUB...
You'll get:
*Access to Exclusive Online Content!
*50% Savings Off the Newsstand Price!
*Exclusive Premiums!
All this available ONLY to Subscribers!
SHONEN JUMP
THE WORLD'S MOST POPULAR MANGA
FILL OUT THE SUBSCRIPTION CARD ON THE OTHER SIDE, OR SUBSCRIBE ONLINE AT:
www.shonenjump.com

JUMP

THE WORLD'S MOST POPULAR MANGA

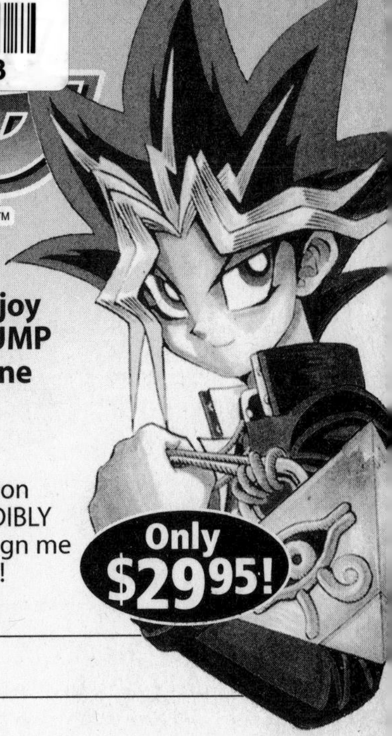

SUBSCRIBE TODAY and SAVE 50% OFF the cover price PLUS enjoy all the benefits of the SHONEN JUMP SUBSCRIBER CLUB, exclusive online content & special gifts ONLY AVAILABLE to SUBSCRIBERS!

☑ **YES!** Please enter my 1 year subscription (12 issues) to *SHONEN JUMP* at the INCREDIBLY LOW SUBSCRIPTION RATE of $29.95 and sign me up for the SHONEN JUMP Subscriber Club!

Only $29⁹⁵!

NAME

ADDRESS

CITY   STATE   ZIP

E-MAIL ADDRESS

☐ MY CHECK IS ENCLOSED   ☐ BILL ME LATER

CREDIT CARD: ☐ VISA   ☐ MASTERCARD

ACCOUNT #   EXP. DATE

SIGNATURE

CLIP AND MAIL TO →

D1019958

Make checks payable to: **SHONEN JUMP**.
Canada add US $12. No foreign orders. Allow 6-8 weeks for delivery.

P6SJGN   YU-GI-OH! © 1996 by Kazuki Takahashi / SHUEISHA Inc.